TASC® Skill Practice!

Test Assessing Secondary Completion Practice Test Questions

Published by

Blue Butterfly Books™

Copyright © 2015, by *Blue Butterfly Books*™, Sheila M. Hynes. ALL RIGHTS RESERVED. No part of this book may be reproduced or transferred in any form or by any means, graphic, electronic, or mechanical, including photocopying, recording, web distribution, taping, or by any information storage retrieval system, without the written permission of the author.

Notice: *Blue Butterfly Books*™ makes every reasonable effort to obtain from reliable sources accurate, complete, and timely information about the tests covered in this book. Nevertheless, changes can be made in the tests or the administration of the tests at any time and *Blue Butterfly Books* ™ makes no representation or warranty, either expressed or implied as to the accuracy, timeliness, or completeness of the information contained in this book. *Blue Butterfly Books* ™ makes no representations or warranties of any kind, express or implied, about the completeness, accuracy, reliability, suitability or availability with respect to the information contained in this document for any purpose. Any reliance you place on such information is therefore strictly at your own risk.

The author(s) shall not be liable for any loss incurred as a consequence of the use and application, directly or indirectly, of any information presented in this work. Sold with the understanding, the author is not engaged in rendering professional services or advice. If advice or expert assistance is required, the services of a competent professional should be sought.

The company, product and service names used in this book are for identification purposes only. All trademarks and registered trademarks are the property of their respective owners. *Blue Butterfly Books* ™ is not affiliate with any educational institution.

We strongly recommend that students check with exam providers for up-to-date information regarding test content.

Please note that TASC® is a registered trademark of McGraw-Hill School Education Holdings LLC which was not involved in the production of, and does not endorse, this product.

We strongly recommend that students check with exam providers for up-to-date information regarding test content.

ISBN-13: 978-1987862065 (Blue Butterfly Books)
ISBN-10: 1987862066

Version 6.5 April 2015

Published by
Blue Butterfly Books
Victoria BC Canada

Printed in the USA

Team Members for this publication

Editor: Sheila M. Hynes, MES York, BA (Hons)
Contributor: Dr. C. Gregory
Contributor: Elizabeta Petrovic MSc (Mathematics)
Contributor: Kelley O'Malley BA (English)

Sustainability and Eco-Responsibility

Here at *Blue Butterfly Books*™, trees are valuable to Mother Earth and the health and wellbeing of everyone. Minimizing our ecological footprint and effect on the environment, we choose Create Space, an eco-responsible printing company.

Electronic routing of our books reduces greenhouse gas emissions, worldwide. When a book order is received, the order is filled at the printing location closest to the client. Using environmentally friendly publishing technology, of the Espresso book printing machine, *Blue Butterfly Books*™ are printed as they are requested, saving thousands of books, and trees over time. This process offers the stable and viable alternative keeping healthy sustainability of our environment.

All paper is acid-free, and interior paper stock is made from 30% post-consumer waste recycled material. Safe for children, Create Space also verifies the materials used in the print process are all CPSIA-compliant.

By purchasing this *Blue Butterfly Books*™, you have supported Full Recovery and Preservation of The Karner Blue Butterfly. Our logo is the Karner Blue Butterfly, Lycaeides melissa samuelis, a rare and beautiful butterfly species whose only flower for propogation is the blue lupin flower. The Karner Butterfly is mostly found in the Great Lakes Region of the U.S.A. Recovery planning is in action, for the return of Karner Blue in Canada led by the National Recovery Strategy. The recovery goals and objectives are aimed at recreating suitable habitats for the butterfly and encourage the growth of blue lupines - the butterfly's natural ideal habitat.

For more info on the Karner Blue Butterfly, feel free to visit:

http://www.albanypinebush.org/conservation/wildlife-management/karner-blue-butterfly-recovery

http://www.wiltonpreserve.org/conservation/karner-blue-butterfly.

Contents

6	**Getting Started**	
	The TASC® Study Plan	7
	Making a Study Schedule	7
13	**Practice Test Questions Set 1**	
	Answer Key	108
171	**Practice Test Questions Set 2**	
	Answer Key	269
337	**Conclusion**	
338	**TASC Test Strategy**	

Getting Started

CONGRATULATIONS! By deciding to take the Test Assessing Secondary Completion (TASC®), you have taken the first step toward a great future! Of course, there is no point in taking this important examination unless you intend to do your very best to earn the highest grade you possibly can. That means getting yourself organized and discovering the best approaches, methods and strategies to master the material. Yes, that will require real effort and dedication on your part but if you are willing to focus your energy and devote the study time necessary, before you know it you will be on you way to a brighter future.

We know that taking on a new endeavour can be a little scary, and it is easy to feel unsure of where to begin. That's where we come in. This study guide is designed to help you improve your test-taking skills, show you a few tricks of the trade and increase both your competency and confidence.

The California High School Proficiency Exam

The TASC® is a large test with five modules, Language Arts (Reading and Writing), Mathematics, Social Studies and Science.

While we seek to make our guide as comprehensive as possible, note that like all entrance exams, the TASC® Exam might be adjusted at some future point. New material might be added, or content that is no longer relevant or applicable might be removed. It is always a good idea to give the materials you receive when you register to take the TASC® a careful review.

The TASC® Study Plan

Now that you have made the decision to take the TASC®, it is time to get started. Before you do another thing, you will need to figure out a plan of attack. The very best study tip is to start early! The longer the time period you devote to regular study practice, the likelier that you will retain the material and be able to access it quickly. If you thought that 1x20 is the same as 2x10, guess what? It really is not, when it comes to study time. Reviewing material for just an hour per day over the course of 20 days is far better than studying for two hours a day for only 10 days. The more often you revisit a particular piece of information, the better you will know it. Not only will your grasp and understanding be better, but your ability to reach into your brain and quickly and efficiently pull out the tidbit you need, will be greatly enhanced as well.

The great Chinese scholar and philosopher Confucius believed that true knowledge could be defined as knowing both what you know and what you do not know. The first step in preparing for the TASC® Exam is to assess your strengths and weaknesses. You may already have an idea of what you know and what you do not know, but evaluating yourself using our Self-Assessment modules for each of the TASC® subject areas will clarify the details.

Making a Study Schedule

To make your study time most productive you will need to develop a study plan. The purpose of the plan is to organize all the bits of pieces of information in such a way that you will not feel overwhelmed. Rome was not built in a day, and learning everything you will need to know to pass the TASC® Exam is going to take time, too. Arranging the material you need to learn into manageable chunks is the best way to go. Each study session should make you feel as though you have succeeded in accomplishing your goal, and your goal is simply to learn what you planned to learn during that particular session. Try to organize the content in such a way that each study session builds on previous ones. That way, you will retain the information, be better able to access it, and review the previous bits and pieces at the same time.

Self-assessment

The Best Study Tip! The very best study tip is to start early! The longer you study regularly, the more you will retain and 'learn' the material. Studying for 1 hour per day for 20 days is far better than studying for 2 hours for 10 days.

What don't you know?

The first step is to assess your strengths and weaknesses. You may already have an idea of where your weaknesses are, or you can take our Self-assessment modules for each of the areas, Math, English, Science and Reading Comprehension.

Exam Component	Rate from 1 to 5
English / Language Arts	
Vocabulary	
Grammar & Usage	
Punctuation	
Capitalization	
Essay Writing	
Reading Comprehension	
Math	
Algebra	
Ratio and Probability	
Quadratics	
Trigonometry	

Social Studies
World History
US History
Civics and Government
Geography
Economics

Science
Physical Sciences
Life Sciences
Earth and Space Science

Making a Study Schedule

The key to making a study plan is to divide the material you need to learn into manageable size and learn it, while at the same time reviewing the material that you already know.

Using the table above, any scores of three or below, you need to spend time learning, going over and practicing this subject area. A score of four means you need to review the material, but you don't have to spend time re-learning. A score of five and you are OK with just an occasional review before the exam.

A score of zero or one means you really do need to work on this and you should allocate the most time and give it the highest priority. Some students prefer a 5-day plan and others a 10-day plan. It also depends on how much time you have until the exam.

Here is an example of a 5-day plan based on an example from the table above:

Vocabulary: 1   Study 1 hour everyday – review on last day
Essay Writing: 3   Study 1 hour for 2 days then ½ hour and then review

Algebra: 4 Review every second day
US History: 2 Study 1 hour on the first day – then ½ hour everyday
Reading Comprehension: 5 Review for ½ hour every other day
Quadratics: 5 Review for ½ hour every other day

Using this example, Quadratics and reading comprehension are good and only need occasional review. Algebra is good and needs 'some' review. Essay Writing needs a bit of work, grammar and usage needs a lot of work and vocabulary is very weak and need most time.   Based on this, here is a sample study plan:

Day	Subject	Time
Monday		
Study	Vocabulary	1 hour
Study	US History	1 hour
	½ hour break	
Study	Essay Writing	1 hour
Review	Algebra	½ hour
Tuesday		
Study	Vocabulary	1 hour
Study	US History	½ hour
	½ hour break	
Study	Essay Writing	½ hour
Review	Algebra	½ hour
Review	Quadratics	½ hour
Wednesday		
Study	Vocabulary	1 hour
Study	US History	½ hour
	½ hour break	
Study	Essay Writing	½ hour
Review	Quadratics	½ hour
Thursday		
Study	Vocabulary	½ hour
Study	US History	½ hour
Review	Essay Writing	½ hour
	½ hour break	

Review	Quadratics	½ hour
Review	Algebra	½ hour
Friday		
Review	Vocabulary	½ hour
Review	US History	½ hour
Review	Essay Writing	½ hour
	½ hour break	
Review	Algebra	½ hour
Review	US History	½ hour

Using this example, adapt the study plan to your own schedule. This schedule assumes 2 ½ - 3 hours available to study everyday for a 5 day period.

First, write out what you need to study and how much. Next figure out how many days you have before the test. Note, do NOT study on the last day before the test. On the last day before the test, you won't learn anything and will probably only confuse yourself.

Make a table with the days before the test and the number of hours you have available to study each day. We suggest working with 1 hour and ½ hour time slots.

Start filling in the blanks, with the subjects you need to study the most, getting the most time and the most regular time slots (i.e. everyday) and the subjects that you know getting the least time (e.g. ½ hour every other day, or every 3rd day).

Tips for making a schedule

Once you make a schedule, stick with it! Make your study sessions reasonable. If you make a study schedule and don't stick with it, you set yourself up for failure. Instead, schedule study sessions that are a bit shorter and set yourself up for success! Make sure your study sessions are do-able. Studying is hard work, but after you pass, you can party and take a break!

Schedule breaks. Breaks are just as important as study time. Work out a rotation of studying and breaks that works for you.

Build up study time. If you find it hard to sit still and study for 1 hour straight through, build up to it. Start with 20 minutes, and then take a break. Once you get used to 20-minute study sessions, increase the time to 30 minutes. Gradually work you way up to 1 hour.

40 minutes to 1 hour is optimal. Studying for longer than this is tiring and not productive. Studying for shorter isn't long enough to be productive.

Studying Math. Studying Math is different from studying other subjects because you use a different part of your brain. The best way to study math is to practice everyday. This will train your mind to think in a mathematical way. If you miss a day or days, the mathematical mind-set is gone and you have to start all over again to build it up.

Study and practice math everyday for at least 5 days before the exam.

Practice Test Questions Set 1

The questions below are not the same as you will find on the TASC® - that would be too easy! And nobody knows what the questions will be and they change all the time. Below are general questions that cover the same subject areas as the TASC®. So, while the format and exact wording of the questions may differ slightly, and change from year to year, if you can answer the questions below, you will have no problem with the TASC®.

For the best results, take these Practice Test Questions as if it were the real exam. Set aside time when you will not be disturbed, and a location that is quiet and free of distractions. Read the instructions carefully, read each question carefully, and answer to the best of your ability.
Use the bubble answer sheets provided. When you have completed the Practice Questions, check your answer against the Answer Key and read the explanation provided.

Do not attempt more than one set of practice test questions in one day. After completing the first practice test, wait two or three days before attempting the second set of questions.

Language Arts - Reading

1. Ⓐ Ⓑ Ⓒ Ⓓ
2. Ⓐ Ⓑ Ⓒ Ⓓ
3. Ⓐ Ⓑ Ⓒ Ⓓ
4. Ⓐ Ⓑ Ⓒ Ⓓ
5. Ⓐ Ⓑ Ⓒ Ⓓ
6. Ⓐ Ⓑ Ⓒ Ⓓ
7. Ⓐ Ⓑ Ⓒ Ⓓ
8. Ⓐ Ⓑ Ⓒ Ⓓ
9. Ⓐ Ⓑ Ⓒ Ⓓ
10. Ⓐ Ⓑ Ⓒ Ⓓ
11. Ⓐ Ⓑ Ⓒ Ⓓ
12. Ⓐ Ⓑ Ⓒ Ⓓ
13. Ⓐ Ⓑ Ⓒ Ⓓ
14. Ⓐ Ⓑ Ⓒ Ⓓ
15. Ⓐ Ⓑ Ⓒ Ⓓ
16. Ⓐ Ⓑ Ⓒ Ⓓ
17. Ⓐ Ⓑ Ⓒ Ⓓ
18. Ⓐ Ⓑ Ⓒ Ⓓ
19. Ⓐ Ⓑ Ⓒ Ⓓ
20. Ⓐ Ⓑ Ⓒ Ⓓ
21. Ⓐ Ⓑ Ⓒ Ⓓ
22. Ⓐ Ⓑ Ⓒ Ⓓ
23. Ⓐ Ⓑ Ⓒ Ⓓ
24. Ⓐ Ⓑ Ⓒ Ⓓ
25. Ⓐ Ⓑ Ⓒ Ⓓ
26. Ⓐ Ⓑ Ⓒ Ⓓ
27. Ⓐ Ⓑ Ⓒ Ⓓ
28. Ⓐ Ⓑ Ⓒ Ⓓ
29. Ⓐ Ⓑ Ⓒ Ⓓ
30. Ⓐ Ⓑ Ⓒ Ⓓ
31. Ⓐ Ⓑ Ⓒ Ⓓ
32. Ⓐ Ⓑ Ⓒ Ⓓ
33. Ⓐ Ⓑ Ⓒ Ⓓ
34. Ⓐ Ⓑ Ⓒ Ⓓ
35. Ⓐ Ⓑ Ⓒ Ⓓ
36. Ⓐ Ⓑ Ⓒ Ⓓ
37. Ⓐ Ⓑ Ⓒ Ⓓ
38. Ⓐ Ⓑ Ⓒ Ⓓ
39. Ⓐ Ⓑ Ⓒ Ⓓ
40. Ⓐ Ⓑ Ⓒ Ⓓ
41. Ⓐ Ⓑ Ⓒ Ⓓ
42. Ⓐ Ⓑ Ⓒ Ⓓ
43. Ⓐ Ⓑ Ⓒ Ⓓ
44. Ⓐ Ⓑ Ⓒ Ⓓ
45. Ⓐ Ⓑ Ⓒ Ⓓ
46. Ⓐ Ⓑ Ⓒ Ⓓ
47. Ⓐ Ⓑ Ⓒ Ⓓ
48. Ⓐ Ⓑ Ⓒ Ⓓ
49. Ⓐ Ⓑ Ⓒ Ⓓ
50. Ⓐ Ⓑ Ⓒ Ⓓ

Language Arts - Writing

1. A B C D
2. A B C D
3. A B C D
4. A B C D
5. A B C D
6. A B C D
7. A B C D
8. A B C D
9. A B C D
10. A B C D
11. A B C D
12. A B C D
13. A B C D
14. A B C D
15. A B C D
16. A B C D
17. A B C D
18. A B C D
19. A B C D
20. A B C D
21. A B C D
22. A B C D
23. A B C D
24. A B C D
25. A B C D
26. A B C D
27. A B C D
28. A B C D
29. A B C D
30. A B C D
31. A B C D
32. A B C D
33. A B C D
34. A B C D
35. A B C D
36. A B C D
37. A B C D
38. A B C D
39. A B C D
40. A B C D
41. A B C D
42. A B C D
43. A B C D
44. A B C D
45. A B C D
46. A B C D
47. A B C D
48. A B C D
49. A B C D
50. A B C D

Mathematics

1. (A) (B) (C) (D)
2. (A) (B) (C) (D)
3. (A) (B) (C) (D)
4. (A) (B) (C) (D)
5. (A) (B) (C) (D)
6. (A) (B) (C) (D)
7. (A) (B) (C) (D)
8. (A) (B) (C) (D)
9. (A) (B) (C) (D)
10. (A) (B) (C) (D)
11. (A) (B) (C) (D)
12. (A) (B) (C) (D)
13. (A) (B) (C) (D)
14. (A) (B) (C) (D)
15. (A) (B) (C) (D)
16. (A) (B) (C) (D)
17. (A) (B) (C) (D)
18. (A) (B) (C) (D)
19. (A) (B) (C) (D)
20. (A) (B) (C) (D)
21. (A) (B) (C) (D)
22. (A) (B) (C) (D)
23. (A) (B) (C) (D)
24. (A) (B) (C) (D)
25. (A) (B) (C) (D)
26. (A) (B) (C) (D)
27. (A) (B) (C) (D)
28. (A) (B) (C) (D)
29. (A) (B) (C) (D)
30. (A) (B) (C) (D)
31. (A) (B) (C) (D)
32. (A) (B) (C) (D)
33. (A) (B) (C) (D)
34. (A) (B) (C) (D)
35. (A) (B) (C) (D)
36. (A) (B) (C) (D)
37. (A) (B) (C) (D)
38. (A) (B) (C) (D)
39. (A) (B) (C) (D)
40. (A) (B) (C) (D)
41. (A) (B) (C) (D)
42. (A) (B) (C) (D)
43. (A) (B) (C) (D)
44. (A) (B) (C) (D)
45. (A) (B) (C) (D)
46. (A) (B) (C) (D)
47. (A) (B) (C) (D)
48. (A) (B) (C) (D)
49. (A) (B) (C) (D)
50. (A) (B) (C) (D)
51. (A) (B) (C) (D)
52. (A) (B) (C) (D)
53. (A) (B) (C) (D)
54. (A) (B) (C) (D)
55. (A) (B) (C) (D)
56. (A) (B) (C) (D)
57. (A) (B) (C) (D)
58. (A) (B) (C) (D)
59. (A) (B) (C) (D)
60. (A) (B) (C) (D)

Social Studies

1. A B C D
2. A B C D
3. A B C D
4. A B C D
5. A B C D
6. A B C D
7. A B C D
8. A B C D
9. A B C D
10. A B C D
11. A B C D
12. A B C D
13. A B C D
14. A B C D
15. A B C D
16. A B C D
17. A B C D
18. A B C D
19. A B C D
20. A B C D
21. A B C D
22. A B C D
23. A B C D
24. A B C D
25. A B C D
26. A B C D
27. A B C D
28. A B C D
29. A B C D
30. A B C D
31. A B C D
32. A B C D
33. A B C D
34. A B C D
35. A B C D
36. A B C D
37. A B C D
38. A B C D
39. A B C D
40. A B C D
41. A B C D
42. A B C D
43. A B C D
44. A B C D
45. A B C D
46. A B C D
47. A B C D
48. A B C D
49. A B C D
50. A B C D

Science

1. Ⓐ Ⓑ Ⓒ Ⓓ
2. Ⓐ Ⓑ Ⓒ Ⓓ
3. Ⓐ Ⓑ Ⓒ Ⓓ
4. Ⓐ Ⓑ Ⓒ Ⓓ
5. Ⓐ Ⓑ Ⓒ Ⓓ
6. Ⓐ Ⓑ Ⓒ Ⓓ
7. Ⓐ Ⓑ Ⓒ Ⓓ
8. Ⓐ Ⓑ Ⓒ Ⓓ
9. Ⓐ Ⓑ Ⓒ Ⓓ
10. Ⓐ Ⓑ Ⓒ Ⓓ
11. Ⓐ Ⓑ Ⓒ Ⓓ
12. Ⓐ Ⓑ Ⓒ Ⓓ
13. Ⓐ Ⓑ Ⓒ Ⓓ
14. Ⓐ Ⓑ Ⓒ Ⓓ
15. Ⓐ Ⓑ Ⓒ Ⓓ
16. Ⓐ Ⓑ Ⓒ Ⓓ
17. Ⓐ Ⓑ Ⓒ Ⓓ
18. Ⓐ Ⓑ Ⓒ Ⓓ
19. Ⓐ Ⓑ Ⓒ Ⓓ
20. Ⓐ Ⓑ Ⓒ Ⓓ
21. Ⓐ Ⓑ Ⓒ Ⓓ
22. Ⓐ Ⓑ Ⓒ Ⓓ
23. Ⓐ Ⓑ Ⓒ Ⓓ
24. Ⓐ Ⓑ Ⓒ Ⓓ
25. Ⓐ Ⓑ Ⓒ Ⓓ
26. Ⓐ Ⓑ Ⓒ Ⓓ
27. Ⓐ Ⓑ Ⓒ Ⓓ
28. Ⓐ Ⓑ Ⓒ Ⓓ
29. Ⓐ Ⓑ Ⓒ Ⓓ
30. Ⓐ Ⓑ Ⓒ Ⓓ
31. Ⓐ Ⓑ Ⓒ Ⓓ
32. Ⓐ Ⓑ Ⓒ Ⓓ
33. Ⓐ Ⓑ Ⓒ Ⓓ
34. Ⓐ Ⓑ Ⓒ Ⓓ
35. Ⓐ Ⓑ Ⓒ Ⓓ
36. Ⓐ Ⓑ Ⓒ Ⓓ
37. Ⓐ Ⓑ Ⓒ Ⓓ
38. Ⓐ Ⓑ Ⓒ Ⓓ
39. Ⓐ Ⓑ Ⓒ Ⓓ
40. Ⓐ Ⓑ Ⓒ Ⓓ
41. Ⓐ Ⓑ Ⓒ Ⓓ
42. Ⓐ Ⓑ Ⓒ Ⓓ
43. Ⓐ Ⓑ Ⓒ Ⓓ
44. Ⓐ Ⓑ Ⓒ Ⓓ
45. Ⓐ Ⓑ Ⓒ Ⓓ
46. Ⓐ Ⓑ Ⓒ Ⓓ
47. Ⓐ Ⓑ Ⓒ Ⓓ
48. Ⓐ Ⓑ Ⓒ Ⓓ
49. Ⓐ Ⓑ Ⓒ Ⓓ
50. Ⓐ Ⓑ Ⓒ Ⓓ

Part I - Reading Comprehension

Questions 1 – 4 refer to the following passage.

Infectious Diseases

An infectious disease is a clinically evident illness resulting from the presence of pathogenic agents, such as viruses, bacteria, fungi, protozoa, multi-cellular parasites, and unusual proteins known as prions. Infectious pathologies are also called communicable diseases or transmissible diseases, due to their potential of transmission from one person or species to another by a replicating agent (as opposed to a toxin).

Transmission of an infectious disease can occur in many different ways. Physical contact, liquids, food, body fluids, contaminated objects, and airborne inhalation can all transmit infecting agents.

Transmissible diseases that occur through contact with an ill person, or objects touched by them, are especially infective, and are sometimes called contagious diseases. Communicable diseases that require a more specialized route of infection, such as through blood or needle transmission, or sexual transmission, are usually not regarded as contagious.

The term infectivity describes the ability of an organism to enter, survive and multiply in the host, while the infectiousness of a disease indicates the comparative ease with which the disease is transmitted. An infection however, is not synonymous with an infectious disease, as an infection may not cause important clinical symptoms. [1]

1. What can we infer from the first paragraph in this passage?

    a. Sickness from a toxin can be easily transmitted from one person to another.

    b. Sickness from an infectious disease can be easily transmitted from one person to another.

    c. Few sicknesses are transmitted from one person to another.

    d. Infectious diseases are easily treated.

2. What are two other names for infections' pathologies?

    a. Communicable diseases or transmissible diseases

    b. Communicable diseases or terminal diseases

    c. Transmissible diseases or preventable diseases

    d. Communicative diseases or unstable diseases

3. What does infectivity describe?

    a. The inability of an organism to multiply in the host

    b. The inability of an organism to reproduce

    c. The ability of an organism to enter, survive and multiply in the host

    d. The ability of an organism to reproduce in the host

4. How do we know an infection is not synonymous with an infectious disease?

    a. Because an infectious disease destroys infections with enough time.

    b. Because an infection may not cause clinical symptoms or impair host function.

    c. We do not. The two are synonymous.

    d. Because an infection is too fatal to be an infectious disease.

Questions 5 – 7 refer to the following passage.

Thunderstorms

The first stage of a thunderstorm is the cumulus stage, or developing stage. In this stage, masses of moisture are lifted upwards into the atmosphere. The trigger for this lift can be insulation heating the ground producing thermals, areas where two winds converge, forcing air upwards, or where winds blow over terrain of increasing elevation. Moisture in the air rapidly cools into liquid drops of water, which appears as cumulus clouds.

As the water vapor condenses into liquid, latent heat is released which warms the air, causing it to become less dense than the surrounding dry air. The warm air rises in an updraft through the process of convection (hence the term convective precipitation). This creates a low-pressure zone beneath the forming thunderstorm. In a typical thunderstorm, approximately 5×10^8 kg of water vapor is lifted, and the amount of energy released when this condenses is about equal to the energy used by a city of 100,000 in a month. [2]

5. The cumulus stage of a thunderstorm is the

    a. The last stage of the storm
    b. The middle stage of the storm formation
    c. The beginning of the thunderstorm
    d. The period after the thunderstorm has ended

6. One way the air is warmed is

    a. Air moving downwards, which creates a high-pressure zone
    b. Air cooling and becoming less dense, causing it to rise
    c. Moisture moving downward toward the earth
    d. Heat created by water vapor condensing into liquid

7. Identify the correct sequence of events.

   a. Warm air rises, water droplets condense, creating more heat, and the air rises farther.

   b. Warm air rises and cools, water droplets condense, causing low pressure.

   c. Warm air rises and collects water vapor, the water vapor condenses as the air rises, which creates heat, and causes the air to rise farther.

   d. None of the above.

Questions 8 – 11 refer to the following passage.

Who Was Anne Frank?

You may have heard mention of the word Holocaust in your History or English classes. The Holocaust took place from 1939-1945. It was an attempt by the Nazi party to purify the human race, by eliminating Jews, Gypsies, Catholics, homosexuals and others they deemed inferior to their "perfect" Aryan race. The Nazis used Concentration Camps, which were sometimes used as Death Camps, to exterminate the people they held in the camps. One of the saddest facts about the Holocaust was the over one million children under the age of sixteen died in a Nazi concentration camp. Just a few weeks before World War II was over, Anne Frank was one of those children to die.

Before the Nazi party began its persecution of the Jews, Anne Frank had a happy live. She was born in June of 1929. In June of 1942, for her 13th birthday, she was given a simple present which would go onto impact the lives of millions of people around the world. That gift was a small red diary that she called Kitty. This diary was to become Anne's most treasured possession when she and her family hid from the Nazi's in a secret annex above her father's office building in Amsterdam.

For 25 months, Anne, her sister Margot, her parents, another family, and an elderly Jewish dentist hid from the Nazis in this tiny annex. They were never permitted to go outside, and their food and supplies were brought to them by Miep Gies and her husband, who did not believe in the Nazi persecution of the Jews. It was a very difficult life for young Anne and she used Kitty as an outlet to describe her life in hiding. After 2 years, Anne and her family were betrayed and arrested by the Nazis. To this day, nobody is exactly sure who betrayed the Frank family and the other annex residents. Anne, her mother, and her sister were separated from Otto Frank, Anne's father. Then, Anne and Margot were separated from their mother. In March of 1945, Margot Frank died of starvation in a Concentration Camp. A few days later, at the age of 15, Anne Frank died of typhus. Of all the people who hid in the Annex, only Otto Frank survived the Holocaust.

Otto Frank returned to the Annex after World War II. It was there that he found Kitty, filled with Anne's thoughts and feelings about being a persecuted Jewish girl. Otto Frank had Anne's diary published in 1947 and it has remained continuously in print ever since. Today, the diary has been published in over 55 languages and more than 24 million copies have been sold around the world. The Diary of Anne Frank tells the story of a brave young woman who tried to see the good in all people.

8. From the context clues in the passage, the word "annex" most nearly means?

    a. Attic

    b. Bedroom

    c. Basement

    d. Kitchen

9. Why do you think Anne's diary has been published in 55 languages?

    a. So everyone could understand it.

    b. So people around the world could learn more about the horrors of the Holocaust.

    c. Because Anne was Jewish but hid in Amsterdam and died in Germany.

    d. Because Otto Frank spoke many languages.

10. From the description of Anne and Margot's deaths in the passage, what can we assume typhus is?

    a. The same as starving to death.

    b. An infection the Germans gave to Anne.

    c. A disease Anne caught in the concentration camp.

    d. Poison gas used by the Germans to kill Anne.

11. In the third paragraph, what does the word outlet most nearly mean?

    a. A place to plug things into the wall

    b. A store where Miep bought cheap supplies for the Frank family

    c. A hiding space similar to an Annex

    d. A place where Anne could express her private thoughts.

Questions 12 – 14 refer to the following passage.

Clouds

A cloud is a visible mass of droplets or frozen crystals floating in the atmosphere above the surface of the Earth or other planetary bodies. Another type of cloud is a mass of material in space, attracted by gravity, called interstellar clouds and nebulae. The branch of meteorology which studies clouds is called nephrology. When we are speaking of Earth clouds, water vapor is usually the condensing substance, which forms small droplets or ice crystal. These crystals are typically 0.01 mm in diameter. Dense, deep clouds reflect most light, so they appear white, at least from the top. Cloud droplets scatter light very efficiently, so the further into a cloud light travels, the weaker it gets. This accounts for the gray or dark appearance at the base of large clouds. Thin clouds may appear to have acquired the color of their environment or background. [4]

12. What are clouds made of?

a. Water droplets.
b. Ice crystals.
c. Ice crystals and water droplets.
d. Clouds on Earth are made of ice crystals and water droplets.

13. The main idea of this passage is

a. Condensation occurs in clouds, having an intense effect on the weather on the surface of the earth.
b. Atmospheric gases are responsible for the gray color of clouds just before a severe storm happens.
c. A cloud is a visible mass of droplets or frozen crystals floating in the atmosphere above the surface of the Earth or other planetary body.
d. Clouds reflect light in varying amounts and degrees, depending on the size and concentration of the water droplets.

14. Why are clouds white on top and grey on the bottom?

a. Because water droplets inside the cloud do not reflect light, it appears white, and the further into the cloud the light travels, the less light is reflected making the bottom appear dark.
b. Because water droplets outside the cloud reflect light, it appears dark, and the further into the cloud the light travels, the more light is reflected making the bottom appear white.
c. Because water droplets inside the cloud reflects light, making it appear white, and the further into the cloud the light travels, the more light is reflected making the bottom appear dark.
d. None of the above.

Questions 15 - 18 refer to the following passage.

Was Dr. Seuss A Real Doctor?

A favorite author for over 100 years, Theodor Seuss Geisel was born on March 2, 1902. Today, we celebrate the birthday of the famous "Dr. Seuss" by hosting Read Across America events throughout the month of March. School children around the country celebrate the "Doctor's" birthday by making hats, giving presentations and holding read aloud circles featuring some of Dr. Seuss' most famous books.

But who was Dr. Seuss? Did he go to medical school? Where was his office? You may be surprised to know that Theodor Seuss Geisel was not a medical doctor at all. He took on the nickname Dr. Seuss when he became a noted children's book author. He earned the nickname because people said his books were "as good as medicine." All these years later, his nickname has lasted and he is known as Dr. Seuss all across the world.

Think back to when you were a young child. Did you ever want to try "green eggs and ham.?" Did you try to "Hop on Pop?" Do you remember learning about the environment from a creature called The Lorax? Of course, you must recall one of Seuss' most famous characters; that green Grinch who stole Christmas. These stories were all written by Dr. Seuss and featured his signature rhyming words and letters. They also featured made up words to enhance his rhyme scheme and even though many of his characters were made up, they sure seem real to us today.

And what of his "signature" book, The Cat in the Hat? You must remember that cat and Thing One and Thing Two from your childhood. Did you know that in the early 1950's there was a growing concern in America that children were not becoming avid readers? This was, book publishers thought, because children found books dull and uninteresting. An intelligent publisher sent Dr. Seuss a book of words that he thought all children should learn as young readers. Dr. Seuss wrote his famous story The Cat in the Hat, using those words. We can see, over the decades, just how much influence his writing has had on very young children. That is why we celebrate this doctor's birthday each March.

15. What does the word "avid" mean in the last paragraph?

    a. Good

    b. Interested

    c. Slow

    d. Fast

16. What can we infer from the statement " His books were like medicine?"

    a. His books made people feel better

    b. His books were in doctor's office waiting rooms

    c. His books took away fevers

    d. His books left a funny taste in readers' mouths.

17. Why is the publisher in the last paragraph referred to as "intelligent?"

    a. The publisher knew how to read.

    b. The publisher knew kids did not like to read.

    c. The publisher knew Dr. Seuss would be able to create a book that sold well.

    d. The publisher knew that Dr. Seuss would be able to write a book that would get young children interested in reading.

18. The theme of this passage is

    a. Dr. Seuss was not a doctor.

    b. Dr. Seuss influenced the lives of generations of young children.

    c. Dr. Seuss wrote rhyming books.

    d. Dr. Suess' birthday is a good day to read a book.

Questions 19 – 22 refer to the following passage.

Frankenstein

Great God! What a scene has just taken place! I am yet dizzy with the remembrance of it. I hardly know whether I shall have the power to detail it; yet the tale which I have recorded would be incomplete without this final and wonderful catastrophe. I entered the cabin where lay the remains of my ill-fated and admirable friend. Over him hung a form which I cannot find words to describe—gigantic in stature, yet uncouth and distorted in its proportions. As he hung over the coffin, his face was concealed by long locks of ragged hair; but one vast hand was extended, in color and apparent texture like that of a mummy. When he heard the sound of my approach, he ceased to utter exclamations of grief and horror and sprung towards the window. Never did I behold a vision so horrible as his face, of such loathsome yet appalling hideousness. I shut my eyes involuntarily and endeavored to recollect what were my duties with regard to this destroyer. I called on him to stay.

He paused, looking on me with wonder, and again turning towards the lifeless form of his creator, he seemed to forget my presence, and every feature and gesture seemed instigated by the wildest rage of some uncontrollable passion.

"That is also my victim!" he exclaimed. "In his murder my crimes are consummated; the miserable series of my being is wound to its close! Oh, Frankenstein! Generous and self-devoted being! What does it avail that I now ask thee to pardon me? I, who irretrievably destroyed thee by destroying all thou lovedst. Alas! He is cold, he cannot answer me."

His voice seemed suffocated, and my first impulses, which had suggested to me the duty of obeying the dying request of my friend in destroying his enemy, were now suspended by a mixture of curiosity and compassion. I approached this tremendous being; I dared not again raise my eyes to his face, there was something so scaring and unearthly in his ugliness. I attempted to speak, but the words died away on my lips. The monster continued to utter wild and incoherent self-reproaches. At length I gathered resolution to address him in a pause of the tempest of his passion.

"Your repentance," I said, "is now superfluous. If you had listened to the voice of conscience and heeded the stings of remorse before you had urged your diabolical vengeance to this extremity, Frankenstein would yet have lived." [7]

19. Who is the "ill-fated and admirable friend" who is lying in the coffin?

    a. Frankenstein's monster

    b. Frankenstein

    c. Mary Shelley

    d. Unknown

20. Why is the speaker 'suspended" from following through on his duty to destroy the monster?

    a. The way the monster looks

    b. The monster's remorse

    c. Curiosity and compassion

    d. Fear the monster might kill him too

21. How does Frankenstein's monster destroy Frankenstein?

    a. By killing Frankenstein

    b. By letting himself be the monster everyone sees him as

    c. By destroying everything Frankenstein loved

    d. All of the above

22. When the Speaker says the monster's repentance is "superfluous, what does he mean?

   a. That it is unnecessary and unused because Frankenstein is already dead and cannot hear him

   b. That he accepts the repentance on behalf of Frankenstein

   c. That the monster does not actually feel remorseful

   d. That his repentance is unneeded because he did not do anything wrong

Questions 23 – 27 refer to the following passage.

Navy Seals

The United States Navy's Sea, Air and Land Teams, commonly known as Navy SEALs, are the U.S. Navy's principal special operations force, and a part of the Naval Special Warfare Command (NSWC) as well as the maritime component of the United States Special Operations Command (USSOCOM).

The unit's acronym ("SEAL") comes from their capacity to operate at sea, in the air, and on land – but it is their ability to work underwater that separates SEALs from most other military units in the world. Navy SEALs are trained and have been deployed in a wide variety of missions, including direct action and special reconnaissance operations, unconventional warfare, foreign internal defence, hostage rescue, counter-terrorism and other missions. All SEALs are members of either the United States Navy or the United States Coast Guard.

In the early morning of May 2, 2011 local time, a team of 40 CIA-led Navy SEALs completed an operation to kill Osama bin Laden in Abbottabad, Pakistan about 35 miles (56 km) from Islamabad, the country's capital. The Navy SEALs were part of the Naval Special Warfare Development Group, previously called "Team 6." President Barack Obama later confirmed the death of bin Laden. The unprecedented media coverage raised the public profile of the SEAL community, particularly the counter-terrorism specialists commonly known as SEAL Team 6. [5]

23. Are Navy SEALs part of USSOCOM?

    a. Yes
    b. No
    c. Only for special operations
    d. No, they are part of the US Navy

24. What separates Navy SEALs from other military units?

    a. Belonging to NSWC
    b. Direct action and special reconnaissance operations
    c. Working underwater
    d. Working for other military units in the world

25. What other military organizations do SEALs belong to?

    a. The US Navy
    b. The Coast Guard
    c. The US Army
    d. The Navy and the Coast Guard

26. What other organization participated in the Bin Laden raid?

    a. The CIA
    b. The US Military
    c. Counter-terrorism specialists
    d. None of the above

27. What is the new name for Team 6?

    a. They were always called Team 6

    b. The counter-terrorism specialists

    c. The Naval Special Warfare Development Group

    d. None of the above

Questions 28 – 30 refer to the following passage.

How To Get A Good Nights Sleep

Sleep is just as essential for healthy living as water, air and food. Sleep allows the body to rest and replenish depleted energy levels. Sometimes we may for various reasons experience difficulty sleeping which has a serious effect on our health. Those who have prolonged sleeping problems are facing a serious medical condition and should see a qualified doctor when possible for help. Here is simple guide that can help you sleep better at night.

Try to create a natural pattern of waking up and sleeping around the same time everyday. This means avoiding going to bed too early and oversleeping past your usual wake up time. Going to bed and getting up at radically different times everyday confuses your body clock. Try to establish a natural rhythm as much as you can.

Exercises and a bit of physical activity can help you sleep better at night. If you are having problem sleeping, try to be as active as you can during the day. If you are tired from physical activity, falling asleep is a natural and easy process for your body. If you remain inactive during the day, you will find it harder to sleep properly at night. Try walking, jogging, swimming or simple stretches as you get close to your bed time.

Afternoon naps are great to refresh you during the day, but they may also keep you awake at night. If you feel sleepy during the day, get up, take a walk and get busy to keep from sleeping. Stretching is a good way to increase blood flow to the brain and keep you alert so that you don't sleep during the day. This will help you sleep better night.

> A warm bath or a glass of milk in the evening can help your body relax and prepare for sleep. A cold bath will wake you up and keep you up for several hours. Also avoid eating too late before bed.

28. How would you describe this sentence?

    a. A recommendation

    b. An opinion

    c. A fact

    d. A diagnosis

29. Which of the following is an alternative title for this article?

    a. Exercise and a good night's sleep

    b. Benefits of a good night's sleep

    c. Tips for a good night's sleep

    d. Lack of sleep is a serious medical condition

30. Which of the following can NOT be inferred from this article?

    a. Biking is helpful for getting a good night's sleep

    b. Mental activity is helpful for getting a good night's sleep

    c. Eating bedtime snacks is not recommended

    d. Getting up at the same time is helpful for a good night's sleep

Questions 31 - 34 refer to the following passage.

The Crusades

In 1095 Pope Urban II proclaimed the First Crusade with the intent and stated goal to restore Christian access to holy places in and around Jerusalem. Over the next 200 years there were 6 major crusades and numerous minor crusades in the fight for control of the "Holy Land." Historians are divided on the real purpose of the Crusades, some believing that it was part of a purely defensive war against Islamic conquest; some see them as part of a long-running conflict at the frontiers of Europe; and others see them as confident, aggressive, papal-led expansion attempts by Western Christendom. The impact of the crusades was profound, and judgment of the Crusaders ranges from laudatory to highly critical. However, all agree that the Crusades and wars waged during those crusades were brutal and often bloody. Several hundred thousand Roman Catholic Christians joined the Crusades, they were Christians from all over Europe.

Europe at the time was under the Feudal System, so while the Crusaders made vows to the Church they also were beholden to their Feudal Lords. This led to the Crusaders not only fighting the Saracen, the commonly used word for Muslim at the time, but also each other for power and economic gain in the Holy Land. This infighting between the Crusaders is why many historians hold the view that the Crusades were simply a front for Europe to invade the Holy Land for economic gain in the name of the Church. Another factor contributing to this theory is that while the army of crusaders marched towards Jerusalem they pillaged the land as they went. The church and feudal Lords vowing to return the land to its original beauty, and inhabitants, this rarely happened though as the Lords often kept the land for themselves. A full 800 years after the Crusades, Pope John Paul II expressed his sorrow for the massacre of innocent people and the lasting damage the Medieval church caused in that area of the World.

31. What is the tone of this article?

    a. Subjective
    b. Objective
    c. Persuasive
    d. None of the Above

32. What can all historians agree on concerning the Crusades?

    a. It achieved great things
    b. It stabilized the Holy Land
    c. It was bloody and brutal
    d. It helped defend Europe from the Byzantine Empire

33. What impact did the feudal system have on the Crusades?

    a. It unified the Crusaders
    b. It helped gather volunteers
    c. It had no effect on the Crusades
    d. It led to infighting, causing more damage than good

34. What does Saracen mean?

    a. Muslim
    b. Christian
    c. Knight
    d. Holy Land

Questions 35 - 36 refer to the following passage.

Scotland's Windy Power Source

The Scottish Government has a targeted plan of generating 100% of Scotland's electricity through renewable energy by 2020. Renewable energy sources include sun, water and wind power. Scotland uses all forms but its fastest growing energy is wind energy. Wind power is generated through the use of wind turbines, placed onshore and offshore. Wind turbines that are grouped together in large numbers are called wind farms. Most Scottish citizens say that the wind farms are necessary to meet current and future energy needs, and would like to see an increase in the number of wind farms. They cite the fact that wind energy does not cause pollution, there are low operational costs, and most importantly due to the definition of renewable energy it cannot be depleted.

35. What is Scotland's fastest growing source of renewable energy?

    a. Solar Panels

    b. Hydroelectric

    c. Wind

    d. Fossil Fuels

36. Why do most Scottish citizens agree with the Government's plan?

    a. Their concern for current and future energy needs

    b. Because of the low operational costs

    c. Because they are out of sight

    d. Because it provides jobs

Questions 37 - 40 refer to the following passage.

Convection

Warm air is less dense than cool air, so warm air rises within cooler air like a hot air balloon or warm water in an ocean current. Clouds form as warm air carrying moisture rises. As the warm air rises, it cools. The moist water vapor begins to condense as the temperature cools. This releases energy that keeps the air warmer than its surroundings. The result is that it continues to rise. If enough instability

is present in the atmosphere, this process will continue long enough for cumulonimbus clouds to form. These clouds support lightning and thunder. All thunderstorms, regardless of type, go through three stages: the cumulus stage, the mature stage, and the dissipation stage. Depending on the conditions in the atmosphere, these three stages can take anywhere from 20 minutes to several hours.
3

37. This passage tells us:

    a. Warm air is denser than cool air

    b. All thunderstorms will go through three stages.

    c. Thunderstorms may occur without clouds present.

    d. The stages of a thunderstorm conclude within just a few minutes.

38. When warm air rises through colder air, it results in:

    a. Evaporation

    b. Humidity

    c. Clear skies

    d. Condensation

39. What is the correct order?

    a. Warm air rises, cools as it gets higher, water condenses, warms the air, and the air rises more.

    b. Warm air rises, warms up more as it get higher, water condenses, warms the air, and the air rises more.

    c. Warm air rises, cools as it gets higher, water condenses, cools the air, and the air rises more.

    d. None of the above.

40. Cumulonimbus clouds are forming now. What must be true?

    a. The process of warm air rising and water condensing hasn't started.

    b. The process of warm air rising and water condensing is just starting now.

    c. The process of warm air rising and water condensing has being going on for some time.

    d. None of the above.

Questions 41 - 44 refer to the following passage.

If You Have Allergies, You're Not Alone

People who experience allergies might joke that their immune systems have let them down or are seriously lacking. Truthfully though, people who experience allergic reactions or allergy symptoms during certain times of the year have heightened immune systems that are, "better" than those of people who have perfectly healthy but less militant immune systems.

Still, when a person has an allergic reaction, they are having an adverse reaction to a substance that is considered normal to most people. Mild allergic reactions usually have symptoms like itching, runny nose, red eyes, or bumps or discoloration of the skin. More serious allergic reactions, such as those to animal and insect poisons or certain foods, may result in the closing of the throat, swelling of the eyes, low blood pressure, inability to breath, and can even be fatal.

Different treatments help different allergies, and which one a person uses depends on the nature and severity of the allergy. It is recommended to patients with severe allergies to take extra precautions, such as carrying an EpiPen, which treats anaphylactic shock and may prevent death, always in order for the remedy to be readily available and more effective. When an allergy is not so severe, treatments may be used just relieve a person of uncomfortable symptoms. Over the counter allergy medicines treat milder symptoms, and can be bought at any grocery store and used in moderation to help people with allergies live normally.

There are many tests available to assess whether a person has allergies or what they may be allergic to, and advances in these tests and the medicine used to treat patients continues to improve. Despite this fact, allergies still affect many people throughout the year or even every day. Medicines used to treat allergies have side effects of their own, and it is difficult to bring the body into balance with the use of medicine. Regardless, many of those who live with allergies are grateful for what is available and find it useful in maintaining their lifestyles.

41. According to this passage, it can be understood that the word "militant" belongs in a group with the words:

- a. a. sickly, ailing, faint
- b. b. strength, power, vigor
- c. c. active, fighting, warring
- d. d. worn, tired, breaking down

42. The author says that "medicines used to treat allergies have side effects of their own" to

a. point out that doctors aren't very good at diagnosing and treating allergies

b. argue that because of the large number of people with allergies, a cure will never be found

c. explain that allergy medicines aren't cures and some compromise must be made

d. argue that more wholesome remedies should be researched and medicines banned

43. It can be inferred that _____ recommend that some people with allergies carry medicine with them.

   a. the author
   b. doctors
   c. the makers of EpiPen
   d. people with allergies

44. The author has written this passage to

   a. inform readers on symptoms of allergies so people with allergies can get help
   b. persuade readers to be proud of having allergies
   c. inform readers on different remedies so people with allergies receive the right help
   d. describe different types of allergies, their symptoms, and their remedies

Questions 45 - 48 refer to the following passage.

When a Poet Longs to Mourn, He Writes an Elegy

Poems are an expressive, especially emotional, form of writing. They have been present in literature virtually from the time civilizations invented the written word. Poets often portrayed as moody, secluded, and even troubled, but this is because poets are introspective and feel deeply about the current events and cultural norms they are surrounded with. Poets often produce the most telling literature, giving insight into the society and mind set they come from. This can be done in many forms.

The oldest types of poems often include many stanzas, may or may not rhyme, and are more about telling a story than experimenting with language or words. The most common types of ancient poetry are epics, which are usually extremely long stories that follow a hero through his journey, or ellegies, which are often solemn in tone and used to mourn or lament something or someone. The Mesopotamians are often said to have invented the written word, and their literature is among the oldest in the world, including the epic poem titled "Epic of Gilgamesh." Similar in style and length to "Gilgamesh" is "Beowulf," an ellegy poem written in Old English and set in Scandinavia. These poems are often used by professors as the earliest examples of literature.

The importance of poetry was revived in the Renaissance. At this time, Europeans discovered the style and beauty of ancient Greek arts, and poetry was among those. Shakespeare is the most well-known poet of the time, and he used poetry not only to write poems but also to write plays for the theater. The most popular forms of poetry during the Renaissance included villanelles, sonnets, as well as the epic. Poets during this time focused on style and form, and developed very specific rules and outlines for how an exceptional poem should be written.

As often happens in the arts, modern poets have rejected the constricting rules of Renaissance poets, and free form poems are much more popular. Some modern poems would read just like stories if they weren't arranged into lines and stanzas. It is difficult to tell which poems and poets will be the most important, because works of art often become more famous in hindsight, after the poet has died and society can look at itself without being in the moment. Modern poetry continues to develop, and will no doubt continue to change as values, thought, and writing continue to change.

Poems can be among the most enlightening and uplifting texts for a person to read if they are looking to connect with the past, connect with other people, or try to gain an understanding of what is happening in their time.

45. In summary, the author has written this passage

    a. as a foreword that will introduce a poem in a book or magazine

    b. because she loves poetry and wants more people to like it

    c. to give a brief history of poems

    d. to convince students to write poems

46. The author organizes the paragraphs mainly by

    a. moving chronologically, explaining which types of poetry were common in that time

    b. talking about new types of poems each paragraph and explaining them a little

    c. focusing on one poet or group of people and the poems they wrote

    d. explaining older types of poetry so she can talk about modern poetry

47. The author's claim that poetry has been around "virtually from the time civilizations invented the written word" is supported by the detail that

    a. Beowulf is written in Old English, which is not really in use any longer

    b. epic poems told stories about heroes

    c. the Renaissance poets tried to copy Greek poets

    d. the Mesopotamians are credited with both inventing the word and writing "Epic of Gilgamesh"

48. According to the passage, it can be understood that the word "telling" means

    a. Speaking

    b. Significant

    c. Soothing

    d. Wordy

Questions 49 – 50 refer to the following passage.

Winged Victory of Samothrace: the Statue of the Gods

Students who read about the "Winged Victory of Samothrace" probably won't be able to picture what this statue looks like. However, almost anyone who knows a little about statues will recognize it when they see it: it is the statue of a winged woman who does not have arms or a head. Even the most famous pieces of art may be recognized by sight but not by name.

This iconic statue is of the Greek goddess Nike, who represented victory and was called Victoria by the Romans. The statue is sometimes called the "Nike of Samothrace." She was often displayed in Greek art as driving a chariot, and her speed or efficiency with the chariot may be what her wings symbolize. It is said that the statue was created around 200 BCE to celebrate a battle that was won at sea. Archaeologists and art historians believe the statue may have originally been part of a temple or other building, even one of the most important temples, Megaloi Theoi, just as many statues were used during that time.

"Winged Victory" does indeed appear to have had arms and a head when it was originally created, and it is unclear why they were removed or lost. Indeed, they have never been discovered, even with all the excavation that has taken place. Many speculate that one of her arms was raised and put to her mouth, as though she was shouting or calling out, which is consistent with the idea of her as a war figure. If the missing pieces were ever to be found, they might give Greek and art historians more of an idea of what Nike represented or how the statue was used.

Learning about pieces of art through details like these can help students remember time frames or locations, as well as learn about the people who occupied them.

49. The author's title says the statue is "of the Gods" because

    a. the statue is very beautiful and even a god would find it beautiful

    b. the statue is of a Greek goddess, and gods were of primary importance to the Greek

    d. Nike lead the gods into war

    d. the statues were used at the temple of the gods and so it belonged to them

50. The third paragraph states that

    a. the statue is related to war and was probably broken apart by foreign soldiers

    b. the arms and head of the statue cannot be found because all the excavation has taken place

    c. speculations have been made about what the entire statue looked like and what it symbolized

    d. the statue has no arms or head because the sculptor lost them

Part II - Language Arts

Directions: Read the essay below, and answer questions 1 - 4.

Alvin Lee's Guitar

Only a few of his contemporaries rocked the rock n' roll era with their guitars like Alvin Lee.[1] Even at the age of 67, just a year before his demise, he produced one of the finest albums of his five-decade long career with *Still on the Road to Freedom.*[2] Strikingly flamboyant with his guitar, Lee gained millions of admirers around the world with hits like *"I'd Love to Change the World," "On the Road to Freedom"* and *"Freedom for the Stallion"* which reflected popular worldviews at the time of their release.[3]

Alvin Lee began playing guitar at an early age, and was influenced by his parents' passion for music and inspired by the likes of Chuck Berry and Scotty Moore.[4] Lee started his career as the lead vocalist and guitarist in a band named the Jaybirds at the famous Marquee Club in London in 1962.[5] A few years later the band changed its name to *Ten Years After* and released its debut album under the new name.[6] Lee's lightning fast guitar playing at the Woodstock Festival gained him instant stardom and Lee was asked to tour the US.[7]

In the coming years, he worked with rock legends like Mylon LeFevre, George Harrison, Steve Winwood, Ronnie Wood and Mick Fleetwood and released the country rock masterpiece *On the Road to Freedom* which brought him overwhelming trans-Atlantic popularity. [8] In subsequent years, he continued addressing social and global issues in albums like *A Space in Time, Pump Iron!, Let It Rock* and *Rocket Fuel*. [9] With many of his songs, such as, "I'd Love to Change the World," Lee used the power of rock music to show his solidarity with ordinary people and their worldviews. [10] He also went on with inspiring the upcoming generations of rock stars by producing expressive and tasteful guitar performances in his 1980s albums *Free Fall, RX5* and *Detroit Diesel*. [11]

1. Which sentence in the second paragraph is the least relevant to the main idea of the second paragraph?

    a. 4

    b. 5

    c. 6

    d. 7

2. Which of the following changes is/are needed in sentence 6?

    a. A few years later, the band changed its name to *Ten Years After* and released its debut album under the new name.

    b. A few years later, the band changed its name to *Ten Years After*, and released its debut album under the new name.

    c. A few years later the band changed its name to *Ten Years After*, and released its debut album under the new name.

    d. A few years later, the band changed its name to *Ten Years After* and, released its debut album under the new name.

3. Which of the following sentences, if inserted before sentence 11, would best illustrate the main idea of the passage?

a. His charismatic personality earned him more fame and led him to perform even better for the sake of his admirers.

b. As he gained popularity because of his artistic creations he tried to implant political motives into his music.

c. At the same time, he thought of doing something for the future generations.

d. With the creative songs he composed, he established himself as an exemplary figure among fellow guitarists and the generations that followed.

4. Which of the following changes are needed to sentence 11?

a. He also went on inspiring the upcoming generations of rock stars by producing expressive and tasteful guitar performances in his 1980s albums *Free Fall, RX5* and *Detroit Diesel*.

b. He also went on to inspire the upcoming generations of rock stars by producing expressive and tasteful guitar performances in his 1980s albums *Free Fall, RX5* and *Detroit Diesel*.

c. He also went with inspiring the upcoming generations of rock stars by producing expressive and tasteful guitar performances in his 1980s albums *Free Fall, RX5* and *Detroit Diesel*. .

d. He also went on to inspiring the upcoming generations of rock stars by producing expressive and tasteful guitar performances in his 1980s albums *Free Fall, RX5* and *Detroit Diesel*.

Read the essay below and answer questions 5 - 6.

Hansel and Gretel

. . . The boy was called Hansel and the girl Gretel. He had little to bite and to break, and once when great dearth fell on the land, he could no longer procure even daily bread. Now when he thought over this by night in his bed, and tossed about in his anxiety, he groaned and said to his wife: 'What is to become of us? How are we to feed our poor children, when we no longer have anything even for ourselves?' 'I'll tell you what, husband,' answered the woman, 'early tomorrow morning we will take the children out into the forest to where it is the thickest; there we will light a fire for them, and give each of them one more piece of bread, and then we will go to our work and leave them alone. They will not find the way home again, and we shall be rid of them.' 'No, wife,' said the man, 'I will not do that; how can I bear to leave my children alone in the forest?—the wild animals would soon come and tear them to pieces.' 'O, you fool!' said she, 'then we must all four die of hunger, you may as well plane the planks for our coffins,' and she left him no peace until he consented . . . .
- from Hansel and Gretel by Jacob and Wilhelm Grimm

5. Which of the following sentences best opens the paragraph above?

    a. There once was a rich man who dwelt in a great forest with his wife and his two children.

    b. Hard by a great forest dwelt a poor wood-cutter with his wife and his two children.

    c. Once upon a time, deep in the forest, dwelt a happy, loving family with two children.

    d. The Black Forest was home to a king and his two children, a boy and a girl.

6. Which of the following sentences best concludes the paragraph above?

    a. "I never had much love for the children," said the man.

    b. "Why give them one last piece of bread when they will soon be torn to pieces by wild animals?" said the man.

    c. "I refuse to be part of this wretched plan of yours," said the man.

    d. "But I feel very sorry for the poor children, all the same," said the man.

Read the paragraph below and answer questions 7 - 8.

Tom Sawyer

. . . Then they cooked some bacon in the frying pan and used up half of their cornbread. It was glorious to feast on an unexplored, uninhabited island. The boys agreed that they never would return to civilization. The fire lit their faces and threw its reddish glare on tree trunks and vines . . . .

    - from The Adventures of Tom Sawyer by Mark Twain

7. Which of the following sentences best opens the paragraph above?

    a. Tom had procured some bacon from his aunt to be used as sustenance for the day's adventure.

    b. Tom and Huck avoided school that morning and went into town for supplies.

    c. They built a fire alongside a large log about twenty steps inside the forest.

    d. They had always enjoyed paddling downriver looking for campsites.

8. Which of the following sentences best concludes the paragraph above?

    a. When the last crisp slice of bacon was gone and the last cornbread devoured, the boys contentedly stretched on the grass.

    b. Aunt Polly scoured the countryside looking for her long lost nephews, worried to death about how they could possibly survive the night.

    c. Then they began the long walk home, with enough bacon, cornbread and coffee to last for the rest of the afternoon.

    d. Tom felt like a king, enjoying the freedom of the newly discovered island, but decided that next time he would invite a companion to accompany him.

Read the paragraph below and answer questions 9 - 10.

The Divide

. . . It is useless for men that have cut hemlocks among the mountains of Sweden for forty years to try to be happy in a country as flat and gray and as naked as the sea. It is not easy for men that have spent their youths fishing in the Northern seas to be content with following a plow, and men that have served in the Austrian army hate hard work and coarse clothing and the loneliness of the plains, and long for marches and excitement and tavern company and pretty barmaids. After a man has passed his fortieth birthday it is not easy for him to change the habits and conditions of his life . . . .
    - from The Divide by Willa Cather

9. Which of the following sentences best opens the paragraph above?

   a. This generation of plains-dwellers finds happiness at every turn.

   b. The Divide brings with it a sense of peace and warmth that acts as a consolation for the rough existence one must lead there.

   c. Canute was overjoyed when he recognized his first hemlock leaves far up in the Swedish mountains as a boy.

   d. It may be that the next generation on the Divide will be very happy, but the present one came too late in life.

10. Which of the following sentences best concludes the paragraph above?

   a. Most men in the Divide were born into this desolate existence, their grandparents having come from far off lands, the scraps of their lives having already been left in all corners of the world.

   b. Most men bring with them to the Divide only the dregs of the lives that they have squandered in other lands and among other peoples.

   c. The opportunity that comes with a new life on the Divide gave these immigrants a youthful energy that they had not sensed in many years.

   d. Canute had carved out for himself a new life here on the Divide, and took pleasure in climbing the Swedish mountains each morning in search of hemlock.

Read the paragraph below and answer questions 11 - 12.

Robert Burns

. . . It is a lovely song about remembering times and people long past. What a great many English-speakers do not know is that the song they sing at the beginning of every New

Year was written by one of the greatest poets that ever lived. Robert Burns lived only 37 years (1759 – 1796), but in that time he became the greatest poet Scotland has ever known. He was a prolific writer whose celebrated career was cut short by his poor health. His work stands out as the voice of an accessible, genuine poet of the common people. Burns' charming and ingenious poetry came out of a centuries-old Scottish folk tradition of songs, poems and stories . . . .

11. Which of the following sentences best opens the paragraph above?

   a. In Scotland and the rest of the English-speaking world, there are few folk songs better known than "Auld Lang Syne."

   b. No one really understands the mystery of the Scottish folk song "Auld Lang Syne."

   c. For a long time, the folk song "Auld Lang Syne" was banned in Scotland.

   d. The anonymous Scottish poet that penned "Auld Lang Syne" would surely be proud of the song's modern popularity.

12. Which of the following sentences best concludes paragraph 6?

   a. In Burn's old age, he remained humble, despite being honored for his many decades of excellent poetry.

   b. Perhaps due to his noble upbringing, Burns could rarely change his stodgy point of view and understand the plight of the common people.

   c. The Scottish folk tradition has been carried on long after Burns' death, and his work has now become a definitive part of that tradition in Scotland.

   d. Burns remains largely unknown, and most of his work goes unread and unnoticed to this very day.

Read the paragraph below and answer questions 13 - 14.

New Orleans

... Wind damage and flood damage could be seen around every corner, but the death and homelessness caused by the storm were the most disheartening consequences. Refugees of Hurricane Katrina lived in hotels, cars, severely damaged homes, and FEMA trailers for months and even years on end after the hurricane. Most estimates put the storm's Louisiana death toll at over 1,500 people. New Orleans has been an historical and cultural center for centuries. It was the site of important battles during the War of 1812 and the American Civil War. Its unique blend of English, French, and Spanish settlers mixed with African slaves has created a culture that brought us all jazz music, voodoo, and creole cuisine . . . .

13. Which of the following sentences best opens the paragraph above?

   a. 1812 was a pivotal year in Louisiana history.

   b. The damage to New Orleans caused by 2005's Hurricane Katrina has been dramatically exaggerated.

   c. When one walked the streets of the old American city of New Orleans in 2006, it was difficult not to be moved by the destruction left by hurricane Katrina in August of the previous year.

   d. The damage to New Orleans caused by Hurricane Katrina was not so much measured in human lives: the main problems were plummeting property values and the high cost of rebuilding the historical city.

14. Which of the following sentences best concludes the paragraph above?

    a. I think that New Orleans would be an interesting place to visit, since it has such a rich history.

    b. The rich history of the city of New Orleans sharpens the agony of the tragic storm's destruction.

    c. The rich history of New Orleans makes it a perfect place for a family vacation or a historical tour.

    d. The 1,500 Louisianans that died in the War of 1812 have left a scar on the city of New Orleans.

15. Which sentence below has an error in punctuation, grammar, usage or capitalization?

    a. To make chicken soup you must first buy a chicken.

    b. To make chicken soup you must first, buy a chicken.

    c. To make chicken soup, you must first buy a chicken.

    d. None of the choices are correct.

16. Which sentence below has an error in punctuation, grammar, usage or capitalization?

    a. To travel around the globe, you have to drive 25000 miles.

    b. To travel around the globe, you have to drive, 25000 miles.

    c. None of the choices are correct.

    d. To travel around the globe, you have to drive 25,000 miles.

17. Which sentence below has an error in punctuation, grammar, usage or capitalization?

    a. The dog loved chasing bones, but never ate them; it was running that he enjoyed.

    b. The dog loved chasing bones; but never ate them, it was running that he enjoyed.

    c. The dog loved chasing bones, but never ate them, it was running that he enjoyed.

    d. None of the choices are correct.

18. Which sentence below has an error in punctuation, grammar, usage or capitalization?

a. None of the choices are correct.

b. He had not paid the rent; therefore, the landlord changed the locks.

c. He had not paid the rent, therefore; the landlord changed the locks.

d. He had not paid the rent therefore, the landlord changed the locks.

19. Which sentence below has an error in punctuation, grammar, usage or capitalization?

a. He would have postponed the camping trip, if he would have known about the forecast.

b. None of the choices are correct.

c. If he have known about the forecast, he would have postponed the camping trip.

d. If he had known about the forecast, he would have postponed the camping trip.

20. Which sentence below has an error in punctuation, grammar, usage or capitalization?

a. The sentence is correct.

b. Although you may not see anyone in the dark, it does not mean that not nobody is there.

c. Although you may not see anyone in the dark, it does not mean that anyone is there.

d. Although you may not see nobody in the dark, it does not mean that not nobody is there.

21. Which sentence below has an error in punctuation, grammar, usage or capitalization?

a. He doesn't have any money to buy clothes and neither do I.

b. He doesn't have any money to buy clothes and neither does I.

c. He don't have any money to buy clothes and neither do I.

d. None of the choices are correct.

22. Choose the sentence with the correct grammar.

a. Because it really don't matter, I don't care if I go there.
b. Because it really doesn't matter, I doesn't care if I go there.
c. Because it really doesn't matter, I don't care if I go there.
d. Because it really don't matter, I don't care if I go there.

23. Which sentence below has an error in punctuation, grammar, usage or capitalization?

a. None of the choices are correct.

b. If you come to the picnic, bring potato salad and wieners.

c. When we go to the picnic, we will bring potato salad and wieners.

d. If you come to the picnic, take potato salad and wieners.

24. Which sentence below has an error in punctuation, grammar, usage or capitalization?

a. The older children have already eat their dinner, but the baby has not yet eaten anything.

b. The older children have already eaten their dinner, but the baby has not yet ate anything.

c. The older children have already eaten their dinner, but the baby has not yet eaten anything.

d. The sentence is correct.

25. Which sentence below has an error in punctuation, grammar, usage or capitalization?

a. Newer cars use fewer gasoline, and produce fewer emissions.

b. None of the choices are correct.

c. Newer cars use less gasoline, and produce fewer emissions.

d. Newer cars fewer less gasoline, and produce less emissions.

26. Which sentence below has an error in punctuation, grammar, usage or capitalization?

a. He should have went to the appointment; instead, he went to the beach.

b. He should have gone to the appointment; instead, he went to the beach.

c. None of the choices are correct.

d. He should have gone to the appointment; instead, he gone to the beach.

27. Which sentence below has an error in punctuation, grammar, usage or capitalization?

a. However, I believe that he didn't really try that hard.

b. However I believe that he didn't really try that hard.

c. None of the choices are correct.

d. However: I believe that he didn't really try that hard.

28. Which sentence below has an error in punctuation, grammar, usage or capitalization?

a. Its important for you to know its official name; its called the Confederate Museum.

b. None of the choices are correct.

c. It's important for you to know its official name; it's called the Confederate Museum.

d. Its important for you to know it's official name; it's called the Confederate Museum.

29. Which sentence below has an error in punctuation, grammar, usage or capitalization?

a. Once the chickens had layed their eggs, they lay on their nests to hatch them.

b. Once the chickens had lay their eggs, they lay on their nests to hatch them.

c. Once the chickens had laid their eggs, they lay on their nests to hatch them.

d. None of the choices are correct.

30. Which sentence below has an error in punctuation, grammar, usage or capitalization?

  a. The mother would not of punished her daughter if she could have avoided it.

  b. The mother would not have punished her daughter if she could of avoided it.

  c. None of the choices are correct.

  d. The mother would not have punished her daughter if she could have avoided it.

31. Which sentence below has an error in punctuation, grammar, usage or capitalization?

  a. Even with an speed limit sign clearly posted, an inattentive driver may drive too fast.

  b. Even with a speed limit sign clearly posted, a inattentive driver may drive too fast.

  c. None of the choices are correct.

  d. Even with a speed limit sign clearly posted, an inattentive driver may drive too fast.

32. Which sentence below has an error in punctuation, grammar, usage or capitalization?

  a. Except for the roses, she did not accept John's frequent gifts.
  b. Accept for the roses, she did not except John's frequent gifts.
  c. None of the choices are correct.
  d. Except for the roses, she did not except John's frequent gifts.

33. Which sentence below has an error in punctuation, grammar, usage or capitalization?

    a. Although he continued to advise me, I no longer took his advice.

    b. Although he continued to advice me, I no longer took his advise.

    c. Although he continued to advise me, I no longer took his advise.

    d. None of the choices are correct.

34. Which sentence below has an error in punctuation, grammar, usage or capitalization?

    a. To adapt to the climate, we had to adapt a different style of clothing.

    b. To adopt to the climate, we had to adopt a different style of clothing.

    c. None of the choices are correct.

    d. To adapt to the climate, we had to adopt a different style of clothing.

35. Which sentence below has an error in punctuation, grammar, usage or capitalization?

    a. None of the choices are correct.

    b. When he's among friends, Robert seems confident, but, among you and me, he is really shy.

    c. When he's between friends, Robert seems confident, but, among you and me, he is really shy.

    d. When he's among friends, Robert seems confident, but, between you and me, he is really shy.

36. Which sentence below has an error in punctuation, grammar, usage or capitalization?

a. I will be finished at ten in the morning, and will be arriving at home at about 6:30.

b. None of the choices are correct.

c. I will be finished at about ten in the morning, and will be arriving at home at about 6:30.

d. I will be finished at ten in the morning, and will be arriving at home at 6:30.

37. Which sentence below has an error in punctuation, grammar, usage or capitalization?

a. Beside the red curtains and pillows, there was a red rug beside the couch.

b. Besides the red curtains and pillows, there was a red rug beside the couch.

c. Besides the red curtains and pillows, there was a red rug besides the couch.

d. None of the choices are correct.

38. Which sentence below has an error in punctuation, grammar, usage or capitalization?

a. Although John can swim very well, the lifeguard may not allow him to swim in the pool.

b. None of the choices are correct.

c. Although John can swim very well, the lifeguard can not allow him to swim in the pool.

d. Although John may swim very well, the lifeguard may not allow him to swim in the pool.

39. Which sentence below has an error in punctuation, grammar, usage or capitalization?

a. Her continuous absences caused a continual disruption at the office.

b. Her continual absences caused a continuous disruption at the office.

c. Her continual absences caused a continual disruption at the office.

d. None of the choices are correct.

40. Which sentence below has an error in punctuation, grammar, usage or capitalization?

a. During the famine, the Irish people had to emigrate to other countries; many of them immigrated to the United States.

b. None of the choices are correct.

c. During the famine, the Irish people had to emigrate to other countries; many of them emigrated to the United States.

d. During the famine, the Irish people had to immigrate to other countries; many of them emigrated to the United States.

41. Which sentence below has an error in punctuation, grammar, usage or capitalization?

a. His home was farther than we expected; farther, the roads were very bad.

b. His home was farther than we expected; further, the roads were very bad.

c. None of the choices are correct.

d. His home was further than we expected; farther, the roads were very bad.

42. Which sentence below has an error in punctuation, grammar, usage or capitalization?

    a. The volunteers brought groceries and toys to the homeless shelter; the latter were given to the staff, while the former were given directly to the children.
    b. The volunteers brought groceries and toys to the homeless shelter; the former was given to the staff, while the latter was given directly to the children.
    c. The volunteers brought groceries and toys to the homeless shelter; the groceries were given to the staff, while the former was given directly to the children.
    d. None of the choices are correct.

43. Read the sentence below.

Mankind's thirst for knowledge about ourselves and the universe has always been insatiable, making curiosity a driving force for human advances through history.

How would you re-write this sentence?

    a. No changes

    b. Mankind's thirst for knowledge has always been insatiable, making curiosity a driving factor for human advances through history.

    c. Mankind's thirst for knowledge is insatiable, making curiosity a driving factor for human advances through history.

    d. Humankind's thirst for knowledge is insatiable, making curiosity a driving force in advances throughout history.

Read the paragraph below and answer question 44.

Curiosity was launched in late November 2011 from Cape Canaveral Air Force Station in Florida. [1] It successfully landed on Mars on August 6, 2012 searching for evidence of life. [2] The car sized robot, weighing about a ton, is equipped with all the technical capacities to carry out its mission to explore our neighbor for biological, geological and geochemical traces of life. [3] It will also test the Martian soil and surface to collect data about its planetary evolution and surface radiation. [4]

44. Which sentence in this paragraph is least relevant to the main idea?

    a. 1
    b. 3
    c. 4
    d. 2

Read the sentence below and answer question 45.

So far, NASA has carried out several exploratory missions to Mars and the rover robot Curiosity is the latest and most sophisticated.

45. What changes are needed to this sentence?

    a. So far, "NASA" has carried out several exploration missions to Mars and the rover robot Curiosity is the latest and most sophisticated of all.

    b. So far, NASA has carried out several exploratory missions to Mars and the rover robot Curiosity is the latest and most sophisticated of all.

    c. So far, NASA has carried out several exploration missions to Mars and the rover robot -Curiosity- is the latest and most sophisticated of all.

    d. So far, NASA has carried out several exploratory missions to Mars and the rover robot "Curiosity" is the latest and most sophisticated of all.

Read the sentence below and answer question 46.

Oleic acid, the main ingredient of olive oil, absorbs infrared radiation is the major component of the Sun's radiation reaching the Earth.

46. Which of the following changes are needed in this sentence?

a. Oleic acid, the main ingredient of olive oil, absorbs infrared radiation is the major component of the Sun's radiation reaching the Earth.

b. Oleic acid, the main ingredient of olive oil, absorbs infrared radiation, which is the major component of the Sun's radiation reaching the Earth.

c. Oleic acid, the main ingredient of olive oil absorbs infrared radiation that is the major component of the Sun's radiation reaching the Earth.

d. Oleic acid, the main ingredient of olive oil, absorbs infrared radiation what is the major component of the Sun's radiation reaching the Earth.

Read the sentence below and answer question 47.

With continued concern over global climate change, environmentalists are urging governments for lowering their dependence on fossil fuels in order for ensuring reduced carbon emission into the atmosphere.

47. Which of the following changes are needed in this sentence?

a. With continued concern over global climate change, environmentalists are urging governments to lowering their dependence on fossil fuels in order to ensuring reduced carbon emission into the atmosphere.

b. With continued concern over global climate change, environmentalists are urging governments lower their dependence on fossil fuels in order for ensuring reduced carbon emission into the atmosphere.

c. With continued concern over global climate change, environmentalists are urging governments to lower their dependence on fossil fuels in order for ensuring reduced carbon emission into the atmosphere.

d. With continued concern over global climate change,

environmentalists are urging governments to lower their dependence on fossil fuels in order to ensure reduced carbon emission into the atmosphere.

Read the paragraph below and answer question 48.

The key feature of the new tool, according to Professor Sarah Parcak, who discovered many cities, temples and pyramids covered under sands and sediment; is that it offers a wider perspective in size and scale of the location under study. [1] Along with the visual information that the satellite images provide, numerous details about the sites can be obtained from infrared (IR) and gravitational field images. [2] This information, coupled with conventional on-site procedures, are vital for archeology. [3]

48. Which of the following changes to sentence 3 would focus attention on the main idea?

    a. These information, along with a supply of some heavy machinery, will help the excavation of every archeological site accomplished within a short period of time.

    b. This information, coupled with conventional on-site procedures, help archeologists plan their excavation carefully and efficiently.

    c. Such details are valuable records of ancient history and are essential assets of any civilization.

    d. Such details, unfortunately, are available to archeological firms who are willing to invest a lot of money on putting satellites into orbit.

49. What changes are needed in sentence 1 of the paragraph above?

    a. The key feature of the new tool- according to Professor Sarah Parcak, who discovered many cities, temples and pyramids covered under sands and sediment- is that it offers a wider perspective in size and scale of the location under study.

    b. The key feature of the new tool- according to Professor Sarah Parcak- who discovered many cities, temples and pyramids covered under sands and sediment, is that it offers a wider perspective in size and scale of the location under study.

c. The key feature of the new tool according to Professor Sarah Parcak- who discovered many cities, temples and pyramids covered under sands and sediment- is that it offers a wider perspective in size and scale of the location under study.

d. The key feature of the new tool, according to Professor Sarah Parcak- who discovered many cities, temples and pyramids covered under sands and sediment is that it offers a wider perspective in size and scale of the location under study.

Read the sentence below and answer question 50.

Malala's dreams were encountered with the obstacles that were also crushing the aspirations of millions of other young girls like her.

50. Which of the following changes are needed to this sentence?

a. Malala's dreams were countered with the obstacles that were also crushing the aspirations of millions of other young girls like her.

b. Malala's dreams were met with the obstacles that were also destroying the aspirations of millions of other young girls like her.

c. Malala's dreams encountered the same obstacles that were also crushing the aspirations of millions of other young girls like her.

d. Malala's dreams were confronted with the obstacles that were also shattering the aspirations of millions of other young girls like her.

Part III - Mathematics

1. Brad has agreed to buy everyone a Coke. Each drink costs $1.89, and there are 5 friends. Estimate Brad's cost.

   a. $7
   b. $8
   c. $10
   d. $12

2. Sarah weighs 25 pounds more than Tony does. If together they weigh 205 pounds, how much does Sarah weigh approximately in kilograms? Assume 1 pound = 0.4535 kilograms.

   a. 41
   b. 48
   c. 50
   d. 52

3. What fraction of $1500 is $75?

   a. 1/14
   b. 3/5
   c. 7/10
   d. 1/20

4. Estimate 16 x 230.

   a. 31,000
   b. 301,000
   c. 3,100
   d. 3,000,000

5. Below is the attendance for a class of 45.

Day	Number of Absent Students
Monday	5
Tuesday	9
Wednesday	4
Thursday	10
Friday	6

What is the average attendance for the week?

    a. 88%
    b. 85%
    c. 81%
    d. 77%

6. John purchased a jacket at a 7% discount. He had a membership which gave him an additional 2% discount on the discounted price. If he paid $425, what is the retail price of the jacket?

    a. $460
    b. $470
    c. $466
    d. $472

7. Estimate 215 x 65.

    a. 1,350
    b. 13,500
    c. 103,500
    d. 3,500

8. 10 x 2 − (7 + 9)

   a. 21
   b. 16
   c. 4
   d. 13

9. 40% of a number is equal to 90. What is the half of the number?

   a. 18
   b. 112.5
   c. 225
   d. 120

10. 1/4 + 3/10 =

   a. 9/10
   b. 11/20
   c. 7/15
   d. 3/40

11. A map uses a scale of 1:2,000   How much distance on the ground is 5.2 inches on the map if the scale is in inches?

   a. 100,400
   b. 10,500
   c. 10,400
   d. 1,400

12. A shop sells a piece of equipment for $545. If 15% of the cost was added to the price as value added tax, what is the actual cost of the equipment?

    a. $490.40
    b. $473.91
    c. $505.00
    d. $503.15

13. What is 0.27 + 0.33 expressed as a fraction?

    a. 3/6
    b. 4/7
    c. 3/5
    d. 2/7

14. 5 men have to share a load weighing 10 kg 550 g equally among themselves. How much will each man have to carry?

    a. 900 g
    b. 1.5 kg
    c. 3 kg
    d. 2 kg 110 g

15. 1/4 + 11/16

    a. 9/16
    b. 1 1/16
    c. 11/16
    d. 15/12

16. A square lawn has an area of 62,500 square meters. What is the cost of building fence around it at a rate of $5.5 per meter?

   a. $4,000
   b. $5,500
   c. $4,500
   d. $5,000

17. A mother is 7 times older than her child. In 25 years, her age will be double that of her child. How old is the mother now?

   a. 35
   b. 33
   c. 30
   d. 25

18. Convert 0.28 to a fraction.

   a. 7/25
   b. 3.25
   c. 8/25
   d. 5/28

19. If a discount of 20% is given for a desk and Mark saves $45, how much did he pay for the desk?

   a. $225
   b. $160
   c. $180
   d. $210

20. In a grade 8 exam, students are asked to divide a number by 3/2, but a student mistakenly multiplied the number by 3/2 and the answer is 5 more than the required one. What was the number?

   a. 4
   b. 5
   c. 6
   d. 8

21. Divide 243 by 3^3

   a. 243
   b. 11
   c. 9
   d. 27

22. Solve the following equation $4(y + 6) = 3y + 30$

   a. y = 20
   b. y = 6
   c. y = 30/7
   d. y = 30

23. Divide $x^2 - y^2$ by $x - y$.

   a. x - y
   b. x + y
   c. xy
   d. y - x

24. Solve for x if, $10^2 \times 100^2 = 1000^x$

   a. x = 2
   b. x = 3
   c. x = -2
   d. x = 0

25. Given polynomials $A = -2x^4 + x^2 - 3x$, $B = x^4 - x^3 + 5$ and $C = x^4 + 2x^3 + 4x + 5$, find $A + B - C$.

    a. $x^3 + x^2 + x + 10$
    b. $-3x^3 + x^2 - 7x + 10$
    c. $-2x^4 - 3x^3 + x^2 - 7x$
    d. $-3x^4 + x^3 + 2 - 7x$

26. Solve the inequality: $(x - 6)^2 \geq x^2 + 12$

    a. $(2, +\infty)$
    b. $[2, +\infty)$
    c. $(-\infty, 2]$
    d. $(12, +\infty)$

27. $7^5 - 3^5 =$

    a. 15,000
    b. 16,564
    c. 15,800
    d. 15,007

28. Divide $x^3 - 3x^2 + 3x - 1$ by $x - 1$.

    a. $x^2 - 1$
    b. $x^2 + 1$
    c. $x^2 - 2x + 1$
    d. $x^2 + 2x + 1$

29. Express 9 x 9 x 9 in exponential form and standard form.

    a. $9^3 = 719$
    b. $9^3 = 629$
    c. $9^3 = 729$
    d. $10^3 = 729$

30. Using the factoring method, solve the quadratic equation: $x^2 - 5x - 6 = 0$

    a. -6 and 1
    b. -1 and 6
    c. 1 and 6
    d. -6 and -1

31. Divide 0.524 by 10^3

    a. 0.0524
    b. 0.000524
    c. 0.00524
    d. 524

32. Factor the polynomial $x^3y^3 - x^2y^8$.

    a. $x^2y^3(x - y^5)$
    b. $x^3y^3(1 - y^5)$
    c. $x^2y^2(x - y^6)$
    d. $xy^3(x - y^5)$

33. Find the solution for the following linear equation:
$5x/2 = (3x + 24)/6$

    a. -1
    b. 0
    c. 1
    d. 2

34. Find 2 numbers whose difference is 11 and product is -24. (There is more than one solution.)

    a. (3,-8)
    b. (-3,8)
    c. (-3,-8)
    d. a and b

35. Solve the system, if a is some real number:

ax + y = 1
x + ay = 1

    a. (1, a)
    b. (1/a + 1, 1)
    c. (1/(a + 1), 1/(a + 1))
    d. (a, 1/a + 1)

36. Draw a reflection of the circle with the center in O with the given mirror line m.

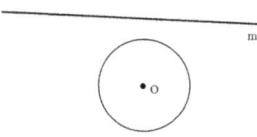

37. Solve the linear equation: 3(x + 2) - 2(1 - x) = 4x + 5

    a. -1
    b. 0
    c. 1
    d. 2

38. Simplify the following expression: $3x^a + 6a^x - x^a + (-5a^x) - 2x^a$

    a. $a^x + x^a$
    b. $a^x - x^a$
    c. a^x
    d. x^a

9. **Add polynomials $-3x^2 + 2x + 6$ and $-x^2 - x - 1$.**

    a. $-2x^2 + x + 5$

    b. $-4x^2 + x + 5$

    c. $-2x^2 + 3x + 5$

    d. $-4x^2 + 3x + 5$

40. **10^4 is NOT equal to which of the following?**

    a. 100,000

    b. 10 x 10 x 10 x 10

    c. 10^2 x 10^2

    d. 10,000

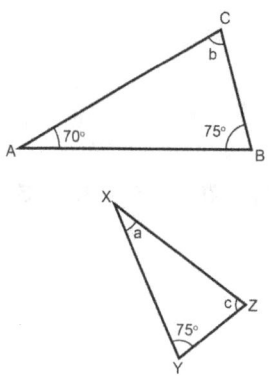

41. **What are the respective values of a, b & c if both triangles are similar?**

    a. 70°, 70°, 35°

    b. 70°, 35°, 70°

    c. 35°, 35°, 35°

    d. 70°, 35°, 35°

42. For what x is the following equation correct:

$$\log_x 125 = 3$$

a. 1
b. 2
c. 3
d. 5

43. What is the value of the expression $(1 - 4\sin^2(\pi/6))/(1 + 4\cos^2(\pi/3))$?

a. -2
b. -1
c. 0
d. 1/2

44. Calculate $(\sin^2 30° - \sin 0°)/(\cos 90° - \cos 60°)$.

a. -1/2
b. 2/3
c. 0
d. 1/2

45. Consider 2 triangles, ABC and A'B'C', where:

BC = B' C'
AC = A' C'
RA = RA'

Are these 2 triangles congruent?

a. Yes
b. No
c. Not enough information

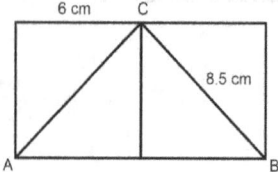

Note: Figure not drawn to scale

46. What is the perimeter of △ABC in the above shape? Assume the quadrangles above are identical rectangles.

    a. 25.5 cm
    b. 27 cm
    c. 30 cm
    d. 29 cm

47. Find the cotangent of a right angle.

    a. -1
    b. 0
    c. 1/2
    d. -1/2

48. If angle a is equal to the expression $3\pi/2 - \pi/6 - \pi - \pi/3$, find sina.

    a. 0
    b. 1/2
    c. 1
    d. 3/2

49. Find x if $\log_x(9/25) = 2$.

    a. 3/5
    b. 5/3
    c. 6/5
    d. 5/6

50. Draw a reflection of the parallelogram ABCD with the given mirror line m.

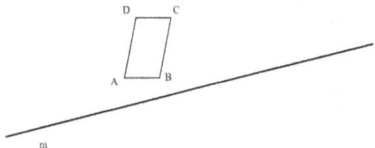

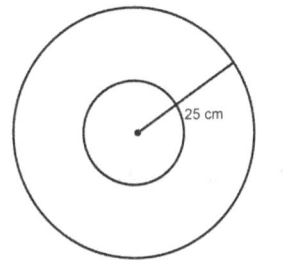

Note: Figure not drawn to scale

51. What is the distance travelled by the wheel above, when it makes 175 revolutions?

    a. 87.5 π m
    b. 875 π m
    c. 8.75 π m
    d. 8750 π m

52. Divide number 21 so that sum of squares of these 2 numbers is 261?

    a. 14 and 7
    b. 15 and 6
    c. 16 and 5
    d. 17 and 4

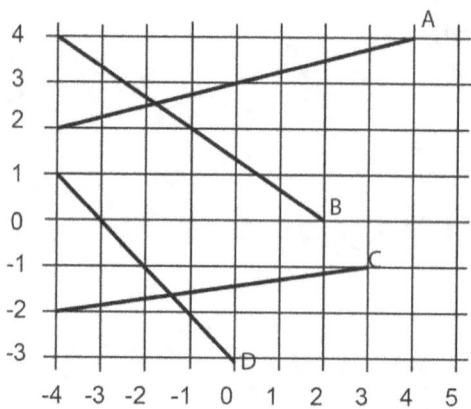

53. Which of the lines above represents the equation 2y − x = 4?

    a. A
    b. B
    c. C
    d. D

54. For any a, find tga•ctga.

    a. -1
    b. 0
    c. 1/2
    d. 1

55. If cosa = 3/5 and b = 24, find side c.

    a. 25
    b. 30
    c. 35
    d. 40

56. Find the sides of a right triangle whose sides are consecutive numbers.

    a. 1, 2, 3
    b. 2, 3, 4
    c. 3, 4, 5
    d. 4, 5, 6

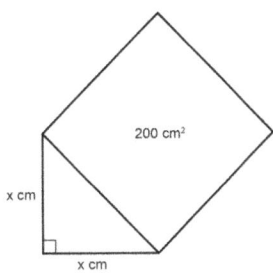

Note: Figure not drawn to scale

57. What is the length of the sides in the triangle above? Assume the quadrangle in the figure above is a square.

    a. 10
    b. 20
    c. 100
    d. 40

58. Calculate $(\cos(\pi/2) + \operatorname{ctg}(\pi/2))/\sin(\pi/2)$.

    a. -2
    b. -1
    c. 0
    d. 1/2

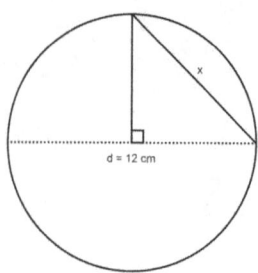

Note: Figure not drawn to scale

59. Calculate the length of side x.

    a. 6.46
    b. 8.48
    c. 3.6
    d. 6.4

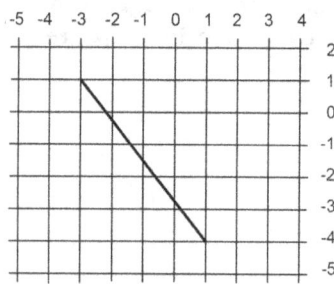

60. What is the slope of the line shown above?

    a. 5/4
    b. -4/5
    c. -5/4
    d. -4/5

Part IV - Social Studies

US History

1. Which one of these was NOT part of the Intolerable Acts?

    a. The Stamp Act

    b. The Townshed Acts

    c. The Tea Act

    d. The Foreign Trade Act

2. The British American colonists revolted because

    a. most colonists wanted to be free from British rule.

    b. most colonists wanted to be represented in Parliament.

    c. most colonists did not want to be taxed.

    d. All of the Above

3. Why did the British Parliament impose the first of the Intolerable Acts?

    a. To raise revenue for British Parliamentary salaries

    b. To pay for the British military in the American Colonies

    c. To make trade with non-British countries more expensive

    d. To fund the British military's ongoing war in India

4. What was the last plea to Great Britain to avert the American Revolutionary War?

    a. The Olive Branch Petition

    b. The Dove Accords

    c. Jefferson's Plea

    d. Adam's Plea

5. Why did the First Continental Congress meet?

    a. Respond to the Intolerable Acts

    b. Establish a military

    c. Establish a federal government

    d. Address issues of states rights

6. Why did the Second Continental Congress meet?

    a. Establish a federal government

    b. Respond to the Intolerable Acts

    c. Ask for aid from the French

    d. Establish a military

7. What document announced a state of war between the British American colonists and Great Britain?

    a. The Articles of Confederation

    b. The Declaration of Independence

    c. The United States Constitution

    d. The Declaration of Hostilities

8. Which of these was NOT considered part of Manifest Destiny?

    a. American people and institutions are special

    b. America had a mission to turn the west into an agrarian landscape

    c. America's destiny was to settle the west

    d. All of the above are correct

9. **What was the start of western expansion?**

   a. The Clermont steamboat

   b. The Mexican American War

   c. The invention of the telegraph

   d. The discovery of gold in California

10. **When did the Gold Rush start in California?**

    a. 1849

    b. 1848

    c. 1855

    d. 1851

World History

11. **What is an early human civilization that smelted copper and alloyed it with tin?**

    a. The Tin Age

    b. The Bronze Age

    c. The Stone Age

    d. The Iron Age

12. **Which of these are NOT a trait of Classical Greece (4th and 5th centuries BCE)?**

    a. The Punic Wars

    b. The Persian Wars

    c. The Parthenon

    d. The philosopher Socrates

13. What political practice, that still influences governments today, was started in Classical Greece?

    a. Dictatorship

    b. Communism

    c. Capitalism

    d. Democracy

14. What are Ares, Aphrodite, Demeter and Athena examples of?

    a. Greek gods

    b. Roman gods

    c. Egyptian gods

    d. Norse gods

15. Which of these did NOT contribute to the fall of the Roman Empire?

    a. The spread of Christianity

    b. Political instability

    c. Invasion by Egyptian forces

    d. Over reliance on slave labor

16. What is/are the Vedas in ancient Indian history?

    a. A time period in which the region saw great economic, social and religious freedom.

    b. The ruling class

    c. A group of people who took over the original Harappan people of India.

    d. Texts discussing the history and religion of Indian peoples and transmitted orally.

17. What was the first recorded Chinese dynasty?

    a. Xia Dynasty

    b. Han Dynasty

    c. Tang Dynasty

    d. Qing Dynasty

18. Which of these inventions were NOT invented by the Chinese?

    a. Paper making

    b. Chemical warfare

    c. Gunpowder

    d. Calculus

19. Which religion allows people to follow the Eightfold Path to Nirvana?

    a. Buddhism

    b. Hinduism

    c. Islam

    d. Taoism

20. What major religion emerged through the prophet Muhammad in Arabia in 7th century CE?

    a. Christianity

    b. Islam

    c. Judaism

    d. Zoroastrianism

Civics and Government

21. What is a political system with a king or queen as leader?

    a. Monarchy

    b. Republic

    c. Democracy

    d. Utopia

22. The concept of voting dates back to

    a. The Enlightenment.

    b. The American Revolution.

    c. Ancient civilizations.

    d. The Renaissance.

23. How is government conducted under a dictatorship?

    a. A strong leader is held responsible to the will of the people

    b. Elected representatives from different parties compromise to create laws

    c. Authority rests with the people

    d. A strong ruler is not held responsible to the will of the people

24. What concept gives a government supreme power within its own territory?

    a. Nationalism

    b. Sovereignty

    c. Justice

    d. Liberty

25. What is a government controlled by the wealthy?

   a. A democracy
   b. A dictatorship
   c. A monarchy
   d. An plutocracy

26. The ancient Romans had a legislative branch of government known as the

   a. Emperor
   b. President
   c. Supreme Court
   d. Senate

27. What is a government controlled by elected representatives?

   a. A Republic
   b. Utopia
   c. A Monarchy
   d. A Oligarchy

28. The primary purpose of the Magna Carta was to

   a. Limit the power of the English peasants.
   b. Limit the power of the English Parliament.
   c. Limit the power of the English Military.
   d. Limit the power of the English King.

29. What is a government controlled by religious leaders based on adherence to a religion?

   a. Plutocracy
   b. Monarchy
   c. Anarchy
   d. Theocracy

30. What is a constitution?

   a. A document that outlines the principles and structure of a government

   b. A document that summons citizens to court

   c. A document that petitions the government for grievances

   d. A document that abolished slavery

Economics

31. As demand increases, supply tends to

   a. decrease.
   b. increase.
   c. remain the same.
   d. fluctuate.

32. As supply increases, prices tend to

   a. rise.
   b. fall.
   c. remain the same.
   d. fluctuate.

33. As economy of scale increase, products are

   a. expensive to produce at first, but eventually become less expensive.

   b. cheap to produce at first, but eventually become more expensive.

   c. expensive to produce because they are customized to individual customers.

   d. sold to the highest bidder.

34. Which of the following is true of a free market economy?

a. The government owns the resources but allows citizens to own private property.

b. The government owns the resources and does not allow citizens to own private property.

c. Resources and private property are owned by citizens.

d. Resources are owned by citizens, but not private property.

35. Which of the following is true of a command economy?

a. The government owns the resources but allows citizens to own private property.

b. The government owns the resources and does not allow citizens to own private property.

c. Resources and private property are both owned by citizens.

d. Resources are owned by citizens, but not private property.

36. What is capital?

a. A measure of individual income.

b. The head of a company, also known as the CEO.

c. The resources needed to start or expand a business.

d. A meeting place for a company's board of directors.

37. What is inflation?

a. An expansion of business

b. An increase in the value of money

c. A decrease in the value of money

d. A growth in unemployment

38. A country's labor force excludes

    a. employees that work as professionals

    b. employees that are not union members

    c. employees that are union members

    d. children that are too young to work

39. Which of the following is a good example of a blue collar occupation?

    a. Miner

    b. Professor

    c. Scientist

    d. Accountant

40. What is consumer confidence?

    a. The optimism held by the general public regarding the economy.

    b. The trust that consumers have that the products they buy are safe.

    c. The demand for a product.

    d. The marketing used to make products seem valuable.

Geography

41. Which of the following is not a reason humans move to urban areas?

    a. Excitement

    b. Education

    c. Open spaces

    d. Job opportunities

42. The era of human existence before writing was developed is known as

    a. Ancient history

    b. Prehistory

    c. Recorded history

    d. Unknown history

43. A thin stretch of land that connects two large areas of land is called

    a. a glacier.

    b. a peninsula.

    c. an isthmus.

    d. an ice sheet.

44. What is an ecosystem?

    a. a group of environmentalists that fight pollution

    b. a group of living organisms and their surrounding environment

    c. a law that delineates city zones

    d. a set of protocols that ensure environmental sustainability

45. Which ocean borders the east coast of Africa?

    a. The Atlantic ocean

    b. The Indian ocean

    c. The Arctic ocean

    d. The Pacific ocean

46. Cuba, Haiti and Puerto Rico are located in the

    a. Caribbean Sea.

    b. North Sea.

    c. Indian Ocean.

    d. Black Sea.

47. The Ural Mountains separate the continents of

    a. North and South America.

    b. Africa and Asia.

    c. Australia and Asia.

    d. Europe and Asia.

48. Australia is a very large

    a. continent.

    b. ocean.

    c. island.

    d. peninsula.

49. A nation is also known as

    a. a country.

    b. a government.

    c. a society.

    d. a utopia.

50. Which of the following is shown most clearly on a physical map?

    a. the borders of countries

    b. the movements of various populations

    c. the ruins of ancient civilizations

    d. features such as mountains, lakes and rivers

Part V - Science

Physical Science

1. The tendency of an atom to attract a shared pair of electrons towards itself is known as

   a. Ionization potential
   b. Electronegativity
   c. Electron affinity
   d. Dipole moment

2. The energy needed to remove an electron from the gaseous state of an atom or molecule is called

   a. Electron affinity
   b. Ionization energy
   c. Lattice energy
   d. Electronegativity

3. The bond formed between elements of low ionization energy and high electronegativity is usually:

   a. Coordinate
   b. Covalent
   c. Metallic
   d. Ionic

4. The ionic compound X+Y- is usually formed when

   a. Ionization energy of X is low.
   b. Electronegativity of D is high.
   c. X is a metal and Y is a non-metal.
   d. All of the above

5. A coordinate covalent bond is formed through

   a. Sharing Of Electrons.
   b. Donation of Electron.
   c. Donation of both electrons by a single atom.
   d. None of These

6. Which of the following only involve ionic bonds.

   a. Li3N
   b. NaCl
   c. NCl3
   d. O2

7. Which of the following involve covalent bonds only:

   a. KF
   b. KCl
   c. CH4
   d. MgCl2

8. Equilibrium is said to be achieved in a Chemical reaction when

   a. Opposing reaction stops
   b. Resultant product is achieved.
   c. Concentration of reactants and products remains constant
   d. Rate constants of opposing reactions are equal.

9. A Reversible Chemical Reaction occurs when

a. Reactants are reactive
b. Reactants are stable
c. Products are stable
d. Products are reactive

10. An increase in temperature during a reversible exothermic reaction will

a. Stop the chemical reaction.
b. Shift the equilibrium towards Reactants side
c. Shift the equilibrium towards Product side
d. None of the above

11. An Increase in temperature during a reversible endothermic reaction will

a. Stop the chemical reaction.
b. Shift the equilibrium towards Reactants side
c. Shift the equilibrium towards Product side
d. None of the above

12. During a reversible exothermic chemical reaction, High value of Kc at equilibrium indicates the presence of

a. More products as compared to Reactants
b. More Reactant as compared to products
c. Same ratio of reactants and products
d. None of the above

13. The solubility of Ca(OH)2 is exothermic. An increase in temperature will cause solubility to

    a. Increase

    b. Decrease

    c. Remain constant

    d. None of the above

14. For the given chemical reaction at equilibrium, which of the following changes will cause production of SO_3 to increase

$2SO_2 + O_2 \rightarrow 2SO_3 + heat$?

    a. Decrease in Pressure

    b. Increase in Temperature

    c. Decrease in Temperature

    d. Addition of SO_3

15. Which of the following is true about "activation energy?"

    a. It is the minimum energy required to activate Atoms/Molecules to undergo Chemical transformation.

    b. It is the Energy content difference between activated/transition-state and initial configuration.

    c. It is calculated through experimental rate constants or diffusion coefficients measured at different temperatures.

    d. All of the above

16. The rate of a Chemical Reaction _____ as the reaction proceeds

    a. Increases

    b. Decreases

    c. Remains constant

    d. Doubles

Practice Test Questions 1

17. The rate of a chemical reaction at _____ is referred as the "instantaneous" rate.

   a. The beginning
   b. The end
   c. Any given time
   d. None of the above

18. What will be the order of chemical reaction if its rate is independent of concentration of reactant molecules?

   a. 1
   b. 0
   c. 2
   d. None of the above

19. A (an) _____ is a substance which retards the rate of a chemical reaction.

   a. Enzyme
   b. Promoter
   c. Inhibitor
   d. Auto catalyst

20. Which of the following statements best explains the Law of Conservation of Mass applied to a burning candle?

   a. Energy released after burning is equal to amount of wax before burning.
   b. The mass of smoke after burning is equal to mass of wick before burning.
   c. The total mass of wick, wax and burnt oxygen before the reaction equals the mass of gases and smoke produced as a result of reaction.
   d. Total mass of molecules of candle before the reaction is equal to the total mass of the candle and burned wick after the reaction

Life Science

21. Fungi lack chlorophyll and their body consists of long and branched thread like filaments called hyphae. This anatomy allows them to absorb organic molecules from digested dead organic matter. Hence, they are considered as:

    a. Phototrophs

    b. Absorptive autotrophs

    c. Absorptive heterotrophs

    d. Lithotrophs

22. 'Autotroph' has Greek origin which means self-nourishing or self-feeding. Organisms from which of the following kingdoms are considered as autotrophs:

    a. Kingdom Protista

    b. Kingdom Fungi

    c. Kingdom Plantae

    d. All except 'b'

23. Which of the statements is true regarding differences among heterotrophs and autotrophs?

    a. Heterotrophs usually contain chlorophyll and prepare their food but autotrophs can't do this.

    b. Autotrophs have machinery for absorbing nutrition from outside environment

    c. Autotrophs and heterotrophs have different energy pathways

    d. Photosynthesis is a characteristic possessed by heterotrophs

24. What is the most common fuel used by the cell to provide energy through cellular respiration?

a. Alcohol
b. Glucose
c. Pyruvate
d. Lactic acid

25. Cellular respiration can be sub-divided into 4 stages, correct sequence for these stages is :

a. Glycolysis, pyruvate oxidation, Kreb's cycle (TCA), Respiratory chain
b. Respiratory chain, Glycolysis, pyruvate oxidation, Kreb's cycle (TCA)
c. Glycolysis, Respiratory chain, pyruvate oxidation, Kreb's cycle (TCA)
d. Respiratory chain, Glycolysis, Kreb's cycle (TCA), pyruvate oxidation

26. What environment does water enter the cell, the cell solution dilutes, and the cell becomes turgid.

a. Hypertonic
b. Hypotonic
c. Isotonic
d. Mesotonic

27. When food is ingested, blood sugar rises. Pancreas releases insulin and blood sugar is lowered to the normal limit. After that, pancreas stops producing insulin. This is an example of:

a. Positive feedback mechanism
b. Afferent pathway
c. Negative feedback mechanism
d. Thermoregulation

28. In a scenario where a red flower (RR) is crossed with a white flower (rr). The progeny (F_1) appeared as: 25% red flowers, 50% pink flowers and 25% white flowers. This is a case of:

    a. Over dominance

    b. Co-dominance

    c. Incomplete dominance

    d. Complete dominance

29. Which case does not obey Mendel's law of independent assortment at times?

    a. Crossing over

    b. Linked genes

    c. Co-dominance

    d. All X-linked genes

30. Which recessive trait will appear as phenotype in progeny in case of heterozygosity?

    a. X-linked in male

    b. Y-linked in male

    c. Autosomal in male

    d. Both a and b

31. Cancer is uncontrolled cell division. This unwanted proliferation of cells leads to a clone of cells called tumor. What process do cancer cells undergo?

    a. mitosis

    b. meiosis

    c. Binary fission

    d. Budding

32. Genetic information remains unchanged after mitotic cell division because of:

   a. No crossing over
   b. Recombination
   c. Controlled cell division
   d. Number of chromosomes remains same

33. What is the critical stage in mitosis ensuring equal distribution of chromosomes in daughter cells?

   a. Prophase
   b. Metaphase
   c. Anaphase
   d. Telophase

34. Meiosis can be related to all the following EXCEPT:

   a. Occurs in diploid cell only
   b. Occurs at time of gamete formation
   c. 2nd meiotic division is like mitosis
   d. None of the above

35. Which of the following is 'reduction phase' in meiosis I:

   a. Prophase I
   b. Metaphase I
   c. Anaphase I
   d. Telophase I

36. What is true regarding natural selection?

a. It is survival of the fittest and better adapted

b. It is survival of the fittest and unrelated to adaptation

c. It is random and unrelated to competitors and environmental factors

d. All of the above

37. Natural selection results in ____.

a. A change in gene pool

b. Adaptation

c. Acclimatization

d. Both a and b

38. In what sequence does natural selection advance?

a. Genetic mutation, adaptation, reproduction, survival, increase in gene pool

b. Adaptation, genetic mutation, reproduction, survival, increase in gene pool

c. Genetic mutation, increase in gene pool, reproduction, adaptation, survival

d. Sequence doesn't matter, it's basically the survival

39. In what sequence does energy flows?

a. Autotrophs, primary consumers, tertiary consumers, secondary consumers, decomposers

b. Autotrophs, decomposers, primary consumers, secondary consumers, tertiary consumers

c. Primary consumers, secondary consumers, tertiary consumers, autotrophs

d. Autotrophs, primary consumers, secondary consumers, tertiary consumers, decomposers

40. What is at the lowest level in energy pyramid?

a. Producers
b. Primary consumer
c. Secondary consumer
d. Decomposer

41. Greenhouse gases absorb infrared radiations and prevent the heat escape from environment. Which of the following is not regarded as greenhouse gas?

a. CO_2
b. O_3
c. CH_4
d. N_2

42. Which of the following statements is false?

a. Green house effect has been increased by human activity
b. More heat from the environment used to escape into space previously
c. Less heat from the environment used to escape into the space now
d. More heat re-emitted into the environment previously

43. Which of the following is NOT a characteristic of green house gases?

a. They absorb heat
b. They allow no heat to escape into space
c. They increases earth's temperature
d. None of the above

44. Which of the following represents the approximate age of our universe?

    a. 13.7×10^{-10} years

    b. 13.7×10^{12} years

    c. 13.7×10^{9} years

    d. 13.7×10^{-9} years

45. Which of the following statements is NOT supported by Big Bang theory:

    a. Expansion of the universe is still going on.

    b. Universe has expanded from initially hot and dense state to present relatively cool and tenuous state.

    c. The theory supports Hubble's law.

    d. Universe is homogeneous and isotropic in space and time

46. The intensity of Microwave background radiation, an after-glow of the big bang, is:

    a. Greatest towards the center of the galaxy

    b. Proportional to the distance from earth

    c. Nearly the same in all directions

    d. Least towards the center of galaxy

47. Two earth plates slip past each other to form:

    a. Divergent plate boundary

    b. Convergent plate boundary

    c. Transform plate boundary

    d. Both b and c

48. What determines the features that will form at a plate boundary after plate movement?

   i. Direction of plate motion

   ii. Type of crust

   iii. Type of ridges

   iv. Type of boundary

a. i and ii
b. i and iv
c. ii and iii
d. iii and iv

49. Oceanic crust is always destroyed in:

   a. Convergence
   b. Divergence
   c. Transformation
   d. Continental rifting

50. _____ can happen between continent-oceanic crust, two oceanic plates and two continents and a crust is destroyed. While, crust is not created nor destroyed after _____

   a. Convergence, divergence
   b. Convergence, transformation
   c. Divergence, transformation
   d. Divergence, convergence

Answer Key

Part 1 – Reading Comprehension

1. B
We can infer from this passage that sickness from an infectious disease can be easily transmitted from one person to another.

From the passage, "Infectious pathologies are also called communicable diseases or transmissible diseases, due to their potential of transmission from one person or species to another by a replicating agent (as opposed to a toxin)."

2. A
Two other names for infectious pathologies are communicable diseases and transmissible diseases.

From the passage, "Infectious pathologies are also called communicable diseases or transmissible diseases, due to their potential of transmission from one person or species to another by a replicating agent (as opposed to a toxin)."

3. C
Infectivity describes the ability of an organism to enter, survive and multiply in the host. This is taken directly from the passage, and is a definition type question.

Definition type questions can be answered quickly and easily by scanning the passage for the word you are asked to define.

"Infectivity" is an unusual word, so it is quick and easy to scan the passage looking for this word.

4. B
We know an infection is not synonymous with an infectious disease because an infection may not cause important clinical symptoms or impair host function.

5. C
The cumulus stage of a thunderstorm is the beginning of the thunderstorm.

This is taken directly from the passage, "The first stage of a thunderstorm is the cumulus, or developing stage."

6. D
The passage lists four ways that air is heated. One of the ways is, heat created by water vapor condensing into liquid.

7. A
The sequence of events can be taken from these sentences:

As the moisture carried by the [1] air currents rises, it rapidly cools into liquid drops of water, which appear as cumulus clouds. As the water vapor condenses into liquid, it [2] releases heat, which warms the air. This in turn, causes the air to become less dense than the surrounding dry air and [3] rise farther.

8. A
We know that an annex is like an attic because the text states the annex was above Otto Frank's building.

Option B is incorrect because an office building doesn't have bedrooms. Option C is incorrect because a basement would be below the office building. Option D is incorrect because there would not be a kitchen in an office building.

9. B
The diary has been published in 55 languages so people all over the world can learn about Anne. That is why the passage says it has been continuously in print.

Option A is incorrect because it is too vague. Option C is incorrect because it was published after Anne died and she did not write in all three languages. Option D is incorrect because the passage does not give us any information about what languages Otto Frank spoke.

10. C
Use the process of elimination to figure this out.

Option A cannot be the correct answer because otherwise the passage would have simply said that Anne and Margot both died of starvation. Options B and D cannot be correct because if the Germans had done something specifically to murder Anne, the passage would have stated that directly. By the process of elimination, Option C has to be the correct answer.

11. D
We can figure this out using context clues. The paragraph is talking about Anne's diary and so, outlet in this instance is a place where Anne can pour her feelings.

Option A is incorrect answer. That is the literal meaning of the word outlet and the passage is using the figurative meaning. Option B is incorrect because that is the secondary literal meaning of the word outlet, as in an outlet mall. Again, we are looking for figurative meaning. Option C is incorrect because there are no clues in the text to support that answer.

12. D
Clouds in space are made of different materials attracted by gravity. Clouds on Earth are made of water droplets or ice crystals.

Choice D is the best answer. Notice also that Choice D is the most specific.

13. C
The main idea is the first sentence of the passage; a cloud is a visible mass of droplets or frozen crystals floating in the atmosphere above the surface of the Earth or other planetary body.

The main idea is very often the first sentence of the paragraph.

14. C
This question asks about the process, and gives choices that can be confirmed or eliminated easily.

From the passage, "Dense, deep clouds reflect most light,

so they appear white, at least from the top. Cloud droplets scatter light very efficiently, so the farther into a cloud light travels, the weaker it gets. This accounts for the gray or dark appearance at the base of large clouds."

We can eliminate choice A, since water droplets inside the cloud do not reflect light is false.

We can eliminate choice B, since, water droplets outside the cloud reflect light, it appears dark, is false.

Choice C is correct.

15. B
When someone is avid about something that means they are highly interested in the subject. The context clues are dull and boring, because they define the opposite of avid.

16. A
The author is using a simile to compare the books to medicine. Medicine is what you take when you want to feel better. They are suggesting that if a person wants to feel good, they should read Dr. Seuss' books.

Option B is incorrect because there is no mention of a doctor's office. Option C is incorrect because it is using the literal meaning of medicine and the author is using medicine in a figurative way. Option D is incorrect because it makes no sense. We know not to eat books.

17. D
The publisher is described as intelligent because he knew to get in touch with a famous author in order to develop a book that children would be interested in reading.

Option A is incorrect because we can assume that all book publishers must know how to read. Option B is incorrect because it says in the article that more than one publisher was concerned about whether or not children liked to read. Option D is incorrect because there is no mention in the article about how well The Cat in the Hat sold when it was first published.

18. B
The passage describes in detail how Dr. Seuss had a great

effect on the lives of children through his writing. It names several of his books, tells how he helped children become avid readers and explains his style of writing.

Option A is incorrect because that is just one single fact about the passage. Option C is incorrect because that is just one single fact about the passage. Option D is incorrect because that is just one single fact about the passage. Again, Option B is correct because it encompasses ALL the facts in the passage, not just one single fact.

19. B
Choice A is incorrect as the monster killed Frankenstein, not the other way around.

Choice C is incorrect; Mary Shelley is the author. Choice D is incorrect, the person is called Frankenstein.

20. C
The speaker 'suspended" from following through on his duty to destroy the monster due to curiosity and compassion. The other choices may seem reasonable, but are not explicitly given in the passage.

21. D
All the choices are correct. Frankenstein's monster destroys Frankenstein by

   a. By killing Frankenstein

   b. By letting himself be the monster everyone sees him as

   c. By destroying everything Frankenstein loved

22. A
Superfluous means unnecessary. Looking at the context of the word as it is used in the passage:

"Your repentance," I said, "is now superfluous. If you had listened to the voice of conscience and heeded the stings of remorse before you had urged your diabolical vengeance to this extremity, Frankenstein would yet have lived."

23. D
SEALs also belong to the Navy and the Coast Guard.

24. A
The CIA also participated. From the passage, the raid was conducted by a "team of 40 *CIA-led* Navy SEALS."

25. C
From the passage, "The Navy SEALs were part of the Naval Special Warfare Development Group, previously called "Team 6."

26. A
The CIA also participated. From the passage, the raid was conducted by a "team of 40 CIA-led Navy SEALS."

27. C
From the passage, "The Navy SEALs were part of the Naval Special

28. A
The sentence is a recommendation.

29. C
Tips for a good night's sleep is the best alternative title for this article.

30. B
Mental activity is helpful for a good night's sleep is can not be inferred from this article.

31. A
Choice B is incorrect; the author did not express their opinion on the subject matter. Choice C is incorrect, the author was not trying to prove a point.

32. C
Choice C is correct; historians believe it was brutal and bloody. Choice A is incorrect; there is no consensus that the Crusades achieved great things. Choice B is incorrect; it did not stabilize the Holy Lands. Choice D is incorrect, some historians do believe this was the purpose but not all historians.

33. D
The feudal system led to infighting. Choice A is incorrect, it

had the opposite effect. Choice B is incorrect, though this is a good answer, it is not the best answer. The Church asked for volunteers not the Feudal Lords. Choice C is incorrect, it did have an effect on the Crusades.

34. A
Saracen was a generic term for Muslims widely used in Europe during the later medieval era.

35. C
Wind is the highest source of renewable energy in Scotland. The other choices are either not mentioned at all or not mentioned in the context for how fast they are growing.

36. A
Most Scottish citizens agree with the Government's plan due to the concern for current and future needs. Choice B is a good choice but not why the majority agree. Choice C is meant to mislead the as they are clearly in sight. Choice D is a good 'common sense' choice but mentioned specifically in the text.

37. B
All thunderstorms will go through three stages. This is taken directly from the text, "All thunderstorms, regardless of type, go through three stages: the cumulus stage, the mature stage, and the dissipation stage."

38. D
Condensation. From the passage, "As the warm air rises, it cools. The moist water vapor begins to condense as the temperature cools."

39. A
The correct order of the process is seen in this passage:

"Clouds form as warm air carrying moisture rises. As the warm air rises, it cools. The moist water vapor begins to condense as the temperature cools. This releases energy that keeps the air warmer than its surroundings. The result is that it continues to rise."

40. C
From the passage, we see that "if enough instability is present in the atmosphere, this process will continue long enough for cumulonimbus clouds to form," where 'this process' is the process of rising air, condensing water drops generating heat, causing the air to rise farther.

41. C
This question tests the reader's vocabulary skills. The uses of the negatives "but" and "less," especially right next to each other, may confuse readers into answering with choices A or D, which list words that are antonyms to "militant." Readers may also be confused by the comparison of healthy people with what is being described as an overly healthy person--both people are good, but the reader may look for which one is "worse" in the comparison, and therefore stray toward the antonym words. One key to understanding the meaning of "militant" if the reader is unfamiliar with it is to look at the root of the word; readers can then easily associate it with "military" and gain a sense of what the word signifies: defense (especially considered that the immune system defends the body). Choice C is correct over choice B because "militant" is an adjective, just as the words in choice C are, whereas the words in choice B are nouns.

42. C
This question tests the reader's understanding of function within writing. The other choices are details included surrounding the quoted text, and may therefore confuse the reader. Choice A somewhat contradicts what is said earlier in the paragraph, which is that tests and treatments are improving, and probably doctors are along with them, but the paragraph doesn't actually mention doctors, and the subject of the question is the medicine. Choice B may seem correct to readers who aren't careful to understand that, while the author does mention the large number of people affected, the author is touching on the realities of living with allergies rather than about the likelihood of curing all allergies. Similarly, while the author does mention the "balance" of the body, which is easily associated with "wholesome," the author is not really making an argument and especially is not making an extreme statement that allergy medicines should be outlawed. Again, because the article's tone is on

living with allergies, choice C is an appropriate choice that fits with the title and content of the text.

43. B
This question tests the reader's inference skills. The text does not state who is doing the recommending, but the use of the "patients," as well as the general context of the passage, lends itself to the logical partner, "doctors," choice B. The author does mention the recommendation but doesn't present it as her own (i.e. "I recommend that"), so choice A may be eliminated. It may seem plausible that people with allergies (choice D) may recommend medicines or products to other people with allergies, but the text does not necessarily support this interaction taking place. Choice C may be selected because the EpiPen is specifically mentioned, but the use of the phrase "such as" when it is introduced is not limiting enough to assume the recommendation is coming from its creators.

44. D
This question tests the reader's global understanding of the text. Choice D includes the main topics of the three body paragraphs, and isn't too focused on a specific aspect or quote from the text, as the other questions are, giving a skewed summary of what the author intended. The reader may be drawn to choice B because of the title of the passage and the use of words like "better," but the message of the passage is larger and more general than this.

45. C
This question tests the reader's summarization skills. The use of the word "actually" in describing what kind of people poets are, as well as other moments like this, may lead readers to selecting choices B or D, but the author is more informational than trying to persuade readers. The author gives no indication that she loves poetry (choice B) or that people, students specifically (D), should write poems. Choice A is incorrect because the style and content of this paragraph do not match those of a foreword; forewords usually focus on the history or ideas of a specific poem to introduce it more fully and help it stand out against other poems. The author here focuses on several poems and gives broad statements. Instead, she tells a kind of story about poems, giving three

very broad time periods in which to discuss them, thereby giving a brief history of poetry, as choice C states.

46. A
This question tests the reader's summarization skills. Key words in the topic sentences of each of the paragraphs ("oldest," "Renaissance," "modern") should give the reader an idea that the author is moving chronologically. The opening and closing sentence-paragraphs are broad and talk generally. B seems reasonable, but epic poems are mentioned in two paragraphs, eliminating the idea that only new types of poems are used in each paragraph. Choice C is also easily eliminated because the author clearly mentions several different poets, groups of people, and poems. Choice D also seems reasonable, considering that the author does move from older forms of poetry to newer forms, but use of "so (that)" makes this statement false, for the author gives no indication that she is rushing (the paragraphs are about the same size) or that she prefers modern poetry.

47. D
This question tests the reader's attention to detail. The key word is "invented"--it ties together the Mesopotamians, who invented the written word, and the fact that they, as the inventors, also invented and used poetry. The other selections focus on other details mentioned in the passage, such as that the Renaissance's admiration of the Greeks (choice C) and that Beowulf is in Old English (choice A). Choice B may seem like an attractive answer because it is unlike the others and because the idea of heroes seems rooted in ancient and early civilizations.

48. B
This question tests the reader's vocabulary and contextualization skills. "Telling" is not an unusual word, but it may be used here in a way that is not familiar to readers, as an adjective rather than a verb in gerund form. A may seem like the obvious answer to a reader looking for a verb to match the use they are familiar with. If the reader understands that the word is being used as an adjective and that choice A is a ploy, they may opt to select choice D, "wordy," but it does not make sense in context. Choice C can be easily eliminated, and doesn't have any connection to the paragraph or

passage. "Significant" (choice B) makes sense contextually, especially relative to the phrase "give insight" used later in the sentence.

49. B

This question tests the reader's summarization skills. Choice A is a very broad statement that may or may not be true, and seems to be in context, but has nothing to do with the passage. The author does mention that the statue was probably used on a temple dedicated to the Greek gods (choice D), but in no way discusses or argues for the gods' attitude toward or claim on these temples or its faucets. Nike does indeed lead the gods into a war (the Titan war), as choice C suggests, but this is not mentioned by the passage and students who know this may be drawn to this answer but have not done a close enough analysis of the text that is actually in the passage. Choice B is appropriately expository, and connects the titular emphasis to the idea that the Greek gods are very important to Greek culture.

50. C

This question tests the reader's summarization skills. The text for choice C is pulled straight from the paragraph, but is not word for word, so it may seem too obvious to be the right answer. The passage does talk about Nike being the goddess of war, as choice A states, but the third paragraph only touches on it and it is an inference that soldiers destroyed the statue, when this question is asking specifically for what the third paragraph actually stated. Choice B is also straight from the text, with a minor but key change: the inclusion of the words "all" and "never" are too limiting and the passage does not suggest that these limits exist. If the reader selects choice D, they are also making an inference that is misguided for this type of question. The paragraph does state that the arms and head are "lost" but does not suggest who lost them.

Part II - Language Arts

1. A
Sentence 4 is least relevant, "Alvin Lee began playing guitar at an early age, and was influenced by his parents' passion for music and inspired by the likes of Chuck Berry and Scotty Moore."

This sentence talks about Lee's source of motivation rather than his achievements, which is actually the main topic of the paragraph. Other sentences are related to a significant extent, but this sentence deviates from the main idea the most.

2. A
The edited version of sentence 6 is, "A few years later, the band changed its name to Ten Years After and released its debut album under the new name."

Option A places a comma after the prepositional phrase "A few years later" that expresses time. No other punctuation is necessary for a coordinate conjunction "and" as proposed by options B and C since the clause "released its debut album under the new name" is a subordinate rather than an independent one. Option D offers an incorrect suggestion, placing a comma after "and."

3. D
The following sentence, if inserted after sentence 11, "With the songs he composed, he established himself as an exemplary figure among fellow guitarists and the immediate generation that followed" best illustrates the main idea of the passage.

This sentence best complements the other sentences and the main idea of the passage which concentrates on the impact Alvin Lee has made on his admirers and contemporaries with his skills and creations. The emphasis of the passage is on how he influenced them with his guitar work and that is complemented best if the sentence by option D before sentence 11.

4. B

Suggested changes to sentence 11 are, "He also went on to inspire upcoming generations of rock stars by producing expressive and tasteful guitar performances in his 1980s albums. *Free Fall*, *RX5* and *Detroit Diesel*."

The correction offered in option B is the only appropriate one since the gerund form of "inspire" is not appropriate when starting the action. In this case, the author expresses initiation of the process of inspiring more than one generation. So, rather than continuing an already started process, this sentence refers to beginning of an additional process of inspiring as indicated by "also." The gerund form is used rather when the action represented by the verb is in a continuous process already in motion. Therefore, the to-infinitive must be used. As a result option A can be eliminated. Options C and D offer no valid gerund or infinitive.

5. B

Choice B matches the rest of the paragraph: a poor family with two children.

Choice A is incorrect because the family is clearly not rich; they are starving. Choice C is incorrect because, although the family and children are right, the parents are neither happy nor loving. Choice D is incorrect because the rest of the paragraph shows that they are not royalty. Although it is plausible because of the flow of "a boy and a girl" into the next sentence.

6. D

The man, who has to be convinced by the woman, goes along with the plan reluctantly.

Choice A is incorrect because the man does seem to care more for the children than the woman does. Choice B is incorrect because it shows a lack of affection on the part of the father. Choice C is incorrect because the previous sentence states that he consented to the plan.

7. C

This sentence is correct because it flows into the rest of the paragraph.

Choice A is incorrect because it does not flow into the rest of the paragraph, although it is plausible because it mentions the same food. Choice B is incorrect because the rest of the paragraph takes place on an uninhabited island, not in town. Choice D is incorrect because it jumps from talking about their mindset on the river right into cooking food on the island.

8. A

Correct because it follows smoothly from the tone and events of the paragraph.

Choice B is incorrect because it jumps from Aunt Polly's actions to the events on the island. Choice C is incorrect because they would not be able to walk home from the island without crossing the river. Choice D is incorrect because Tom was clearly not alone on the island.

9. D

This sentence flows into the paragraph and mentions the unhappiness of the people living in the Divide.

Choice A is incorrect because the people being described are not happy. Choice B is incorrect because there is nothing comforting about the Divide mentioned in the paragraph, but plausible because it does mention the rough existence.

10. B

This is the best choice because it flows from the rest of the paragraph and does not contradict anything.

Choice A is incorrect because the paragraph speaks about immigrants, not native-born people. Choice C is incorrect because, although it talks about immigrants, it is incorrect that they are full of youthful energy. Choice D is incorrect because it abruptly changes the point of view and the story does not take place in the mountains.

11. A

This sentence flows into the rest of the paragraph and does not contradict anything in it.

Choice B is incorrect because the paragraph mentions

that the song is well known. Choice C is incorrect because the rest of the paragraph mentions nothing of this, on the contrary the song and its author are described as popular Choice C is incorrect because the song's author is not anonymous.

12. C
Correct because it flows from the rest of the paragraph and does not contradict anything.

Choice A is incorrect because the paragraph states that he died at age 37; he had no old age. Choice B is incorrect because he was not a noble and had the sensibility of the common people. Choice D is incorrect because the paragraph explains that Burns is well known and popular.

13. C
This sentence introduces the topic and transitions into the rest of the paragraph.

Choice A is incorrect because, although the paragraph mentions the War of 1812, it really does not concern it at all. Choice B is incorrect because the paragraph does not go on to claim that the damage was exaggerated. Choice C is incorrect because the paragraph does speak of human lives and not about the cost of rebuilding or property values.

14. B
Correct because it ties together the two topics of the paragraph: the hurricane's damage and the history of the area.

Choice A is incorrect because it abruptly changes the subject from the hurricane to a first person opinion. Choice C is incorrect because it abruptly changes the subject to tourism. Choice C is incorrect because although the number 1,500 and the War of 1812 are mentioned, they are not related.

15. C
Comma separate phrases.

16. D
The comma separates clauses and numbers are separated

with a comma. The correct sentence is,
'To travel around the globe, you have to drive 25,000 miles.'

17. A
The dog loved chasing bones, but never ate them; it was running that he enjoyed.

18. B
The semicolon links independent clauses with a conjunction (therefore).

19. D
The third conditional is used for talking about an unreal situation (that did not happen) in the past. For example, "If I had studied harder, [if clause] I would have passed the exam [main clause]. Which is the same as, "I failed the exam, because I didn't study hard enough."

20. C
Double negative sentence. In double negative sentences, one of the negatives is replaced with "any."

21. A
Disagreeing with a negative statement uses "neither." Disagreeing with a negative statement uses "neither." Use "I do" and "He does."

22. C
"Doesn't," "does not," and "does" are used with the third person singular--words like he, she, and it. Don't, do not, or do is used for other subjects.

23. C
Bring vs. Take. Usage depends on your location. Something coming your way is brought to you. Something going away is taken from you.

24. C
Present perfect. You cannot use the Present Perfect with specific time expressions such as: yesterday, one year ago, last week, when I was a child, at that moment, that day, one day, etc. The Present Perfect is used with unspecific expres-

sions such as: ever, never, once, many times, several times, before, so far, already, yet, etc.

25. C
Fewer vs. Less. 'Fewer' is used with countables and 'less' is used with uncountables.

26. B
Went vs. Gone. Went is the simple past tense. Gone is used in the past perfect.

27. A
When using 'however,' place a comma before and after, except when however begins the sentence.

28. C
Its vs. It's. 'It's' is a contraction for it is or it has. 'Its' is a possessive pronoun meaning, more or less, of it or belonging to it.

29. C
Lay vs. Lie. Lie requires an object and lay does not. Laid is the past tense of lay.

30. D
The third conditional is used for talking about an unreal situation (that did not happen) in the past. For example, "If I had studied harder, [if clause] I would have passed the exam [main clause]. Which is the same as, "I failed the exam, because I didn't study hard enough."

31. D
A vs. An. The article 'a' come before a consonant and 'an' comes before a vowel.

32. A
Accept vs. Except. To accept is to receive or to say yes. Except is a preposition that means excluding.

33. A
Advise vs. Advice. To advise is to give advice. Advice is an opinion that someone offers.

34. C
Adapt vs. Adopt.
Adapt means "to change." Usually we adapt to someone or something. Adopt means "to take as one's own."

35. D
Among vs. Between. 'Among' is for more than 2 items, and 'between' is only for 2 items. Replace "in order to," with "to."

When he's among friends (many or more than 2), Robert seems confident, but, between you and me (two), he is very shy.

36. D
At vs. About. At refers to a specific time and about refers to a more general time. A common usage is 'at about 10,' but it isn't proper grammar.

37. B
Beside vs. Besides. 'Beside' means next to, and 'besides' means in addition to.

38. A
Can vs. May. 'Can' refers to ability and 'may' refers to permission.

Although John can swim (is able to. very well, he may not (permission. be allowed to swim in the pool.

39. B
Continual vs. Continuous. 'Continuous' means a time with no interruption and 'continual' means a time with interruption.

Her continual absences (with interruption – not always absent) caused a continuous disruption (the disruption was ongoing without interruption) at the office.

40. A
Emigrate vs. Immigrate. To emigrate means to leave one's country and to immigrate means to come to a country.

41. B

Further vs. Farther. 'Farther' is used for physical distance, and 'further' is used for figurative distance.

42. B

Former vs. Latter. 'Former' refers to the first of two things, 'latter' to the second.

43. D

Suggested revision of this sentence, "Humankind's thirst for knowledge is insatiable, making curiosity a driving force for advances throughout history."

Use the gender neutral "humankind." Replace the past perfect "has always been" with the present tense to make a simpler and more direct sentence. "Though history" is incorrect. Use "throughout" when referring to a time period. Replace the preposition "for" with "in."

44. A

Sentence 1 is the least relevant. "Curiosity was launched in late November 2011 from Cape Canaveral Air Force Station in Florida."

This paragraph talks about the objectives of the rover. All sentences other than sentence 2 mention the objectives. This sentence, however, informs about when the spacecraft was launched.

45. D

The changes needed to this sentence are, "So far, NASA has carried out several exploratory missions to Mars and the rover robot "Curiosity" is the latest and most sophisticated of all."

"Curiosity" is the name of a spacecraft that was assigned the particular name because of its association of its mission to satisfy our curiosity about the planet Mars. In this respect, the name bears a special meaning and emphasis, which must be reflected in representing it using the quotation mark.

Use of the adjective "exploratory" to describe the missions is correct.

Option D offers these changes.

46. B
Suggested corrections to this sentence are, "Oleic acid, the main ingredient of olive oil, absorbs infra-red radiation, which is the major component of the Sun's radiation reaching the Earth."

The sentence is missing the subordinate conjunction "which" or "that" necessary to construct the subordinate clause, with a comma before "which." Options B and C suggest these changes, but since option C contains a punctuation error, only B is has the valid answer.

47. D
Suggested changes to this sentence are, "With continued concern over global climate change, environmentalists are urging governments to lower their dependence on fossil fuels in order to ensure reduced carbon emission into the atmosphere."

This sentence contains inappropriate use of gerunds and infinitives. To-infinitives are preferred when the continuous form of a main verb is used right before or after them. Here, "urging" should be followed by the to-infinitive of "lower," Farther in the sentence, the linking phrase "in order to," has only one acceptable form; itself. Therefore, the verb which is linked to must contain the infinitive form. The gerund form must be discarded. The only valid option is D.

48. B
Suggested changes to sentence 3 are, "This information, coupled with conventional on-site procedures, help archeologists plan their excavation carefully and efficiently."

The second paragraph points out the significance of satellite imaging for archeological studies. The original sentence only makes a general claim. Option A contradicts excavation principles by adding "along with a supply of heavy machinery" which would destroy the site. Option B, more appropriately, adds the aspects of archeological excavation that are going to be boosted by the technology. Options C and D offer very little relevance to satellite imaging and the dimensions of excavation that are going to be affected.

49. A
Suggested changes to sentence 1 are, "The key feature of the new tool- according to Professor Sarah Parcak, who discovered many cities, temples and pyramids covered under sands and sediment- is that it offers a wider perspective in size and scale of the location."

The changes in this sentence are related to punctuation. The original sentence contains a semicolon before a verbal phrase which is not justifiable with its standard use. The sentence can be modified using parenthetic dashes since using parenthetic commas makes the sentence very complicated as the sentence contains several clauses and a list.

50. C
Suggested changes to this sentence are, "Malala's dreams encountered the same obstacles that were also crushing the aspirations of millions of other young girls like her."

The changes needed are related to usage. "Were encountered with the obstacles," can be replaced with "encountered the same obstacles."

Part III - Mathematics

1. C
If there are 5 friends and each drink costs $1.89, we can round up to $2 per drink and estimate the total cost at, 5 X $2 = $10.
The actual, cost is 5 X $1.89 = $9.45.

2. D
If we subtract 25 pounds from the total 205, then in remaining 180 pounds, their weights are equal. So Sarah's weight will be = 90 + 25 = 115 pounds.

In kilograms it will be = 115×0.4535 = 52.15 Kg.

Sarah will weigh approximately 52 Kg.

3. D
75/1500 = 15/300 = 3/60 = 1/20

4. C
16 X 230 is about 3,100. The actual number is 3680.

5. B

Day	Number of Absent Students	Number of Present Students	% Attendance
Monday	5	40	88.88%
Tuesday	9	36	80.00%
Wednesday	4	41	91.11%
Thursday	10	35	77.77%
Friday	6	39	86.66%

To find the average or mean, sum the series and divide by the number of items.

(88.88 + 80.00 + 91.11 + 77.77 + 86.66/5
424.42)/5 = 84.88
Round up to 85%.

Percentage attendance will be 85%

6. C
Let the original price be 100x.

At the rate of 7% discount, the discount will be 100x•7/100 = 7x. So, the discounted price will be = 100x - 7x = 93x.

Over this price, at the rate of 2% additional discount, the discount will be 93x•2/100 = 1.86x. So, the additionally discounted price will be = 93x - 1.86x = 91.14x.

This is the amount which John has paid for the jacket:

91.14x = 425

x = 425 / 91.14 = 4.6631

The jacket costs 100x. So, 100x = 100•4.6631 = $466.31.

When rounded to the nearest whole number, this is equal to $466.

7. B
215 X 65 is about 13,500. The exact answer is 13,975.

8. C
10 x 2 − (7 + 9). This is an order of operations question. Do brackets first, then multiplication and division, then addition and subtraction.

10 X 2 - 16

20

9. B
40/100 X = 90
40X = (90 * 100) = 9000
x = 9000/40 = 900/4 = 225
Half of 225 = 112.5

10. B
First, see if you can eliminate any choices. 1/4 + 1/3 is going to equal about 1/2.

Choice A, 9/10 is very close to 1, so it can be eliminated.
Choices B and C are very close to 1/2 so they should be considered.
Choice D is less than half and very close to zero, so it can be eliminated.

Looking at the denominators, Choice C has denominator of 15, and Choice B has denominator of 20. Right away, notice that 20 is common multiple of 4 and 10, and 15 is not.

Confirming - 1/4 + 1/3 = 5/20 + 6/20 = 11/20.

11. C
1 inch on map = 2,000 inches on ground. So, 5.2 inches on map = 5.2•2,000 = 10,400 inches on ground.

12. B
Actual cost = X, therefore, 545 = x + 0.15x, 545 = 1x + 0.15x, 545 = 1.15x, x = 545/1.15 = 473.9

Practice Test Questions 1

13. C
0.27 + 0.33 = 0.60 and 0.60 = 60/100 = 3/5

14. D
First, we need to convert all units to grams. Since 1000 g = 1 kg:

10 kg 550 g = 10•1000 g + 550 g = 10,000 g + 550 g = 10,550 g.

10,550 g is shared between 5 men. So each man will have to carry 10,550/5 = 2,110 g

2,110 g = 2,000 g + 110 g = 2 kg 110 g

15. D
A common denominator is needed, a number which both 4 and 16 will divide into. So, 4+11/16 = 15/16

16. B
As the lawn is square shaped, the length of one side will be the square root of the area. √62,500 = 250 meters. So, the perimeter is found by 4 times the length of the side of the square:

250•4 = 1000 meters.

Since each meter costs $5.5, the total cost of the fence will be 1000•5.5 = $5,500.

17. A
The easiest way to solve age problems is to use a table:

	Mother	Child
Now	7x	x
25 years later	7x + 25	x + 25

Now, mother is 7 times older than her child. So, if we say that the child is x years old, mother is 7x years old. In 25 years, 25 will be added to their ages. We are told that in 25 years, mother's age will double her child's age. So,

7x + 25 = 2(x + 25) ... by solving this equation, we reach x that is the child's age:

7x + 25 = 2x + 50

$7x - 2x = 50 - 25$

$5x = 25$

$x = 5$

Mother is 7x years old: $7x = 7 \cdot 5 = 35$

18. A
$0.28 = 28/100 = 7/25$

19. C
By the given information given, we understand that the discounted part is the saved amount. If we say that the original price of the desk is 100x; by 20% discount rate, 20x will be the discounted part:

$20x = 45$

We know that Mark paid 20% less than the original price. So, he paid $100x - 20x = 80x$. We are asked to find 80x. With a simple direct proportion, we can find the result:

$20x = 45$

$80x = ?$

By cross multiplication, we find the result:

$? = 80x \cdot 45 / 20x = 4 \cdot 45 = \$180$

20. C
Let the number be x.

$x/(3/2)$ is the required result.

$x \cdot (3/2)$ is the operation the student does mistakenly. We are told that the multiplication result is 5 more than the division result that is the required one:

$x \cdot (3/2) = x/(3/2) + 5$ ... by solving this equation, we find x.

$3x/2 = 2x/3 + 5$

$3x/2 - 2x/3 = 5$ ... by equating the denominators to 6:

$9x/6 - 4x/6 = 5$

$(9x - 4x)/6 = 5$

$5x/6 = 5$

$5x = 30$

$x = 6$

21. C
$243/3 \times 3 \times 3 = 243/27 = 9$

22. B
$4y + 24 = 3y + 30$, $= 4y - 3y + 24 = 30$, $= y + 24 = 30$, $= y = 30 - 24$, $= y = 6$

23. B
$(x^2 - y^2) / (x - y) = x + y$

$\underline{-(x^2 - xy)}$
$\quad xy - y^2$

$\underline{-(xy - y^2)}$
$\quad\quad 0$

24. A
$10 \times 10 \times 100 \times 100 = 1000^x$, $= 100 \times 10,000 = 1000^x$, $= 1,000,000 = 1000^x = x = 2$

25. C
We are asked to find A + B - C. By paying attention to the sign distribution; we write the polynomials and operate:

$A + B - C = (-2x^4 + x^2 - 3x) + (x^4 - x^3 + 5) - (x^4 + 2x^3 + 4x + 5)$

$= -2x^4 + x^2 - 3x + x^4 - x^3 + 5 - x^4 - 2x^3 - 4x - 5$

$= -2x^4 + x^4 - x^4 - x^3 - 2x^3 + x^2 - 3x - 4x + 5 - 5$ ... similar terms written together to ease summing/substituting.

$= -2x^4 - 3x^3 + x^2 - 7x$

26. C
To find the solution for the inequality, we need to simplify it first:

$(x - 6)^2 \geq x^2 + 12$ ... we can write the open form of the left side:

$x^2 - 12x + 36 \geq x^2 + 12$ ... x^2 terms on both sides cancel each other:

$-12x + 36 \geq 12$ ... Now, we aim to have x alone on one side. So, we subtract 36 from both sides:

$-12x + 36 - 36 \geq 12 - 36$

$-12x \geq -24$ ... We divide both sides by -12. This means that the inequality will change its direction:

$x \leq 2$ ... x can be 2 or a smaller value.

This result is shown by $(-\infty, 2]$.

Note: The square parenthesis means that the limit on its side is included to the solution and in our solution, 2 is included.

27. B
$(7 \times 7 \times 7 \times 7 \times 7) - (3 \times 3 \times 3 \times 3 \times 3) = 16{,}807 - 243 = 16{,}564$.

28. C
$(x^3 - 3x^2 + 3x - 1) / (x - 1) = x^2 - 2x + 1$
$\underline{-(x^3 - x^2)}$
$\quad -2x^2 + 3x - 1$
$\quad \underline{-(-2x^2 + 2x)}$
$\quad\quad\quad x - 1$

$\underline{-(x - 1)}$
0

29. C
Exponential form is 9^3 and standard from is 729

30. B
$x^2 - 5x - 6 = 0$

We try to separate the middle term -5x to find common factors with x^2 and -6 separately:

$x^2 - 6x + x - 6 = 0$ ... Here, we see that x is a common factor for x^2 and -6x:

x(x - 6) + x - 6 = 0 ... Here, we have x times x - 6 and 1 time x - 6 summed up. This means that we have x + 1 times x - 6:

(x + 1)(x - 6) = 0 ... This is true when either or both of the expressions in the parenthesis are equal to zero:

x + 1 = 0 ... x = -1

x - 6 = 0 ... x = 6

-1 and 6 are the solutions for this quadratic equation.

31. B
0.524/ (10•10•10) = 0.524/1000 ... This means that we need to carry the decimal point 3 decimals left from the point it is now:

= 0.0.0.0.524 = 0.000524

32. A
We need to find the greatest common divisor of the two terms to factor the expression. We should remember that if the bases of exponent numbers are the same, the multiplication of two terms is found by summing the powers and writing on the same base. Similarly; when dividing, the power of the divisor is subtracted from the power of the divided. Both x^3y^3 and x^2y^8 contain x^2 and y^3. So;

$x^3y^3 - x^2y^8 = x \cdot x^2y^3 - y^5 \cdot x^2y^3$ ... We can carry x^2y^3 out as the factor:

$= x^2y^3(x - y^5)$

33. D
Our aim is to collect the knowns on one side, and the unknowns (x terms) on the other side:

5x/2 = (3x + 24)/6 ... First, we can simplify the denominators of both sides by 2:

5x = (3x + 24)/3 ... Now, we can do cross multiplication:

15x = 3x + 24

15x - 3x = 24

12x = 24

$x = 24/12 = 2$

34.

a. and b. are correct. $(3,-8)$ and $(-3,8)$

$x - y = 11$
$x = 11 - y$
$xy = -24$
$(11 + y)y = -24$
$11y + y^2 = -24$

$y^2 + 11y + 24 = 0$

$y_{1,2} = (-11 \pm \sqrt{(121 - 96)})/2$

$y_{1,2} = (-11 \pm \sqrt{25})/2$

$y_{1,2} = (-11 \pm 5)/2$

$y_1 = -8$
$y_2 = -3$

$x_1 = 11 + y_1 = 11 - 8 = 3$

$x_2 = 11 + y_2 = 11 - 3 = 8$

35. C
Solving the system means finding x and y. Since we also have a in the system, we will find x and y depending on a.

We can obtain y by using the equation $ax + y = 1$:

$y = 1 - ax$ ... Then, we can insert this value into the second equation:

$x + a(1 - ax) = 1$

$x + a - a^2x = 1$

$x - a^2x = 1 - a$

$x(1 - a^2) = 1 - a$ ... We need to obtain x alone:

$x = (1 - a)/(1 - a^2)$ ... Here, $1 - a^2 = (1 - a)(1 + a)$ is used:

x = (1 - a)/((1 - a)(1 + a)) ... Simplifying by (1 - a):

x = 1/(a + 1) ... Now we know the value of x. By using either of the equations, we can find the value of y. Let us use y = 1 - ax:

y = 1 - a•1/(a + 1)

y = 1 - a/(a + 1) ... By writing on the same denominator:

y = ((a + 1) - a)/(a + 1)

y = (a + 1 - a)/(a + 1) ... a and -a cancel each other:

y = 1/(a + 1) ... x and y are found to be equal.

The solution of the system is (1/(a + 1), 1/(a + 1))

36. We reflect the center O against the mirror line m at right angle and we use a compass to draw the circle with the same radius as the original circle.

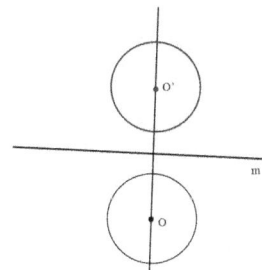

37. C
To solve the linear equation, we operate the knowns and unknowns within each other and try to obtain x term (which is the unknown) alone on one side of the equation:

3(x + 2) - 2(1 - x) = 4x + 5 ... We remove the parenthesis by distributing the factors:

3x + 6 - 2 + 2x = 4x + 5

5x + 4 = 4x + 5

5x - 4x = 5 - 4

x = 1

38. C
Here, we use the commutative property of multiplication, meaning that xa = ax:

3xa + 6ax - xa + (-5ax) - 2xa = 3ax + 6ax - ax - 5ax - 2ax

= (3 + 6 - 1 - 5 - 2)ax

= (9 - 8)ax

= ax

39. B
By paying attention to the sign distribution; we write the polynomials and operate:

$(-3x^2 + 2x + 6) + (-x^2 - x - 1)$

$= -3x^2 + 2x + 6 - x^2 - x - 1$

$= -3x^2 - x^2 + 2x - x + 6 - 1$ ... similar terms written together to ease summing/substituting.

$= -4x^2 + x + 5$

40. A
10^4 is not equal to 100,000
$10^4 = 10 \times 10 \times 10 \times 10 = 10^2 \times 10^2 = 10,000$

41. D
Comparing angles on similar triangles, a, b and c will be 70°, 35°, 35°

42. D
$\log_x 125 = 3$ ... we use the property that $\log_a a^b = b \cdot \log_a a = b$

$\log_x 125 = 3 \cdot \log_x x$

$\log_x 125 = \log_x x^3$ ... We can cancel the $\log_x$ function on both sides:

$125 = x^3$

$5^3 = x^3$

5 = x

So; x = 5

43. C
$(1 - 4\sin^2(\pi/6))/(1+4\cos^2(\pi/3)) = (1 - 4\sin^2(30°))/(1 + 4\cos^2(60°))$

We know that $\sin 30° = \cos 60° = 1/2$

$(1 - 4\sin^2(30°))/(1 + 4\cos^2(60°)) = (1 - 4\cdot(1/2)^2)/(1 + 4\cdot(1/2)^2)$

$= (1 - 4\cdot(1/4))/(1 + 4\cdot(1/4))$

$= (1 - 1)/(1 + 1) = 0/2 = 0$

44. A
We know that $\sin 30° = \cos 60° = 1/2$, $\sin 0° = \cos 90° = 0$
$(\sin^2 30° - \sin 0°)/(\cos 90° - \cos 60°) = ((1/2)^2 - 0)/(0 - (1/2))$

$= (1/4)/(-1/2) = -1/2$

45. A
Yes the triangles are congruent.

46. D
Perimeter of triangle ABC is asked.
Perimeter of a triangle = sum of all three sides.

Here, Perimeter of △ABC = |AC| + |CB| + |AB|.

Since the triangle is located in the middle of two adjacent and identical rectangles, we find the side lengths using these rectangles:

|AB| = 6 + 6 = 12 cm

|CB| = 8.5 cm

|AC| = |CB| = 8.5 cm

Perimeter = |AC| + |CB| + |AB| = 8.5 + 8.5 + 12 = 29 cm

47. B
a=90°

$\cot 90° = \cos 90°/\sin 90° = 0/1 = 0$

48. A

First, we need to simplify the value of angle α:

α = 3π/2 - π/6 - π - π/3 ... by equating the denominators at 6:

α = 9π/6 - π/6 - 6π/6 - 2π/6

α = (9 - 1 - 6 - 2)π/6

α = 0•π /6

α = 0

sinα = sin0° = 0

49. A

$\log_x(9/25) = 2$ ... we use the property that $\log_a a^b = b \cdot \log_a a = b$

$\log_x(9/25) = 2 \cdot \log_x x$

$\log_x(9/25) = \log_x x^2$ ... We can cancel the $\log_x$ function on both sides:

$9/25 = x^2$

$(3/5)^2 = x^2$ ... We can remove the power 2 in both sides:

$3/5 = x$

So; x = 3/5

50.

We reflect points A, B, C and D against the mirror line m at right angle and we connect the new points A', B',C' and D'.

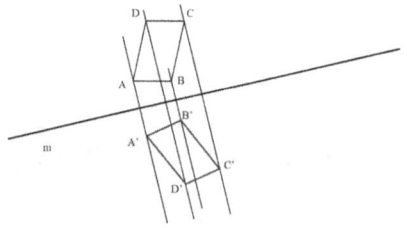

51. A

The wheel travels $2\pi r$ distance when it makes one revolution. Here, r stands for the radius. The radius is given as 25 cm in the figure. So,

$2\pi r = 2\pi \cdot 25 = 50\pi$ cm is the distance travelled in one revolution.

In 175 revolutions: $175 \cdot 50\pi = 8750\pi$ cm is travelled.

We are asked to find the distance in meter.

1 m = 100 cm So;

8750π cm = 8750π / 100 = 87.5π m

52. B
$x + y = 21$
$x = 21 - 7$
$x^2 + y^2 = 261$

$(21 - y)^2 + y^2 = 261$
$441 - 42y + y^2 + y^2 = 261$
$2y^2 - 42y + 180 = 0$
$y^2 - 21y + 90 = 0$

$y_{1,2} = (21 \pm \sqrt{441 - 3600})/2$

$y_{1,2} = (21 \pm \sqrt{81})/2$

$y_{1,2} = (21 \pm 9)/2$

$y_1 = 15$
$y_2 = 6$

$x_1 = 21 - y_1 = 21 - 15 = 6$

$x_2 = 21 = y_2 = 21 = 6 = 15$

53. A
If a line represents an equation, all points on that line should satisfy the equation. Meaning that all (x, y) pairs

present on the line should be able to verify that 2y - x is equal to 4. We can find out the correct line by trying a (x, y) point existing on each line. It is easier to choose points on the intersection of the grid lines:

Try the point (4, 4) on line A:

2•4 - 4 = 4

8 - 4 = 4

4 = 4 ... this is a correct result, so the equation for line A is 2y - x = 4.

Try other points to check the other lines:

Point (-1, 2) on line B:

2•2 - (-1) = 4

4 + 1 = 4

5 = 4 ... this is a wrong result, so the equation for line B is not 2y - x = 4.

Point (3, -1) on line C:

2•(-1) - 3 = 4

-2 - 3 = 4

-5 = 4 ... this is a wrong result, so the equation for line C is not 2y - x = 4.

Point (-2, -1) on line D:

2•(-1) - (-2) = 4

-2 + 2 = 4

0 = 4 ... this is a wrong result, so the equation for line D is not 2y - x = 4.

54. D
We know that;

tga = sina/cosa

ctga = cosa/sina

So;

tga/ctga = (sina/cosa)•(cosa/sina) = (sina • cosa)/(sina • cosa)

sina terms and cosa terms cancel each other in the nominator and the denominator:

tga/ctga = 1

55. D
To understand this question better, let us draw a right triangle by writing the given data on it:

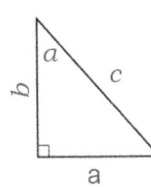

The side opposite to angle a is named by a. cos a = length of the adjacent side / length of the hypotenuse = b/c

cos a = 3/5 is given. This means that b/c = 3/5

b = 24 is also given:

24/c = 3/5 ... By cross multiplication:

24•5 = 3c ... Simplifying both sides by 3:

8•5 = c

c = 40

56. C
In a right angle, Pythagorean Theorem is applicable:
$a^2 + b^2 = c^2$ ... Here, a and b represent the adjacent and opposite sides, c represents the hypotenuse. Hypotenuse is larger than the other two sides.

In this question, we need to try each answer choice by applying $a^2 + b^2 = c^2$ to see if it is satisfied; by inserting the largest number into c:

a. 1, 2, 3:

$1^2 + 2^2 = 3^2$

$1 + 4 = 9$

$5 = 9$ ... This is not correct, so answer choice does not represent a right angle whose sides are consecutive numbers.

b. 2, 3, 4:

$2^2 + 3^2 = 4^2$

$4 + 9 = 16$

$13 = 16$ ... This is not correct, so this answer choice does not represent a right angle whose sides are consecutive numbers.

c. 3, 4, 5:

$3^2 + 4^2 = 5^2$

$9 + 16 = 25$

$25 = 25$ ... This is correct, 3, 4, 5 are also consecutive numbers; so this answer choice represents a right angle whose sides are consecutive numbers.

d. 4, 5, 6:

$4^2 + 5^2 = 6^2$

$16 + 25 = 36$

$41 = 36$ ... This is not correct, so this answer choice does not represent a right angle whose sides are consecutive numbers.

57. A
If we call one side of the square "a," the area of the square will be a^2.

We know that $a^2 = 200$ cm².

On the other hand; there is an isosceles right triangle. Using the Pythagorean Theorem:

(Hypotenuse)² = (Adjacent Side)² + (Opposite Side)² Where the hypotenuse is equal to one side of the square. So,

$a^2 = x^2 + x^2$

$200 = 2x^2$

$200/2 = 2x^2/2$

$100 = x^2$

$x = \sqrt{100}$

$x = 10$ cm

58. C

We know that π/2 = 90°

cos90° = 0, sin90° = 1

ctg90° = cos90°/sin90° = 0/1 = 0 So;

(cos(π/2) + ctg(π/2))/sin(π/2) = (cos90° + ctg90°)/sin90° = (0 + 0)/1 = 0

59. B

In the question, we have a right triangle formed inside the circle. We are asked to find the length of the hypotenuse of this triangle. We can find the other two sides of the triangle by using circle properties:

The diameter of the circle is equal to 12 cm. The legs of the right triangle are the radii of the circle; so they are 6 cm long.

Using the Pythagorean Theorem:

(Hypotenuse)² = (Adjacent Side)² + (Opposite Side)²

$x^2 = r^2 + r^2$

$x^2 = 6^2 + 6^2$

$x^2 = 72$

$x = \sqrt{72}$

$x = 8.48$

60. C
Slope (m) = change in y / change in x

$(x_1, y_1) = (-3, 1)$ & $(x_2, y_2) = (1, -4)$
Slope = $[-4 - 1]/[1-(-3)] = -5/4$

Part IV - Social Studies

US History

1. D
The Foreign Trade Act did not take place until centuries after the American Revolutionary War. All the Intolerable Acts took place in the lead-up to the American Revolutionary War.

Choice A is incorrect; the Stamp Act imposed a tax on the colonies by forcing them to use paper produced in Britain for many printed materials. This was the first of the Intolerable Acts or taxes that were placed on British American subjects without their consent.

Choice B is incorrect; the Townshed Acts were also part of the Intolerable Acts that were meant to raise revenue in the colonies for the employment of judges and governors. These were also used to punish colonists and force compliance with the numerous other taxes being levied against the colonies.

Choice C is incorrect; the Tea Act allowed the British East India Company to sell tea directly to the colonies, thus making it cheaper. Many colonists hated this act because a small tax was added without their consent, which resulted in the Boston Tea Party.

2. B
The British imposed taxes through the Intolerable Acts either without representation from the colonies at all, or with representatives that effectively had no say in the matter.

Choice A is incorrect; even during the American Revolutionary War, most of the colonists did not decisively want to be free from British rule; they either wanted to stay under British rule, or were undecided.

Choice C is incorrect; while Colonists and people everywhere do not like to be taxed, most realized taxes were what allowed government to function and the colonists made no statements against ALL taxes, just some of them.

3. B
After the Seven Years War with France, Great Britain had a lot of debt and Parliament wanted the colonies to pay for some of the military expenditures and the cost of maintaining a military presence in the colonies.

Choice A is incorrect; None of the Intolerable Acts were used to raise revenue for the British Parliament salaries. The Intolerable Acts were used to pay off war debt, punish the colonies, and a variety of other things.

Choice C is incorrect; the Navigation Acts kept most trade in the British Colonies strictly between the colonies and Great Britain.

Choice D is incorrect; while the East India Company was fighting in India at this time, the British military was not involved there yet.

4. A
The Second Continental Congress tried to avert war even though the battles of Lexington and Concord had already been fought. This was known as the Olive Branch Petition. King James would not receive the petition because it came from what he perceived as an illegal and illegitimate assembly.

Choice C is false; because while Thomas Jefferson wrote the first draft of the petition, most of it was redrafted, and it was never called Jefferson's Plea.

Choice D is false; neither Samuel nor John Adams thought the Plea would help, and contributed nothing to the process.

The plea was never called Adam's Plea.

5. A
The First continental Congress met to discuss various ways of getting rid of the Intolerable Acts and petition the King of England for a redress of grievances.

Choice B is incorrect; this is the purpose of the Second Continental Congress.

Choice C is incorrect; the federal government was set up with the Articles of Confederation.

Choice D is incorrect; all the "states" at this point were not states yet, instead they were colonies that firmly belonged to Great Britain.

6. D
While many other things were achieved, the main purpose of the Second Continental Congress was to establish a Continental Army.

Choice A is incorrect; the federal government was set up with the Articles of Confederation

Choice B is incorrect; Responding to the Intolerable Acts was the purpose of the First Continental Congress

Choice C is incorrect; asking for French aid was officially done after the Second Continental Congress was over, though Benjamin Franklin and others hinted at this possibility with many French officials.

7. B
With the Declaration of Independence, the colonies disavowed the rule of Great Britain, effectively announcing a state of war between the colonists and Great Britain.

Choice A is incorrect; the Articles of Confederation Established a federal government and occurred after there was a state of war between Great Britain and the Colonies.

Choice C is incorrect; the United States Constitution was a

document that strengthened the federal government and, provided more effective ways of raising revenue.

Choice D is incorrect; while a declaration of hostilities does announce a state of war, there was no such document called the Declaration of Hostilities.

8. D
All the reasons listed were part of Manifest Destiny,

- Many Americans believed that they were special and could use the land better than anyone else.

- The agrarian ideal was a very popular idea at the time, many dreamed that America should be populated by self-sufficient farmers. With all the "open" land in the west this seemed like a real possibility.

- Many Americans believed that God had set America a destiny to bring civilization to the west, and that America would one day stretch across the continent.

9. A
The Clermont steamboat's maiden voyage between New York and Albany took 32 hours, much less time than the four days it would take the average sloop. This showed that distances between areas were shrinking time-wise.

Choice B is incorrect; while the Mexican American War brought many people west it was not the start of western expansion.

Choice C is incorrect; the invention of the telegraph greatly helped communication across the country, but it was not invented until long after western expansion had started.

Choice D is incorrect; gold in California brought more people west faster than ever before, but western expansion had already started decades before.

10. B
Gold was discovered in California in 1848, and the Gold Rush commenced.

Choice A is incorrect; while the miners were called 49ers after the year that most people started mining for gold in California, this was not when the Gold Rush started.

Choice C is incorrect; this was the year that the Gold Rush ended in California.

Choice D is incorrect; this was the year that California was admitted to the Union, not when the Gold Rush started.

World History

11. B
The Bronze Age was a period of time between the Stone Age and the Iron Age when bronze was used widely to make tools, weapons, and other implements. Bronze is made when copper is heated and mixed with tin, creating a stronger metal than copper.

Choice A is incorrect; there is no Tin Age.

Choice C is incorrect; The Stone Age came before The Bronze Age and is known for its use of stone, not metal.

Choice D is incorrect; The Iron Age came after The Bronze Age and is known for its use of iron.

12. A
The Punic Wars happened in Rome in the 3rd century BCE.

Choice B is incorrect; the Persian Wars happened in the 5th century BCE.

Choice C is incorrect; the Parthenon was constructed during the 5th century BCE.

Choice D is incorrect; Socrates lived in Greece during the 5th century BCE.

Practice Test Questions 1

13. D
Democracy was first introduced in Athens in the 6th century.

Choice A is incorrect; dictatorships were first introduced in Rome in the 6th century.

Choice B is incorrect; Communism was first introduced in Russia in the 19th century.
Choice C is incorrect; Capitalism was first introduced in Europe in the MIddle Ages.

14. A
Ares, Aphrodite, Demeter and Athena are the names of four ancient Greek gods.

Choice B is incorrect; when Rome overtook Greece, they adopted some of their gods, but called them by different names.

Choices C is incorrect, Egyptian and Norse gods had different names.

15. C
Egypt attacking Rome at that time did not contribute to the fall of the Roman Empire. All the other choice were contributing factors.

Choice A is incorrect; the spread of Christianity displaced Roman religion.

Choice B is incorrect; Rome had grown very large and difficult to govern leading to civil war.

Choice D is incorrect; as Rome stopped expanding they were no longer gaining slaves and were unable to support themselves.

16. D
Vedas are ancient texts composed in Vedic Sandskrit.

Choice A is incorrect; this was not a time period in history.

Choice B is incorrect; this was not the name of the ruling class.

Choice C is incorrect; it is not known what happened to the Harappans, and the next invaders were the Aryans.

17. A
There is some doubt as to whether the Xia Dynasty existed, however, some recorded and archeological evidence that hints that it did.

Choice B is incorrect; the Han dynasty was a golden age in Chinese history where Imperial China started, but it was not the first dynasty.

Choice C is incorrect; the Tang dynasty is another golden age of culture and society of Chinese history, Chang'an the capital of China was the largest city in the world at the time.

Choice D is incorrect; the Qing Dynasty was the last imperial dynasty of China, not the first.

18. D
Both Isaac Newton and Gottfried Leibniz discovered calculus independently - it was not invented by the Chinese.

The other choices are all inventions by the Chinese. Paper making was invented by the Chinese around 200 BCE, the Chinese first used chemical warfare during about 400 BCE, using the smoke of burnt mustard plants to kill their enemies, and the first use of gunpowder by the Chinese was before 1000 CE.

19. A
Buddhism maintains anyone can follow the Eightfold path to correct behavior and reach Nirvana.

Choice B is incorrect; in Hinduism, someone must go through a series of reincarnations before they can reach enlightenment.

Choice C is incorrect; Islam follows the teachings of the Qur'an.

Choice D is incorrect; Taoism is a Chinese philosophy of living.

20. B
Islam emerged in Arabia in 7th century CE. Some archaeologists prefer to use the terms Before the Common Era (B.C.E.) and the Common Era (C.E.), which are exactly the same as B.C. and A.D. but have nothing to do with Christianity.

Choice A is incorrect; Christianity emerged in Rome in 1st century CE.

Choice C is incorrect; Judaism emerged in Israel in 6th century BCE.

Choice D is incorrect; Zoroastrianism emerged in Indo-Iran in 2nd century BCE.

Civics and Government

21. A
A political system with a king or queen as leader is a monarchy.

Choices B and C are incorrect by definition, it would need to be "republican monarchy" or "constitutional monarchy" to be closer to the correct answer.

Choice D is clearly incorrect, since Utopia is a fictional place

22. C
The concept of voting dates back to ancient civilization.

Choices A is incorrect because voting existed before the Enlightenment.

Choice B is incorrect because voting existed before the American Revolution.
Choice D is incorrect because voting existed before the Renaissance.

23. D
Dictatorships have strong leaders and the people have virtually no power.

Choice A is partly correct as dictatorships have strong leaders, but the leader is not held responsible to the will of the people.

Choice B is incorrect; dictatorships normally only have one political party. The answer is a good definition of a republic.

Choice C is incorrect because in a dictatorship, virtually no power rests with the people.

24. B
Choice A is incorrect because nationalism is similar to patriotism.

Choice C is incorrect because justice is about punishing criminals, although selecting this answer does show some good thinking.

Choice D is incorrect because liberty is irrelevant to the question.

25. D
A plutocracy is a country or society governed by the wealthy.

26. D
The ancient Romans had a legislative branch of government known as the Senate.

Choice A is incorrect because the Roman Emperor was not the legislative branch.

Choice B is incorrect because a president not a legislator and the term "president" was not used in ancient Roman government.

Choice C is incorrect because a court is not a legislative branch.

27. A
A government controlled by elected representatives is known as a Republic.

Choice B is incorrect; since a Utopia is a fictional place.

Choice C is incorrect by definition; it would need to be "constitutional monarchy" to be closer to a correct answer.

28. D
The primary purpose of the Magna Carta was to take power from the king and give it to Parliament.

Choice A is incorrect; it had little to do with the peasants.

Choice B is incorrect; it took power from the king and gave it to Parliament.

Choice C is incorrect; it had little to do with the military.

29. D
A theocracy is a government controlled by religious leaders based on adherence to a religion.

Choices A and B are incorrect by definition.

Choice C is clearly incorrect because anarchy refers to a lack of government.

30. A
A constitution a document that outlines the principles and structure of a government.

Choice B is the definition of a subpoena.

Choice C is the definition of a petition.

Choice D is the definition of the Emancipation Proclamation.

Economics

31. A
As demand increases, supply tends to decrease.

Choice B is incorrect; supply and demand tend to be inversely related.

Choice C is clearly incorrect; demand has a strong influence on supply.

Choice D is incorrect; demand has a predictable effect on supply.

32. B
As supply increases, prices tend to decrease.

Choice A is incorrect; more supply lowers prices

Choices C and D are incorrect; supply has a predictable effect on prices.

33. A
As economies of scale increase, products are expensive to produce at first, but eventually become less expensive. This usually applies to large items, such as airplanes and cars.

Choice C is incorrect; here products are not customized to individual customers.

Choice D is incorrect; bidding is irrelevant to production.

34. C
In a free market economy, citizens own resources and private property.

Choices A and D are incorrect by definition.

Choice B is the definition of a command economy.

35. B
In a command economy, the government owns the resources and does not allow citizens to own private property.

Choices A and D are incorrect by definition.

Choice C is incorrect; this is the definition of a free market economy.

36. C
Capital is the resource (namely money) needed to start or expand a business.

Choice A is incorrect; per capita income is a measure of individual income.

Choices B and D are incorrect but may sound plausible.

37. C
Inflation is an increase in the value of money, or more precisely, a general increase in prices and fall in the purchasing value of money.

Choice A is incorrect; inflation refers to currency, not business.

Choice B is incorrect; this is the definition of deflation.

Choice D is incorrect; unemployment is not a cause of inflation.

38. D
A country's labor force excludes children who are too young to work and are not calculated as part of the job market.

Choice A is incorrect; professionals are included.

Choices B and C are incorrect but the word "labor" makes them seem plausible.

39. A
A miner is a physical laborer and a good example of a blue collar occupation.

Choices B, C and D are incorrect; a professor, a scientist and an accountant are all professionals.

40. A
Consumer confidence is an economic indicator which measures the degree of optimism consumers feel about the overall state of the economy and their personal financial situation.
Choices B and C are incorrect but sound plausible.

Geography

41. C
Open spaces is not a reason that humans move to urban areas.

Choice A is incorrect; people move to cities for excitement.

Choice B is incorrect; most universities are located in cities.

Choice D is incorrect; cities normally have more job opportunities than rural areas.

42. B
The era of human existence before writing was developed is known as prehistory.

Choices A and B are incorrect; ancient and recorded history are written.

Choice D is incorrect; unknown history is not a real term.

43. C
A thin stretch of land that connects two large areas of land is called an isthmus.

44. B
An ecosystem is a group of living organisms and their surrounding environment.

All the other choices are incorrect, but plausible, due to the eco- prefix.

45. B
The Indian ocean borders the east coast of Africa.

Choice A is incorrect; the Atlantic borders the west coast.

Choices C and D are clearly incorrect; the pacific doesn't border Africa.

46. A
Cuba, Haiti and Puerto Rico are located in the Caribbean Sea.

Choice B is incorrect; the North Sea borders Europe.

Choice C is incorrect; the Indian Ocean borders Asia and Africa.

Choice D is incorrect; the Black Sea is adjacent to the Mediterranean.

47. D
The Ural Mountains separate the continents of Europe and Asia.
Choice A is incorrect; North and South America are not separated by mountains.

Choice B is incorrect; Africa and Asia are not separated by mountains.

Choice C is incorrect; Australia is an island.

48. A
Australia is a contintent, though not a large one.

Continents have the following characteristics:

- Areas of geologically stable continental crust, or cratons, tectonically independent from other continents
- Biological distinctiveness, with unique animal and plant life
- Cultural uniqueness
- Local belief in separate continental status

49. A
A nation is also known as a country; nation and country are

interchangeable terms.

Choice B is incorrect; although nations have governments, they are not interchangeable.

Choice C is incorrect; a society does not have to be a nation.

Choice D is clearly incorrect; a utopia is a fictional place.

50. D
Physical maps show features such as mountains, lakes and rivers.

Choice A is incorrect; a political map shows borders of countries.

Choice B is incorrect; movements of populations are not shown on a physical map.

Choice C is incorrect; ruins are not shown on a physical map.

Part V Science

Physical Science

1. B
Ionization potential and Electron affinity are energies required/released on removal/addition of electrons and dipole moment is measure of separation of positive and negative charges.

2. B
Electron Affinity is the energy released when an electron is added to an atom. Electronegativity is the tendency of an atom to attract a shared pair of electron. Lattice energy is the energy of formation of the crystal from infinitely separated ions.

3. D
Ionic bond requires transfer of electron from valence shell of a metal (Low ionization energy required. to that of non-metal (Preferably High tendency to gain electron)

4. D All mentioned criteria fulfill the formation of an ionic bond.

    a. Ionization energy of X is low.

    b. Electronegativity of D is high.

    c. X is a metal and Y is a non-metal.

5. D
Ionic bond is formed by simple donation of electron. Covalent bond is formed by sharing of electrons. Coordinate covalent bond is formed by donation of both electrons by single atom.

6. A
An Ionic bond is formed between a metal and non-metal. Lithium is a metal while N is a non-metal. No other option has the same case, hence option A is the best possible answer.

7. C
Covalent bond involves sharing of electron. CH4 is formed from sharing of electrons.

Options A, B and C are incorrect because potassium is an alkali metal, magnesium is also a metal, while Cl and F are non-metals hence, an ionic bond is formed between these compounds.

8. C
In a chemical reaction, chemical equilibrium is the state in which both reactants and products are present in concentrations which have no further tendency to change with time. Usually, this state results when the forward reaction proceeds at the same rate as the reverse reaction.

9. D
In a reversible chemical reaction, reactants are reacting to

yield the products, as the products are reacting to produce the reactants.

10. B
In an exothermic reaction, an increase in temperature favors the reaction to occur in the backward direction.

11. C
In an endothermic reaction, an increase in temperature favors the reaction to occur in the forward direction.

12. A
For exothermic reaction, Kc increases with the decrease in temperature and a decrease in temperature favors the reaction to occur in the forward direction.

13. B
In an exothermic reaction, an increase in temperature favors the reaction to occur in the backward direction

14. C
Emission of heat on products side indicates that it is an exothermic reaction. In an exothermic reaction, a decrease in temperature favors the reaction to occur in the forward direction.

15. D
Activation energy is the difference in energy content between atoms or molecules in an activated or transition-state configuration and the corresponding atoms and molecules in their initial configuration, the minimum amount of energy that is required to activate atoms or molecules to a condition in which they can undergo chemical transformation.

16. B
The rate of reaction is not constant throughout the activity but decreases with time due to decrease in the concentration of reactants. All other options are incorrect.

17. C
when there is a chance of rate of reaction being changed at the time of measured. Infinitesimally small amount is measure for infinitesimally short period of time. It means, instantaneous rate of reaction measured at any given time is

instantaneous. All other options are incorrect

18. B
A zero-order reaction is independent of concentration of reactant molecules.

Options A and C are incorrect as first order reaction is when the rate depends linearly on one reactant and a 2nd order reaction is when the sum of the exponents in the rate law is equal to two.

19. C
As the name indicates, an inhibitor decrease the rate of reaction, or can even prevent the chemical reaction from occurring.

Option A is incorrect as enzyme are biological catalysts that help complex reactions to occur.

Option C is incorrect as promoter means an agent which might promote an event. While auto catalyst is when product of the reaction acts as a catalysis.

20. D
According to law of conservation of mass, which states that for any system closed to all transfers of matter and energy (both of which have mass), the mass of the system must remain constant over time. Therefore, when a candle burns, the wax and wick both give off energy.

Life Science

21. C
Absorptive heterotrophs: as they absorb nutrition from organic sources.

Fungi cannot prepare their own food by absorbing light, hence choices A and B are incorrect. They do not use reduced inorganic matter as H-donor, so choice D is also incorrect.

22. D
All choices except B are correct organisms belonging to kingdom Protista and Plantae have ability to produce their own food. Fungi are heterotrophs hence choice B is incorrect.

23. C
Autotrophs and heterotrophs have different energy pathways: it means their bodies are designed to obtain energy from different energy sources. For example, heterotrophs obtain organic compounds from outside, and utilize it while autotrophs prepare complex organic compounds within their own system.

Choices A and D are incorrect; heterotrophs don't contain chlorophyll and can't prepare their own food.

Choice B is incorrect; autotrophs prepare their own food and don't need to absorb it from outside.

24. B
Glucose splits into two molecules of pyruvic acid through glycolysis and provides energy to the cell. Glycolysis is the most common metabolic pathway for providing energy to the cell and glucose is initial substrate for glycolysis.

Choices A, C, and D are incorrect because: glucose breaks down to give pyruvate via glycolysis and then alcohol, and lactic acid are produced by breakdown of pyruvate by enzymatic metabolism.

25. A
Glycolysis, pyruvate oxidation, Kreb's cycle (TCA), Respiratory chain: glucose is converted to pyruvate by glycolysis, pyruvate is converted to Acetyl CoA which enters Kreb's cycle. Finally NADH enters the respiratory chain.

All other choices are incorrect.

26. B
A hypotonic environment is an environment which is more diluted than the cell's environment, hence, water will move to the area of lower concentration i.e. cell.

Choice A is incorrect because a hypertonic environment is concentrated as compared to the cell, and water from the cell will move outside and it will shrink.

Choice C is incorrect because an isotonic environment is when cell's internal environment resembles outside environment.

Choice D is incorrect because mesotonic is not a term used in homeostasis.

27. C
A negative feedback mechanism reduces the original effect of stimulus, as insulin reduces the sugar level to normal

Choice A is incorrect because positive feedback increases the original effect of the stimulus.

Choice B is incorrect because afferent pathway is related to carrying nerve impulses to brain as a result of stimulus.

Choice D is incorrect because thermoregulation is the temperature maintaining mechanism of the body.

28. C
Incomplete dominance. 'R' (red color) is not completely dominant over the white color 'r' and an intermediate phenotype 'pink' (Rr) is observed for heterozygous progeny.

Choice A is incorrect because in over dominance, the phenotype is intense as compared to parental generation.

Choice B is incorrect because in co-dominance, both alleles express independently.

Choice D is incorrect because in complete dominance, R would completely dominate the recessive r trait, and heterozygous progeny would appear as red flowers.

29. B
Linked genes. linked genes form a linkage group on human chromosomes. Linked genes whose loci are close to each other don't follow the law of independent assortment be-

cause they can't assort independently during meiosis.

Choice A is incorrect because crossing over leads to independent assortment of alleles. Different linked genes can be separated by crossing over.

Choice C is incorrect because co-dominance is a case when both alleles express in heterozygous condition.
Choice D is incorrect because all X-linked genes don't disobey law of independent assortment.

30. A
X-linked in male : Y chromosomes doesn't contain all genes present on X chromosome, hence, many diseases like hemophilia are recessive but appear in a male child, moreover, male progeny is heterozygous (XY) for sex-linked alleles.

Choice B is incorrect because Y-linked traits are not considered as recessive, they appear in father and son and are not transferred to female progeny. Moreover, sex linked recessives mostly refer to X-linked recessive.

Choice C is incorrect because autosomal chromosomes of male and female progeny behave similarly, hence, are recessive traits for heterozygosity, and will not appear in both.

31. A
Cancer cells undergo mitosis. In mitosis same number of chromosomes are present in daughter cells. Cancer cells have problem with regulation of mitotic cell division.

Choice B is incorrect because in meiosis number of chromosomes is reduced to half than that of parent cell.

Choice C is incorrect because binary fission is an asexual cell division mechanism for bacteria and other prokaryotes.

Choice D is incorrect because budding is a asexual cell division mechanism for yeast etc.

32. A
Genetic information remains unchanged after mitotic cell division because of no crossing over. Crossing over leads to

the appearance of new traits in the offspring due to recombination. Alleles may assort independently and different phenotype can be observed in the progeny.

Choice B is incorrect because recombination leads to formation of new genetic combinations that are different than that of parents.

Choice C is incorrect because controlled cell division is not related to change in genetic information.

Choice D is incorrect because when an egg fertilizes with sperm, the number of chromosome in the fertilized egg is the same, but the genetic makeup is different than both parents.

33. C
Anaphase is the critical stage in mitosis ensuring equal distribution of chromosomes in daughter cells. During anaphase, the spindle fibers contract and chromosomes move towards the opposite poles. An Equal number of chromosomes should reach at each pole.

Choice A is incorrect because during prophase chromosomes condense and nuclear envelop disappears.

Choice B is incorrect because chromosomes arrange at the equator by kinetochore fibers.

Choice D is incorrect because when chromosomes reach opposite poles, telophase begins.

34. D
None of the above. All choices are related to meiosis. The choices given are:

    a. Occurs in diploid cell only
    b. Occurs at time of gamete formation
    c. 2nd meiotic division is like mitosis

35. C
Anaphase I: as each pole receive half the total number of chromosomes.

All other options are incorrect because division of chromosomes occurs in anaphase as (1/2 number of) chromosomes move to the opposite poles in anaphase I.

36. A
Natural selection is survival of the fittest and better adapted. Fitness is a comparative trait, the one who survives and better adapts, survives and is thus selected by nature.
Choice B is incorrect as adaptation is a major factor in natural selection.

Choice C is incorrect; natural selection is highly influenced by environmental factors.

37. D
Both A and B are results of natural selection. Natural selection changes the gene pool leaving behind the best adapted individuals.

Choice C is incorrect because acclimatization is when organism adjust to the changing environment, no change in gene pool occurs.

38. A
Natural selection advances in the following sequence: genetic mutation, adaptation, reproduction, survival, increase in gene pool. A genetic mutation will make an individual different. This difference will make the individual better adapted to the environment, this trait (aided better adaptation) will be passed onto the next generation by reproduction. The better adapted will survive and reproduce hence, there will be increase in gene pool.

39. D
Energy flows in the following sequence: autotrophs, primary consumers, secondary consumers, tertiary consumers, decomposers. Autotrophs are producers, then comes primary, secondary and tertiary consumers, and at the end of the chain, decomposers.

40. A
Producers are at the lowest level of the energy pyramid, as they prepare their own food from solar energy and can pass

on energy.

Choices B, C and D are placed above producers respectively.

Earth and Space Sciences

41. D
Carbon dioxide, ozone and methane are all greenhouse gases, however, nitrogen N_2 is not a green house gas. Nitrous oxide N_2O also known as laughing gas is a compound of nitrogen which acts as greenhouse gas.

42. D
Choice D is false because less heat re-emitted into the environment previously as compared to now, as less heat escapes into the space and rest of the heat is re-emitted into the environment due to green house gases.

Choice A is true, as human activity has increased green house gases like CO_2 etc, and green house effect has increased as a result.

Choice B is true because more heat escaped from the earth environment to outer space.

Choice C is true because less heat escapes now to the outer space from the earth's environment.

43. B
Green house gases allow less heat to escape into the environment, they do not block the heat escape completely hence, this choice is not correct.

Choices A and C are correct because these gases absorb heat, and as a result increase the temperature of the earth.

44. C
Studies based on cosmic background radiation suggest that the universe is about 13.7 billion years old. 1 billion=10^9. Hence the correct answer is 13.7 x 10^9 years.

45. D
Choices A, B and C are supported by Big bang theory however the last option adheres to "Steady-state theory" and is not part of Big Bang explanations.

46. C
The Cosmic Microwave Background radiation, or CMB for short, is a faint glow of light that fills the universe, falling on Earth from every direction with nearly uniform intensity.

47. D
Gravitational force between the two bodies provides the required centripetal force which makes the moon move in a circular orbit around the earth.

48. A
The direction of plate motion and type of crust will determine the features at the new plate boundary for example appearance of an ocean or disappearance will be determined by these two.

All other combination are incorrect as type of ridges and type of boundary will not play role in features of a new plate boundary.

49. A
Convergence of plates leads to collision and oceanic crust is destroyed. Actions listed in the other choices form oceanic crust.

50. B
Convergence can occur between continent-ocean, continent-continent, ocean-ocean but the crust will be destroyed. After transformation no crust is created or destroyed.

All other combinations are incorrect as divergence can occur in ocean and on land and crust will be formed.

Practice Test Questions Set 2

THE PRACTICE TEST PORTION PRESENTS QUESTIONS THAT ARE REPRESENTATIVE OF THE TYPE OF QUESTION YOU SHOULD EXPECT TO FIND ON THE TASC®. However, they are not intended to match exactly what is on the TASC®.

For the best results, take this Practice Test as if it were the real exam. Set aside time when you will not be disturbed, and a location that is quiet and free of distractions. Read the instructions carefully, read each question carefully, and answer to the best of your ability.

Use the bubble answer sheets provided. When you have completed the Practice Test, check your answer against the Answer Key and read the explanation provided.

Reading Answer Sheet

1. (A) (B) (C) (D)
2. (A) (B) (C) (D)
3. (A) (B) (C) (D)
4. (A) (B) (C) (D)
5. (A) (B) (C) (D)
6. (A) (B) (C) (D)
7. (A) (B) (C) (D)
8. (A) (B) (C) (D)
9. (A) (B) (C) (D)
10. (A) (B) (C) (D)
11. (A) (B) (C) (D)
12. (A) (B) (C) (D)
13. (A) (B) (C) (D)
14. (A) (B) (C) (D)
15. (A) (B) (C) (D)
16. (A) (B) (C) (D)
17. (A) (B) (C) (D)
18. (A) (B) (C) (D)
19. (A) (B) (C) (D)
20. (A) (B) (C) (D)
21. (A) (B) (C) (D)
22. (A) (B) (C) (D)
23. (A) (B) (C) (D)
24. (A) (B) (C) (D)
25. (A) (B) (C) (D)
26. (A) (B) (C) (D)
27. (A) (B) (C) (D)
28. (A) (B) (C) (D)
29. (A) (B) (C) (D)
30. (A) (B) (C) (D)
31. (A) (B) (C) (D)
32. (A) (B) (C) (D)
33. (A) (B) (C) (D)
34. (A) (B) (C) (D)
35. (A) (B) (C) (D)
36. (A) (B) (C) (D)
37. (A) (B) (C) (D)
38. (A) (B) (C) (D)
39. (A) (B) (C) (D)
40. (A) (B) (C) (D)
41. (A) (B) (C) (D)
42. (A) (B) (C) (D)
43. (A) (B) (C) (D)
44. (A) (B) (C) (D)
45. (A) (B) (C) (D)
46. (A) (B) (C) (D)
47. (A) (B) (C) (D)
48. (A) (B) (C) (D)
49. (A) (B) (C) (D)
50. (A) (B) (C) (D)

English and Language Arts Answer Sheet

1. Ⓐ Ⓑ Ⓒ Ⓓ
2. Ⓐ Ⓑ Ⓒ Ⓓ
3. Ⓐ Ⓑ Ⓒ Ⓓ
4. Ⓐ Ⓑ Ⓒ Ⓓ
5. Ⓐ Ⓑ Ⓒ Ⓓ
6. Ⓐ Ⓑ Ⓒ Ⓓ
7. Ⓐ Ⓑ Ⓒ Ⓓ
8. Ⓐ Ⓑ Ⓒ Ⓓ
9. Ⓐ Ⓑ Ⓒ Ⓓ
10. Ⓐ Ⓑ Ⓒ Ⓓ
11. Ⓐ Ⓑ Ⓒ Ⓓ
12. Ⓐ Ⓑ Ⓒ Ⓓ
13. Ⓐ Ⓑ Ⓒ Ⓓ
14. Ⓐ Ⓑ Ⓒ Ⓓ
15. Ⓐ Ⓑ Ⓒ Ⓓ
16. Ⓐ Ⓑ Ⓒ Ⓓ
17. Ⓐ Ⓑ Ⓒ Ⓓ
18. Ⓐ Ⓑ Ⓒ Ⓓ
19. Ⓐ Ⓑ Ⓒ Ⓓ
20. Ⓐ Ⓑ Ⓒ Ⓓ
21. Ⓐ Ⓑ Ⓒ Ⓓ
22. Ⓐ Ⓑ Ⓒ Ⓓ
23. Ⓐ Ⓑ Ⓒ Ⓓ
24. Ⓐ Ⓑ Ⓒ Ⓓ
25. Ⓐ Ⓑ Ⓒ Ⓓ
26. Ⓐ Ⓑ Ⓒ Ⓓ
27. Ⓐ Ⓑ Ⓒ Ⓓ
28. Ⓐ Ⓑ Ⓒ Ⓓ
29. Ⓐ Ⓑ Ⓒ Ⓓ
30. Ⓐ Ⓑ Ⓒ Ⓓ
31. Ⓐ Ⓑ Ⓒ Ⓓ
32. Ⓐ Ⓑ Ⓒ Ⓓ
33. Ⓐ Ⓑ Ⓒ Ⓓ
34. Ⓐ Ⓑ Ⓒ Ⓓ
35. Ⓐ Ⓑ Ⓒ Ⓓ
36. Ⓐ Ⓑ Ⓒ Ⓓ
37. Ⓐ Ⓑ Ⓒ Ⓓ
38. Ⓐ Ⓑ Ⓒ Ⓓ
39. Ⓐ Ⓑ Ⓒ Ⓓ
40. Ⓐ Ⓑ Ⓒ Ⓓ
41. Ⓐ Ⓑ Ⓒ Ⓓ
42. Ⓐ Ⓑ Ⓒ Ⓓ
43. Ⓐ Ⓑ Ⓒ Ⓓ
44. Ⓐ Ⓑ Ⓒ Ⓓ
45. Ⓐ Ⓑ Ⓒ Ⓓ
46. Ⓐ Ⓑ Ⓒ Ⓓ
47. Ⓐ Ⓑ Ⓒ Ⓓ
48. Ⓐ Ⓑ Ⓒ Ⓓ
49. Ⓐ Ⓑ Ⓒ Ⓓ
50. Ⓐ Ⓑ Ⓒ Ⓓ

Mathematics Answer Sheet

1. (A) (B) (C) (D)
2. (A) (B) (C) (D)
3. (A) (B) (C) (D)
4. (A) (B) (C) (D)
5. (A) (B) (C) (D)
6. (A) (B) (C) (D)
7. (A) (B) (C) (D)
8. (A) (B) (C) (D)
9. (A) (B) (C) (D)
10. (A) (B) (C) (D)
11. (A) (B) (C) (D)
12. (A) (B) (C) (D)
13. (A) (B) (C) (D)
14. (A) (B) (C) (D)
15. (A) (B) (C) (D)
16. (A) (B) (C) (D)
17. (A) (B) (C) (D)

18. (A) (B) (C) (D)
19. (A) (B) (C) (D)
20. (A) (B) (C) (D)
21. (A) (B) (C) (D)
22. (A) (B) (C) (D)
23. (A) (B) (C) (D)
24. (A) (B) (C) (D)
25. (A) (B) (C) (D)
26. (A) (B) (C) (D)
27. (A) (B) (C) (D)
28. (A) (B) (C) (D)
29. (A) (B) (C) (D)
30. (A) (B) (C) (D)
31. (A) (B) (C) (D)
32. (A) (B) (C) (D)
33. (A) (B) (C) (D)
34. (A) (B) (C) (D)

35. (A) (B) (C) (D)
36. (A) (B) (C) (D)
37. (A) (B) (C) (D)
38. (A) (B) (C) (D)
39. (A) (B) (C) (D)
40. (A) (B) (C) (D)
41. (A) (B) (C) (D)
42. (A) (B) (C) (D)
43. (A) (B) (C) (D)
44. (A) (B) (C) (D)
45. (A) (B) (C) (D)
46. (A) (B) (C) (D)
47. (A) (B) (C) (D)
48. (A) (B) (C) (D)
49. (A) (B) (C) (D)
50. (A) (B) (C) (D)

Social Studies Answer Sheet

1. Ⓐ Ⓑ Ⓒ Ⓓ
2. Ⓐ Ⓑ Ⓒ Ⓓ
3. Ⓐ Ⓑ Ⓒ Ⓓ
4. Ⓐ Ⓑ Ⓒ Ⓓ
5. Ⓐ Ⓑ Ⓒ Ⓓ
6. Ⓐ Ⓑ Ⓒ Ⓓ
7. Ⓐ Ⓑ Ⓒ Ⓓ
8. Ⓐ Ⓑ Ⓒ Ⓓ
9. Ⓐ Ⓑ Ⓒ Ⓓ
10. Ⓐ Ⓑ Ⓒ Ⓓ
11. Ⓐ Ⓑ Ⓒ Ⓓ
12. Ⓐ Ⓑ Ⓒ Ⓓ
13. Ⓐ Ⓑ Ⓒ Ⓓ
14. Ⓐ Ⓑ Ⓒ Ⓓ
15. Ⓐ Ⓑ Ⓒ Ⓓ
16. Ⓐ Ⓑ Ⓒ Ⓓ
17. Ⓐ Ⓑ Ⓒ Ⓓ

18. Ⓐ Ⓑ Ⓒ Ⓓ
19. Ⓐ Ⓑ Ⓒ Ⓓ
20. Ⓐ Ⓑ Ⓒ Ⓓ
21. Ⓐ Ⓑ Ⓒ Ⓓ
22. Ⓐ Ⓑ Ⓒ Ⓓ
23. Ⓐ Ⓑ Ⓒ Ⓓ
24. Ⓐ Ⓑ Ⓒ Ⓓ
25. Ⓐ Ⓑ Ⓒ Ⓓ
26. Ⓐ Ⓑ Ⓒ Ⓓ
27. Ⓐ Ⓑ Ⓒ Ⓓ
28. Ⓐ Ⓑ Ⓒ Ⓓ
29. Ⓐ Ⓑ Ⓒ Ⓓ
30. Ⓐ Ⓑ Ⓒ Ⓓ
31. Ⓐ Ⓑ Ⓒ Ⓓ
32. Ⓐ Ⓑ Ⓒ Ⓓ
33. Ⓐ Ⓑ Ⓒ Ⓓ
34. Ⓐ Ⓑ Ⓒ Ⓓ

35. Ⓐ Ⓑ Ⓒ Ⓓ
36. Ⓐ Ⓑ Ⓒ Ⓓ
37. Ⓐ Ⓑ Ⓒ Ⓓ
38. Ⓐ Ⓑ Ⓒ Ⓓ
39. Ⓐ Ⓑ Ⓒ Ⓓ
40. Ⓐ Ⓑ Ⓒ Ⓓ
41. Ⓐ Ⓑ Ⓒ Ⓓ
42. Ⓐ Ⓑ Ⓒ Ⓓ
43. Ⓐ Ⓑ Ⓒ Ⓓ
44. Ⓐ Ⓑ Ⓒ Ⓓ
45. Ⓐ Ⓑ Ⓒ Ⓓ
46. Ⓐ Ⓑ Ⓒ Ⓓ
47. Ⓐ Ⓑ Ⓒ Ⓓ
48. Ⓐ Ⓑ Ⓒ Ⓓ
49. Ⓐ Ⓑ Ⓒ Ⓓ
50. Ⓐ Ⓑ Ⓒ Ⓓ

Science Answer Sheet

1. (A) (B) (C) (D)
2. (A) (B) (C) (D)
3. (A) (B) (C) (D)
4. (A) (B) (C) (D)
5. (A) (B) (C) (D)
6. (A) (B) (C) (D)
7. (A) (B) (C) (D)
8. (A) (B) (C) (D)
9. (A) (B) (C) (D)
10. (A) (B) (C) (D)
11. (A) (B) (C) (D)
12. (A) (B) (C) (D)
13. (A) (B) (C) (D)
14. (A) (B) (C) (D)
15. (A) (B) (C) (D)
16. (A) (B) (C) (D)
17. (A) (B) (C) (D)
18. (A) (B) (C) (D)
19. (A) (B) (C) (D)
20. (A) (B) (C) (D)
21. (A) (B) (C) (D)
22. (A) (B) (C) (D)
23. (A) (B) (C) (D)
24. (A) (B) (C) (D)
25. (A) (B) (C) (D)
26. (A) (B) (C) (D)
27. (A) (B) (C) (D)
28. (A) (B) (C) (D)
29. (A) (B) (C) (D)
30. (A) (B) (C) (D)
31. (A) (B) (C) (D)
32. (A) (B) (C) (D)
33. (A) (B) (C) (D)
34. (A) (B) (C) (D)
35. (A) (B) (C) (D)
36. (A) (B) (C) (D)
37. (A) (B) (C) (D)
38. (A) (B) (C) (D)
39. (A) (B) (C) (D)
40. (A) (B) (C) (D)
41. (A) (B) (C) (D)
42. (A) (B) (C) (D)
43. (A) (B) (C) (D)
44. (A) (B) (C) (D)
45. (A) (B) (C) (D)
46. (A) (B) (C) (D)
47. (A) (B) (C) (D)
48. (A) (B) (C) (D)
49. (A) (B) (C) (D)
50. (A) (B) (C) (D)

Reading and Language Arts

Questions 1-4 refer to the following passage.

The Respiratory System

The respiratory system's function is to allow oxygen exchange through all parts of the body. The anatomy or structure of the exchange system, and the uses of the exchanged gases, varies depending on the organism. In humans and other mammals, for example, the anatomical features of the respiratory system include airways, lungs, and the respiratory muscles. Molecules of oxygen and carbon dioxide are passively exchanged, by diffusion, between the gaseous external environment and the blood. This exchange process occurs in the alveolar region of the lungs.

Other animals, such as insects, have respiratory systems with very simple anatomical features, and in amphibians even the skin plays a vital role in gas exchange. Plants also have respiratory systems but the direction of gas exchange can be opposite to that of animals.

The respiratory system can also be divided into physiological, or functional, zones. These include the conducting zone (the region for gas transport from the outside atmosphere to just above the alveoli), the transitional zone, and the respiratory zone (the alveolar region where gas exchange occurs). [6]

1. What can we infer from the first paragraph in this passage?

    a. Human and mammal respiratory systems are the same

    b. The lungs are an important part of the respiratory system

    c. The respiratory system varies in different mammals

    d. Oxygen and carbon dioxide are passive exchanged by the respiratory system

2. What is the process by which molecules of oxygen and carbon dioxide are passively exchanged?

    a. Transfusion

    b. Affusion

    c. Diffusion

    d. Respiratory confusion

3. What organ plays an important role in gas exchange in amphibians?

    a. The skin

    b. The lungs

    c. The gills

    d. The mouth

4. What are the three physiological zones of the respiratory system?

    a. Conducting, transitional, respiratory zones

    b. Redacting, transitional, circulatory zones

    c. Conducting, circulatory, inhibiting zones

    d. Transitional, inhibiting, conducting zones

Questions 5 - 8 refer to the following passage.

The Life of Helen Keller

Many people have heard of Helen Keller. She is famous because she was unable to see or hear, but learned to speak and read and went onto attend college and earn a degree. Her life is a very interesting story, one that she developed into an autobiography, which was then adapted into both a stage play and a movie. How did Helen Keller overcome her disabilities to become a famous woman? Read onto find out.

Helen Keller was not born blind and deaf. When she was a

small baby, she had a very high fever for several days. As a result of her sudden illness, baby Helen lost her eyesight and her hearing. Because she was so young when she went deaf and blind, Helen Keller never had any recollection of being able to see or hear. Since she could not hear, she could not learn to talk. Since she could not see, it was difficult for her to move around. For the first six years of her life, her world was very still and dark.

Imagine what Helen's childhood was like. She could not hear her mother's voice. She could not see the beauty of her parent's farm. She could not recognize who was giving her a hug, or a bath or even where her bedroom was each night. More sad, she could not communicate with her parents in any way. She could not express her feelings or tell them the things she wanted. It must have been a very sad childhood.

When Helen was six years old, her parents hired her a teacher named Anne Sullivan. Anne was a young woman who was almost blind. However, she could hear and she could read Braille, so she was a perfect teacher for young Helen. At first, Anne had a very hard time teaching Helen anything. She described her first impression of Helen as a "wild thing, not a child." Helen did not like Anne at first either. She bit and hit Anne when Anne tried to teach her. However, the two of them eventually came to have a great deal of love and respect.

Anne taught Helen to hear by putting her hands on people's throats. She could feel the sounds that people made. In time, Helen learned to feel what people said. Next, Anne taught Helen to read Braille, which is a way that books are written for the blind. Finally, Anne taught Helen to talk. Although Helen did learn to talk, it was hard for anyone but Anne to understand her.

As Helen grew older, she amazed people with her story. She went to college and wrote books about her life. She gave talks to the public, with Anne at her side, translating her words. Today, both Anne Sullivan and Helen Keller are famous women who are respected for their lives' work.

5. Helen Keller could not see and hear and so, her biggest problem in childhood was her inability to do what?

   a. Communicate
   b. Walk
   c. Play
   d. Eat

6. Helen learned to hear by feeling the vibrations people made when they spoke. What were these vibrations were felt through?

   a. Mouth
   b. Throat
   c. Ears
   d. Lips

7. From the passage, we can infer that Anne Sullivan was a patient teacher. We can infer this because

   a. Helen hit and bit her and Anne remained her teacher.
   b. Anne taught Helen to read only.
   c. Anne was hard of hearing too.
   d. Anne wanted to be a teacher.

8. Helen Keller learned to speak but Anne translated her words when she spoke in public. The reason Helen needed a translator was because

   a. Helen spoke another language.
   b. Helen's words were hard for people to understand.
   c. Helen spoke very quietly.
   d. Helen did not speak but only used sign language.

Questions 9 - 12 refer to the following passage.

Low Blood Sugar

As the name suggest, low blood sugar is low sugar levels in the bloodstream. This can occur when you have not eaten properly and undertake strenuous activity, or when you are very hungry. When Low blood sugar occurs regularly and is ongoing, it is a medical condition called hypoglycemia. This condition can occur in diabetics and in healthy adults.

Causes of low blood sugar can include excessive alcohol consumption, metabolic problems, stomach surgery, pancreas, liver or kidneys problems, as well as a side-effect of some medications.

Symptoms

There are different symptoms depending on the severity of the case.

Mild hypoglycemia can lead to feelings of nausea and hunger. The patient may also feel nervous, jittery and have fast heart beats. Sweaty skin, clammy and cold skin are likely symptoms.

Moderate hypoglycemia can result in a short temper, confusion, nervousness, fear and blurring of vision. The patient may feel weak and unsteady.

Severe cases of hypoglycemia can lead to seizures, coma, fainting spells, nightmares, headaches, excessive sweats and severe tiredness.

Diagnosis of low blood sugar

A doctor can diagnosis this medical condition by asking the patient questions and testing blood and urine samples. Home testing kits are available for patients to monitor blood sugar levels. It is important to see a qualified doctor though. The doctor can administer tests to ensure that will safely rule out other medical conditions that could affect blood sugar levels.

Treatment

Quick treatments include drinking or eating foods and drinks with high sugar contents. Good examples include soda, fruit juice, hard candy and raisins. Glucose energy tablets can also help. Doctors may also recommend medications and well as changes in diet and exercise routine to treat chronic low blood sugar.

9. Based on the article, which of the following is true?

    a. Low blood sugar can happen to anyone.

    b. Low blood sugar only happens to diabetics.

    c. Low blood sugar can occur even.

    d. None of the statements are true.

10. Which of the following are the author's opinion?

    a. Quick treatments include drinking or eating foods and drinks with high sugar contents.

    b. None of the statements are opinions.

    c. This condition can occur in diabetics and also in healthy adults.

    d. There are different symptoms depending on the severity of the case

11. What is the author's purpose?

    a. To inform

    b. To persuade

    c. To entertain

    d. To analyze

12. Which of the following is not a detail?

    a. A doctor can diagnosis this medical condition by asking the patient questions and testing.

    b. A doctor will test blood and urine samples.

    c. Glucose energy tablets can also help.

    d. Home test kits monitor blood sugar levels.

Questions 13 - 16 refer to the following passage.

Myths, Legend and Folklore

Cultural historians draw a distinction between myth, legend and folktale simply as a way to group traditional stories. However, in many cultures, drawing a sharp line between myths and legends is not that simple. Instead of dividing their traditional stories into myths, legends, and folktales, some cultures divide them into two categories. The first category roughly corresponds to folktales, and the second is one that combines myths and legends. Similarly, we can not always separate myths from folktales. One society might consider a story true, making it a myth. Another society may believe the story is fiction, which makes it a folktale. In fact, when a myth loses its status as part of a religious system, it often takes on traits more typical of folktales, with its formerly divine characters now appearing as human heroes, giants, or fairies. Myth, legend, and folktale are only a few of the categories of traditional stories. Other categories include anecdotes and some kinds of jokes. Traditional stories, in turn, are only one category within the larger category of folklore, which also includes items such as gestures, costumes, and music. [7]

13. The main idea of this passage is that

  a. Myths, fables, and folktales are not the same thing, and each describes a specific type of story

  b. Traditional stories can be categorized in different ways by different people

  c. Cultures use myths for religious purposes, and when this is no longer true, the people forget and discard these myths

  d. Myths can never become folk tales, because one is true, and the other is false

14. The terms myth and legend are

  a. Categories that are synonymous with true and false

  b. Categories that group traditional stories according to certain characteristics

  c. Interchangeable, because both terms mean a story that is passed down from generation to generation

  d. Meant to distinguish between a story that involves a hero and a cultural message and a story meant only to entertain

15. Traditional story categories not only include myths and legends, but

  a. Can also include gestures, since some cultures passed these down before the written and spoken word

  b. In addition, folklore refers to stories involving fables and fairy tales

  c. These story categories can also include folk music and traditional dress

  d. Traditional stories themselves are a part of the larger category of folklore, which may also include costumes, gestures, and music

16. This passage shows that

 a. There is a distinct difference between a myth and a legend, although both are folktales

 b. Myths are folktales, but folktales are not myths

 c. Myths, legends, and folktales play an important part in tradition and the past, and are a rich and colorful part of history

 d. Most cultures consider myths to be true

Questions 17 - 20 refer to the following passage.

What Is Mardi Gras?

Mardi Gras is fast becoming one of the South's most famous and most celebrated holidays. The word Mardi Gras comes from the French and the literal translation is "Fat Tuesday." The holiday has also been called Shrove Tuesday, due to its associations with Lent. The purpose of Mardi Gras is to celebrate and enjoy before the Lenten season of fasting and repentance begins.

What originated by the French Explorers in New Orleans, Louisiana in the 17th century is now celebrated all over the world. Panama, Italy, Belgium and Brazil all host large scale Mardi Gras celebrations, and many smaller cities and towns celebrate this fun loving Tuesday as well. Usually held in February or early March, Mardi Gras is a day of extravagance, a day for people to eat, drink and be merry, to wear costumes, masks and to dance to jazz music.

The French explorers on the Mississippi River would be in shock today if they saw the opulence of the parades and floats that grace the New Orleans streets during Mardi Gras these days. Parades in New Orleans are divided by organizations. These are more commonly known as Krewes.

Being a member of a Krewe is a task because Krewes are responsible for overseeing the parades. Each Krewe's parade is ruled by a Mardi Gras "King and Queen." The role of the

King and Queen is to "bestow" gifts on their adoring fans as the floats ride along the street. They throw doubloons, which is fake money and usually colored green, purple and gold, which are the colors of Mardi Gras. Beads in those color shades are also thrown and cups are thrown as well. Beads are by far the most popular souvenir of any Mardi Gras parade, with each spectator attempting to gather as many as possible.

17. The purpose of Mardi Gras is to

    a. Repent for a month.

    b. Celebrate in extravagant ways.

    c. Be a member of a Krewe.

    d. Explore the Mississippi.

18. From reading the passage we can infer that "Kings and Queens"

    a. Have to be members of a Krewe.

    b. Have to be French.

    c. Have to know how to speak French.

    d. Have to give away their own money.

19. Which group of people began to hold Mardi Gras celebrations?

    a. Settlers from Italy

    b. Members of Krewes

    c. French explorers

    d. Belgium explorers

20. In the context of the passage, what does the word spectator most nearly mean?

    a. Someone who participates actively

    b. Someone who watches the parade's action

    c. Someone on one of the parade floats

    d. Someone who does not celebrate Mardi Gras

Questions 21 - 24 refer to the following passage.

The Civil War

The Civil War began on April 12, 1861. The first shots of the Civil War were fired in Fort Sumter, South Carolina. Note that even though more American lives were lost in the Civil War than in any other war, not one person died on that first day. The war began because eleven Southern states seceded from the Union and tried to start their own government, The Confederate States of America.

Why did the states secede? The issue of slavery was a primary cause of the Civil War. The eleven southern states relied heavily on their slaves to foster their farming and plantation lifestyles. The northern states, many of whom had already abolished slavery, did not feel that the southern states should have slaves. The north wanted to free all the slaves and President Lincoln's goal was to both end slavery and preserve the Union. He had Congress declare war on the Confederacy on April 14, 1862. For four long, blood soaked years, the North and South fought.

From 1861 to mid 1863, it seemed as if the South would win this war. However, on July 1, 1863, an epic three day battle was waged on a field in Gettysburg, Pennsylvania. Gettysburg is remembered for being the bloodiest battle in American history. At the end of the three days, the North turned the tide of the war in their favor. The North then went onto dominate the South for the remainder of the war. Most well remembered might be General Sherman's "March to The Sea," where he famously led the Union Army through Georgia and the Carolinas, burning and destroying everything in their path.

In 1865, the Union army invaded and captured the Confederate capital of Richmond Virginia. Robert E. Lee, leader of the Confederacy surrendered to General Ulysses S. Grant, leader of the Union forces, on April 9, 1865. The Civil War was over, and the Union was preserved.

21. What does the word secede most nearly mean?

    a. To break away from

    b. To accomplish

    c. To join

    d. To lose

22. Which of the following statements summarizes a FACT from the passage?

    a. Congress declared war and then the Battle of Fort Sumter began.

    b. Congress declared war after shots were fired at Fort Sumter.

    c. President Lincoln was pro slavery

    d. President Lincoln was at Fort Sumter with Congress

23. Which event finally led the Confederacy to surrender?

    a. The battle of Gettysburg

    b. The battle of Bull Run

    c. The invasion of the confederate capital of Richmond

    d. Sherman's March to the Sea

24. The word abolish as used in this passage most nearly means?

    a. To ban
    b. To polish
    c. To support
    d. To destroy

Questions 25 - 28 refer to the following passage.

**The Daffodils
by William Wordsworth**

I wandered lonely as a cloud
That floats on high o'er vales and hills,
When all at once I saw a crowd,
A host, of golden daffodils;
Beside the lake, beneath the trees,
Fluttering and dancing in the breeze.

Continuous as the stars that shine
And twinkle on the Milky Way,
They stretched in never-ending line
Along the margin of a bay:
Ten thousand saw I at a glance,
Tossing their heads in sprightly dance.

The waves beside them danced, but they
Out-did the sparkling waves in glee:
A Poet could not but be gay,
In such a jocund company:
I gazed--and gazed--but little thought
What wealth the show to me had brought:

For oft, when on my couch I lie
In vacant or in pensive mood,
They flash upon that inward eye
Which is the bliss of solitude;
And then my heart with pleasure fills,
And dances with the daffodils.

25. Is the author of this poem a lover of nature?

   a. Yes

   b. No

   c. Uncertain. There isn't enough information

26. What is the general mood of this poem?

   a. Sad

   b. Thoughtful

   c. Happy

   d. Excited

27. What does sprightly mean?

   a. Growing very fast

   b. Sad and melancholy

   c. Weak and slow

   d. Happy and full of life

28. What is jocund company?

   a. Sad

   b. Happy

   c. Joyful

   d. Boring

Questions 29 - 32 refer to the following passage.

Ways Characters Communicate in Theater

Playwrights give their characters voices in a way that gives depth and added meaning to what happens on stage during their play. There are different types of speech in scripts that allow characters to talk with themselves, with other characters, and even with the audience.

It is very unique to theater that characters may talk "to themselves." When characters do this, the speech they give is called a soliloquy. Soliloquies are usually poetic, introspective, moving, and can tell audience members about the feelings, motivations, or suspicions of an individual character without that character having to reveal them to other characters on stage. "To be or not to be" is a famous soliloquy given by Hamlet as he considers difficult but important themes, such as life and death.

The most common type of communication in plays is when one character is speaking to another or a group of other characters. This is generally called dialogue, but can also be called monologue if one character speaks without being interrupted for a long time. It is not necessarily the most important type of communication, but it is the most common because the plot of the play cannot really progress without it.

Lastly, and most unique to theater (although it has been used somewhat in film) is when a character speaks directly to the audience. This is called an aside, and scripts usually specifically direct actors to do this. Asides are usually comical, an inside joke between the character and the audience, and very short. The actor will usually face the audience when delivering them, even if it's for a moment, so the audience can recognize this move as an aside.

All three of these types of communication are important to the art of theater, and have been perfected by famous playwrights like Shakespeare. Understanding these types of communication can help an audience member grasp what is artful about the script and action of a play.

29. According to the passage, characters in plays communicate to

    a. move the plot forward

    b. show the private thoughts and feelings of one character

    c. make the audience laugh

    d. add beauty and artistry to the play

30. When Hamlet delivers "To be or not to be," he can most likely be described as

    a. solitary

    b. thoughtful

    c. dramatic

    d. hopeless

31. The author uses parentheses to punctuate "although it has been used somewhat in film"

    a. to show that films are less important

    b. instead of using commas so that the sentence is not interrupted

    c. because parenthesis help separate details that are not as important

    d. to show that films are not as artistic

32. It can be understood that by the phrase "give their characters voices," the author means that

    a. playwrights are generous.

    b. playwrights are changing the sound or meaning of characters' voices to fit what they had in mind.

    c. dialogue is important in creating characters.

    d. playwrights may be the parent of one of their actors and give them their voice.

Questions 33 - 36 refer to the following two passages.

**Annabelle Lee First and Third Stanza
by Edgar Allan Poe**

It was many and many a year ago,
In a kingdom by the sea,

That a maiden there lived whom you may know
By the name of Annabel Lee;
And this maiden she lived with no other thought
Than to love and be loved by me.

But our love it was stronger by far than the love
Of those who were older than we
Of many far wiser than we
And neither the angels in heaven above,
Nor the demons down under the sea,
Can ever dissever my soul from the soul
Of the beautiful Annabel Lee.
For the moon never beams without bringing me dreams
Of the beautiful Annabel Lee;
And the stars never rise but I feel the bright eyes
Of the beautiful Annabel Lee;
And so, all the night-tide, I lie down by the side
Of my darling, my darling, my life and my bride,
In the sepulcher there by the sea,
In her tomb by the sounding sea.

War and Peace
Leo Tolstoy

"Yes, love, ...but not the love that loves for something, to gain something, or because of something, but that love that I felt for the first time, when dying, I saw my enemy and yet loved him. I knew that feeling of love which is the essence of the soul, for which no object is needed. And I know that blissful feeling now too. To love one's neighbours; to love one's enemies. To love everything - to Love God in all His manifestations. Some one dear to one can be loved with human love; but an enemy can only be loved with divine love. And that was why I felt such joy when I felt that I loved that man. What happened to him? Is he alive? ...Loving with human love, one may pass from love to hatred; but divine love cannot change. Nothing, not even death, can shatter it. It is the very nature of the soul. And how many people I have hated in my life. And of all people none I have loved and hated more than her.... If it were only possible for me to see her once more... once, looking into those eyes to say..."

33. What is the difference between the two kinds of love described in these passages?

    a. One speaks to romantic love and the other Divine love

    b. There is no difference

    c. Young love, and old love

    d. Both a and c.

34. In the poem, the author refers to Annabelle Lee in the past tense, why?

    a. Because she no longer loves him

    b. Because she has died

    c. For stylistic reasons

    d. None of the above

35. Agape is Greek for "unconditional love," which passage better describes unconditional love?

    a. The Poem by Edgar Allen Poe

    b. The Excerpt from War and Peace by Leo Tolstoy

    c. Neither passage

    d. Both passages

36. The dying man in the second passage, how many people does he specifically say he loves in the passage?

    a. One

    b. Two

    c. Three

    d. Four

Questions 37 - 40 refer to the following passage.

Women and Advertising

Only in the last few generations have media messages been so widespread and so readily seen, heard, and read by so many people. Advertising is an important part of both selling and buying anything from soap to cereal to jeans. For whatever reason, more consumers are women than are men. Media message are subtle but powerful, and more attention has been paid lately to how these message affect women. Of all the products that women buy, makeup, clothes, and other stylistic or cosmetic products are among the most popular. This means that companies focus their advertising on women, promising them that their product will make her feel, look, or smell better than the next company's product will. This competition has resulted in advertising that is more and more ideal and less and less possible for everyday women. However, because women do look to these ideals and the products they represent as how they can potentially become, many women have developed unhealthy attitudes about themselves when they have failed to become those ideals.

In recent years, more companies have tried to change advertisements to be healthier for women. This includes featuring models of more sizes and addressing a huge outcry against unfair tools such as airbrushing and photo editing. There is debate about what the right balance between real and ideal is, because fashion is also considered art and some changes are made to purposefully elevate fashionable products and signify that they are creative, innovative, and the work of individual people. Artists want their freedom protected as much as women do, and advertising agencies are often caught in the middle.

Some claim that the companies who make these changes are not doing enough. Many people worry that there are still not enough models of different sizes and different ethnicities. Some people claim that companies use this healthier type of advertisement not for the good of women, but because they would like to sell products to the women who are looking for these kinds of messages. This is also a hard balance to find: companies do need to make money, and women do need to feel respected.

While the focus of this change has been on women, advertising can also affect men, and this change will hopefully be a lesson on media for all consumers.

37. The second paragraph states that advertising focuses on women

    a. to shape what the ideal should be

    b. because women buy makeup

    c. because women are easily persuaded

    d. because of the types of products that women buy

38. According to the passage, fashion artists and female consumers are at odds because

    a. there is a debate going on and disagreement drives people apart

    b. both of them are trying to protect their freedom to do something

    c. artists want to elevate their products above the reach of women

    d. women are creative, innovative, individual people

39. The author uses the phrase "for whatever reason" in this passage to

    a. keep the focus of the paragraph on media messages and not on the differences between men and women

    b. show that the reason for this is unimportant

    c. argue that it is stupid that more women are consumers than men

    d. show that he or she is tired of talking about why media messages are important

40. This passage suggests that

a. advertising companies are still working on making their messages better

b. all advertising companies seek to be more approachable for women

c. women are only buying from companies that respect them

d. artists could stop producing fashionable products if they feel bullied

Questions 41 - 44 refer to the following passage.

FDR, the Treaty of Versailles, and the Fourteen Points

At the conclusion of World War I, both those who had won the war and those who were forced to admit defeat welcomed the end of the war and anticipated that a peace treaty would be signed. The American president, Franklin D. Roosevelt, played an important part in proposing what the agreements should be and did so through his Fourteen Points.

World War I had begun in 1914 when an Austrian archduke was assassinated, leading to a domino effect that pulled the world's most powerful countries into war on a large scale. The war catalyzed the creation and use of deadly weapons that had not previously existed, resulting in a great loss of soldiers on both sides of the fighting. More than 9 million soldiers were killed.

The United States agreed to enter the war right before it ended, and it is believed that its decision to finally become involved brought on the end of the war. FDR made it very clear that the U.S. was entering the war for moral reasons and had an agenda focused on world peace. The Fourteen Points were individual goals and ideas (focused on peace, free trade, open communication, and self reliance) that FDR wanted the power nations to strive for now that the war had concluded. He was optimistic and had many ideas about what could be accomplished through and during the post-war peace. However, FDR's fourteen points were poorly received when he presented them to the leaders of other world powers, many of whom wanted only to help their own countries and to punish the Germans for fueling the war, and they fell by the wayside. World War II was imminent, for Germany lost everything.

Some historians believe that the other leaders who participated in the Treaty of Versailles weren't receptive to the Fourteen Points because World War I was fought almost entirely on European soil, and the United States lost much less than did the other powers. FDR was in a unique position to help determine the fate of the war, but doing it on his own terms did not help accomplish his goals. This is only one historical example of how the United State has tried to use its power as an important country, but found itself limited because of geological or ideological factors.

41. The main idea of this passage is that

    a. World War I was unfair because no fighting took place in America

    b. World War II happened because of the Treaty of Versailles

    c. the power the United States has to help other countries also prevents it from helping other countries

    d. Franklin D. Roosevelt was one of the United States' smartest presidents

42. According to the second paragraph, World War I started because

    a. an archduke was assassinated

    b. weapons that were more deadly had been developed

    c. a domino effect of allies agreeing to help each other

    d. the world's most powerful countries were large

43. The author includes the detail that 9 million soldiers were killed

    a. to demonstrate why European leaders were hesitant to accept peace

    b. to show the reader the dangers of deadly weapons

    c. to make the reader think about which countries lost the most soldiers

    d. to demonstrate why World War II was imminent

44. According to this passage, it can be understood that the word catalyzed means

    a. analyzed

    b. sped up

    c. invented

    d. funded

Questions 45 - 49 refer to the following passage.

A Day That Will Live in Infamy! Attack on Pearl Harbor

In 1941, the world was at war. The United States was trying very hard to keep itself out of the conflict. In Europe, the countries of Germany and Italy had formed an alliance to expand their land and territory. Germany had already taken over Poland, Denmark, and parts of France. They were heading next toward England and due to all the fighting in Europe, there were battles taking place as far south as North Africa, where the German and Italian armies were fighting the British.

This got even worse when the Asian nation of Japan formed an alliance with Germany and Italy. Together, the three countries called themselves, the AXIS. Now, the war was in the Pacific as well as in Europe and Northern Africa. A great deal of Americans felt that perhaps now was the time for the United States to join with its ally, Great Britain and stop the Axis from taking over more regions of the world.

In 1941, Franklin Roosevelt was President of the United States. His fear at the time was that Japan would try to take over many countries in Asia. He did not want to see that happen, so he moved some of the United States warships that had been stationed in San Diego, to the military base at Pearl Harbor, in Honolulu, Hawaii.

Japan quietly plotted their attack. They waited until the early hours of the morning on Sunday, December 7, 1941. Then, 350 Japanese war plans began to drop bombs on the U.S. ships at Pearl Harbor. The first bombs fell at 7:48am and a mere 90 minutes later, the attack was over. Pearl Harbor was decimated. 8 battleships were damaged. Eleven ships were sunk and 300 U.S. planes were destroyed. Most devastating was the loss of life 2,400 U.S. military members was killed in the attack and 1,282 were injured.

President Roosevelt addressed the country via the radio and said "Today is a day that will live in infamy." He asked Congress to declare war on Japan. War was declared on Japan on December 8th and on Germany and Italy on December 11th. The United States had entered World War Two.

46. After reading the passage, we can infer that the word infamy most nearly means what?

    a. Famous

    b. Remembered in a good way

    c. Remembered in a bad way

    d. Easily forgotten

47. What three countries formed the Axis?

    a. Italy, England, Germany

    b. United States, England, Italy

    c. Germany, Japan, Italy

    d. Germany, Japan, United States

48. What do you think was President Roosevelt's reason for moving warships to Pearl Harbor?

    a. He feared Japan would bomb San Diego

    b. He knew Japan was going to attack Pearl Harbor

    c. He was planning to attack Japan

    d. He wanted to try and protect Asian countries from Japanese takeover

49. Why do you think Japan chose a Sunday morning at 7:48am for their attack?

    a. They knew the military slept late

    b. There is a law against bombing countries on a Sunday

    c. They wanted the attack to catch people by surprise

    d. That was the only free time they had to attack.

Question 50 refers to the following passage.

Trees

With an estimated 100,000 species, trees represent 25 percent of all living plant species. The majority of tree species grow in tropical regions of the world and many of these areas have not been surveyed by botanists, making species diversity poorly understood. The earliest trees were tree ferns and horsetails, which grew in forests in the Carboniferous period. Tree ferns still survive, but the only surviving horsetails are no longer in tree form. Later, in the Triassic period, conifers and ginkgos, appeared, followed by flowering plants after that in the Cretaceous period. [8]

50. Choose the correct list below, ranked from oldest to youngest trees.

    a. Flowering plants, conifers and ginkgos, tree ferns and horsetails

    b. Tree ferns and horsetails, conifers and ginkgos, flowering plants

    c. Tree ferns and horsetails, flowering plants, conifers and ginkgos

    d. Conifers and ginkgos, tree ferns and horsetails, flowering plants

Part II - Language Arts

Read the paragraph below and answer questions 1 - 2.

. . . Since he disappeared during a storm, it was supposed that the ill-fated man went to the very edge of the small, rocky island on which the light house stood, and was swept out by a wave. This supposition seemed the more likely as his boat was not found next day in its rocky niche. The place of light house keeper had become vacant. It was necessary to fill this place at the earliest moment possible, since the light house had no small significance for the local movement as well as for vessels going from New York to Panama. Mosquito Bay abounds in sandbars and banks. Among these navigation, even in the daytime, is difficult; but at night, especially with the fogs which are so frequent on those waters warmed by the sun of the tropics, it is nearly impossible.
    - from The Light House Keeper of Aspinwall by Henryk Sienkiewicz

Practice Test Questions 2 203

1. Which of the following sentences best opens the paragraph above?

  a. Once upon a time it happened that the couple who kept the Aspinwall light house, not far from Panama, disappeared without a trace.

  b. Once upon a time it happened that a ship wrecked into the rocks below the Aspinwall light house, not far from Panama.

  c. Once upon a time it happened that the light house keeper in Aspinwall, not far from Panama, disappeared without a trace.

  d. Once upon a time it happened that the light house keeper in Aspinwall, not far from Panama, escaped his imprisonment on the rocky island and disappeared without a trace.

2. Which of the following sentences best concludes the paragraph above?

  a. The light house itself was a monstrosity along the bay, made even more so by its insignificance in helping ships practically navigate the waters.

  b. The only guide at that time for the numerous vessels is the light house.

  c. The local Panamanians regarded the light house with disdain.

  d. The numerous vessels guided themselves through the bay and found that they had no need to fill the vacant place of the light house keeper.

Read the paragraph below and answer questions 3 - 4.

. . . These parts of the opposing armies were two long waves that pitched upon each other madly at dictated points. To and fro they swelled. Sometimes, one side by its yells and cheers would proclaim decisive blows, but a moment later the other side would be all yells and cheers. Once the youth saw a spray of light forms go in houndlike leaps toward the waving blue lines. There was much howling, and presently it went away with a vast mouthful of prisoners. Again, he saw a blue wave dash with such thunderous force against a gray obstruction that it seemed to clear the earth of it and leave nothing but trampled sod. And always in their swift and deadly rushes to and fro the men screamed and yelled like maniacs. Particular pieces of fence or secure positions behind collections of trees were wrangled over, as gold thrones or pearl bedsteads. There were desperate lunges at these chosen spots seemingly every instant, and most of them were bandied like light toys between the contending forces . . . .

- from The Red Badge of Courage by Stephen Crane

3. Which of the following sentences best opens the paragraph above?

a. On an incline over which a road wound he saw wild and desperate rushes of men perpetually backward and forward in riotous surges.

b. The battalion charged onward, wildly whelming the ambushed opposition and driving the desperate survivors off into the wood.

c. I looked and watched the riotous battle rage on wildly.

d. The riotous, bandying battle overwhelmed the youth and he scampered over the incline during a surge, proceeding to disguise himself thoroughly and steal away homeward.

4. Which of the following sentences best concludes the paragraph above?

a. In all my dreams I have not witnessed a scene more gruesome and sickly to recount.

b. The youth was pleased to witness the decisive direction of the crimson battle flags, as their westward lunging indicated a complete victory.

c. The youth could not tell from the battle flags flying like crimson foam in many directions which color of cloth was winning.

d. Escaping the scene as fast as could be, the youth found an abandoned cabin nearby and proceeded to live in it as if it were his own, building a new life as a farmer.

Read the paragraph below and answer questions 5 - 6.

. . . The original inhabitants of the enormous island came there from Asia and had a fairly isolated existence. They developed their own culture and spoke hundreds of different languages. The first known European contact with Australia was with Dutch explorers in the 17th Century, but the English were the first to explore and colonize the continent later on. English settlers arrived in Australia and English became the dominant language and Christianity the dominant religion. The 19th Century saw the development of the territory into a modern power and an important part of the enormous British Empire, and the 20th Century saw its independence from Great Britain and emergence as a powerful nation. Native Australians now make up only three percent of the Australian population; most Australians now have European ancestry . . . .

5. Which of the following sentences best opens the paragraph above?

a. When Europeans discovered the empty island of Australia, they found it perfectly suited to their needs.

b. Have you ever wondered why French is the official language of Australia?

c. The violent Australian struggle for independence dealt a huge blow to the country's native inhabitants.

d. The continent of Australia has been inhabited for thousands of years.

6. Which of the following sentences best concludes the paragraph above?

   a. Nowadays, most Australians speak English, Dutch and at least two native Australian languages.

   b. The continent remained largely unchanged for millennia, but in the last 250 years it has undergone drastic upheavals due to European colonization.

   c. We will never know what really happened during the European colonization of Australia, since no written records exist.

   d. Since the majority of Australians are natives, Christianity and the English language never really caught on.

Read the paragraph below and anwser questions 7 - 8.

. . . In the early 1800s, John Dalton theorized that matter is composed of tiny individual units. In the late 1897, J. J. Thomson discovered that atoms contain both positive and negative charges and visualized the negative charges as immersed within positively charged material. In 1909, Ernest Rutherford discovered that atoms have a positively charged nucleus at their center. Neils Bohr theorized in 1913 that negatively charged electrons orbit the positively charged nucleus in fixed paths, like planets around the sun. In the 1920s, several scientists modified Bohr's ideas of the orbital paths of electrons by demonstrating that electrons do not behave like other particles and that their location as they orbit the nucleus is difficult to predict. The rest of the 20th Century saw the discovery of other sub-atomic particles such as neutrons, quarks and gluons . . . .

7. Which of the following sentences best opens the paragraph above?

   a. The modern understanding of atomic structure is the product of the hard work of many scientists.

   b. Atomic structure is easy to understand because it boils down to common sense.

   c. 1913 was an important year in physics.

   d. Neils Bohr is considered the "father of modern physics" due to his work on atomic structure.

8. Which of the following sentences best concludes the paragraph above?

a. Ernest Rutherford is now widely considered to have been misguided and his work fraudulent.

b. Scientists now have a solid understanding of atomic structure, but new discoveries will surely be made in the future.

c. Now that scientists have completely understood the atom for about 100 years, they have turned their attention toward other pursuits and rarely study atomic structure.

d. Each new discovery changes what scientists thought they knew, forcing them to completely discard their previous ideas.

Read the paragraph below and anwser questions 9 - 10.

. . . Goalie Violet Jackson had her work cut out for her, enduring a barrage of shots in the first half, but letting none through. In the ninth minute of the game, Minnesota State defender Diana Smith stole the ball and vaulted it up the field for a waiting Melissa Welch, whose soft touch popped the ball over the head of the opposing goalie to find the back of the net. Though there was a tough battle through the rest of the match, things kept getting bogged down at midfield and no other goals were scored. The final was 1-0 Minnesota State. With this victory, Minnesota State will get an automatic berth in the national tournament, where they will face stiff competition. "We are already mentally preparing for the tournament," said the head coach after the game. "We can't afford to make mistakes there." The win is the women's soccer team's fifteenth of the season, giving them their first winning record in more than three years . . . .

9. Which of the following sentences best opens the paragraph above?

a. Despite winning the final game of the season, Minnesota State's record will not be enough to warrant an invitation to the national tournament.

b. After losing the last game of the season, the Minnesota State women's soccer team now advances to the national tournament.

c. A devastating one-goal loss put an end to Minnesota State's difficult season last night.

d. The Minnesota State women's soccer team won a close one today to earn a spot in the upcoming national tournament.

10. Which of the following sentences best concludes the paragraph above?

a. This hard-won victory marks the beginning of a new era of success for Minnesota State soccer.

b. Minnesota State fans are used to winning, so they will expect the team to go far in the tournament.

c. Next week the team will wait to see if they are invited to the upcoming national tournament.

d. This loss marks a new low for the Minnesota State soccer program.

Practice Test Questions 2

Directions: Each questions below may contain an error in capitalization, punctuation, grammar or usage. Choose the correct version.

11. Jessica's father was in the Navy, so she attended schools in Newark; New Jersey, Key West; Florida, San Diego, California, and Fairbanks, Alaska.

    a. Jessica's father was in the Navy, so she attended schools in Newark, New Jersey, Key West, Florida, San Diego, California, and Fairbanks, Alaska.

    b. Jessica's father was in the Navy, so she attended schools in: Newark, New Jersey, Key West, Florida, San Diego, California, and Fairbanks, Alaska.

    c. Jessica's father was in the Navy, so she attended schools in Newark, New Jersey; Key West, Florida; San Diego, California; and Fairbanks, Alaska.

    d. None of the choices are correct.

12. George wrecked John's car; that was the end of their friendship.

    a. George wrecked John's car that was the end of their friendship.

    b. George wrecked John's car. that was the end of their friendship.

    c. The sentence is correct.

    d. None of the choices are correct.

13. The dress was not Gina's favorite, however, she wore it to the dance.

    a. The dress was not Gina's favorite; however, she wore it to the dance.

    b. None of the choices are correct.

    c. The dress was not Gina's favorite, however; she wore it to the dance.

    d. The dress was not Gina's favorite however, she wore it to the dance.

14. Chris showed his dedication to golf in many ways; for example, he watched all the tournaments on television.

    a. Chris showed his dedication to golf in many ways, for example, he watched all the tournaments on television.

    b. The sentence is correct.

    c. Chris showed his dedication to golf in many ways, for example; he watched all the tournaments on television.

    d. Chris showed his dedication to golf in many ways for example he watched all the tournaments on television.

15. There was scarcely no food in the pantry, because not nobody ate at home.

    a. There was scarcely no food in the pantry, because nobody ate at home.

    b. There was scarcely any food in the pantry, because nobody ate at home.

    c. There was scarcely any food in the pantry, because not nobody ate at home.

    d. The sentence is correct.

16. Choose the sentence with the correct grammar.

    a. If Joe had told me the truth, I wouldn't have been so angry.

    b. If Joe would have told me the truth, I wouldn't have been so angry.

    c. I wouldn't have been so angry if Joe would have told the truth.

    d. If Joe would have telled me the truth, I wouldn't have been so angry.

17. Michael have lived in that house for forty years, while I has owned this one for only six weeks.

   a. Michael has lived in that house for forty years, while I has owned this one for only six weeks.

   b. Michael have lived in that house for forty years, while I have owned this one for only six weeks.

   c. None of the choices are correct.

   d. Michael has lived in that house for forty years, while I have owned this one for only six weeks.

18. Until you take the overdue books to the library, you can't take any new ones home.

   a. Until you take the overdue books to the library, you can't take any new ones home
   b. Until you take the overdue books to the library, you can't bring any new ones home.
   c. Until you bring the overdue books to the library, you can't take any new ones home.
   d. None of the choices are correct.

19. If they had gone to the party, he would have gone too.

   a. The sentence is correct.

   b. If they had went to the party, he would have gone too.

   c. If they had gone to the party, he would have went too.

   d. If they had went to the party, he would have went too.

20. His doctor suggested that he eat fewer snacks and do fewer lounging on the couch.

    a. His doctor suggested that he eat less snacks and do fewer lounging on the couch.

    b. His doctor suggested that he eat fewer snacks and do less lounging on the couch.

    c. His doctor suggested that he eat less snacks and do less lounging on the couch.

    d. None of the choices are correct.

21. Lee pronounced it's name incorrectly; it's an impatiens, not an impatience.

    a. The sentence is correct.

    b. Lee pronounced its name incorrectly; its an *impatiens*, not an *impatience*.

    c. Lee pronounced it's name incorrectly; its an *impatiens*, not an *impatience*.

    d. Lee pronounced its name incorrectly; it's an *impatiens*, not an *impatience*.

22. There was, however very little difference between the two.

    a. There was however, very little difference between the two.

    b. None of the choices are correct.

    c. There was; however, very little difference between the two.

    d. There was, however, very little difference between the two.

23. The Ford Motor Company was named for Henry Ford

    a. which had founded the company.

    b. who founded the company.

    c. whose had founded the company.

    d. whom had founded the company.

Fill in the blank.

24. Thomas Edison _____ after he invented the light bulb, television, motion pictures, and phonograph.

    a. has always been known as the greatest inventor

    b. was always been known as the greatest inventor

    c. must have had been always known as the greatest inventor

    d. will had been known as the greatest inventor

25. The weatherman on Channel 6 said that this has been the _____.

    a. most hottest summer on record.

    b. hottest summer on record.

    c. hotter summer on record.

    d. None of the above

26. Although Joe is tall for his age, his brother Elliot is _____ of the two.

    a. the tallest

    b. more tallest

    c. the tall

    d. the taller

27. I can never remember how to use those two common words, "sell," meaning to trade a product for money, or _____ meaning an event where products are traded for less money than usual.

   a. sale-
   b. "sale,"
   c. "sale
   d. "to sale,"

28. His father is _____

   a. a poet and novelist
   b. poet and novelist
   c. a poet and a novelist
   d. none of the above

29. The class just finished reading , _____ a short story by Carl Stephenson about a plantation owner's battle with army ants.

   a. -"Leinengen versus the Ants,"
   b. Leinengen versus the Ants,
   c. "Leinengen versus the Ants,"
   d. Leinengen versus the Ants

30. After the car was fixed it _____ again.

   a. ran good
   b. ran well
   c. would have run well
   d. ran more well

31. "Where does the sun go during the _____ asked little Kathy.

   a. night,"
   b. night"?,
   c. night,?"
   d. night?"

Questions 32 - 33 are based on the short essay below.

The Legend of Alexandre Pato

Although well known among his fans for the "duck dance" he performs after scoring, Alexandre Rodrigues da Silva has earned the name "Pato" for his ducky skills with the ball he uses to out-class his opponent in the field. [1] Already a promising talent in his early teens, Pato came into the limelight at the 2006 Club World Cup after becoming the youngest player, at 17 years and 102 days, to score a goal in a FIFA organized event- a feat previously held for decades by his legendary compatriot Pele. [2]

Alexandro started his soccer career at the age of 16 in the Brazilian club Sports Club, Internacional, from Rio Grande do Sul, and soon established himself as the main striker (forward). [3] Not only that; being the youngest recruit and the point of focus of his team fans, he led Internacional to their first title in the Recopa Sudamericana with his goals in the 2005-06 Season. [4]

At the age of only 17, Pato was transferred to the Italian giant AC Milan, and after a year, became the team's top scorer, with 18 goals in the 2008-09 Season. [5] The same year, he made his first international appearance and triumphed over Pele, once again by scoring the fastest goal in an international debut by a Brazilian. [6] The following season, Pato won the 2009 Series A Young Player of the Year award. [7] Still a teenager, he became the talk of Europe alongside the likes of Cristiano Ronaldo, Lionel Messi and Kaka. [8]

32. Which of the following changes to sentence 7 would focus attention on the main idea of the third paragraph?

a. The following season, Pato accomplished what he was yearning for throughout his life by winning the 2009 Series A Young Player of the Year award.

b. The following season, Pato conquered Europe by winning the 2009 Series A Young Player of the Year award.

c. The following season, Pato won the 2009 Series A Young Player of the Year award and proved his worth.

d. The following season, Pato accomplished his first European ambition by winning the 2009 Series A Young Player of the Year award.

33. Which of the following change(s) is/are needed in sentence 1?

a. He is well known among his fans for the "duck dance" he performs after scoring, but Alexandre Rodrigues da Silva has earned the name "Pato" for his ducky skills with the ball that he uses to outclass his opponent in the field.

b. Although well-known among his fans for the "duck-dance" he performs after scoring, Alexandre Rodrigues da Silva has earned the name "Pato" for his ducky skills with the ball that he uses to outclass his opponent in the field.

c. He is well known among his fans for the "duck-dance" he performs after scoring, but Alexandre Rodrigues da Silva has earned the name "Pato" for his ducky skills with the ball that he uses to out-class his opponent in the field.

d. He is well-known among his fans for the duck-dance he performs after scoring, but Alexandre Rodrigues da Silva has earned the name "Pato" for his ducky skills with the ball that he uses to out-class his opponent in the field.

Questions 34 - 35 are based on the short essay below.

The Future of Augmented Reality

In just a few years, Facebook has became popular worldwide, bringing with it other social media sites like Twitter.[1] Telecommunications has entered its third generation, and with unprecedented marketing from companies around the world, smartphones have become a 'must-have' accessory for everyone in the developed world. [2] In 2010, Information Technology experienced a renaissance called "the Apps Revolution"- a phenomena that is generating applications for every computing device imaginable, in every available language. [3] This has solicited application developers to explore more avant-garde concepts that offer the capacity to be integrated into their applications. [4] Developers integrated augmented reality into their applications and created applications like MapLens, SiteLens, Layar and the AR game ARhrrrr! [5]

These applications are only a few demonstrations of the true potential of augmented reality. [6] They are, in fact, just the "tip of the iceberg" to developer firms like Layar, who are getting ready to release APPs that do real-time underwater exploration. [7] And more and more APP developers are joining this race chasing after the huge profits available in this new industry. [8]

34. Which of the following change(s) to sentence 5 would focus attention on the main idea of the first paragraph?

a. Developers incorporated augmented reality with their applications and created applications like MapLens, SiteLens, Layar and the AR game ARhrrrr!

b. Augmented reality has turned out to be one such idea that soon was incorporated into applications like MapLens, SiteLens, Layar and the AR game ARhrrrr!

c. Augmented reality offered intense opportunity to developers in this regard.

d. Augmented reality started to fuel the blooming apps industry.

35. Which of the following changes are needed in sentence 4?

    a. This has lead application developers to explore more avant-garde concepts that offer the capacity to be integrated into their applications.

    b. This has tempted application developers to explore more avant-garde concepts that offer the possibility to be integrated into their applications.

    c. This has caused application developers to explore more avant-garde concepts that offer the potential to be integrated into their applications.

    d. This aftermath caused application developers to explore more avant-garde concepts that offer the capacity to be integrated into their applications.

Questions 36 - 38 are based on the short essay below.

Spring in Bengali

The days get warmer and the cool nights shorter. [1] There is dryness in the air and a drowsiness that suggests an afternoon nap. [2] Spring in the Bengali calendar, from the middle of February to the middle of April, are the months of Phalgoon and Chaitra. [3]

In the early days of spring, the trees, bereft of the leaves, look gaunt and ungainly. [4] But soon there are green shoots and the trees are covered with luxurious greenery. [5] Spring may witness the arrival of season's first rain and a nor'wester. [6]

The mango trees that start to spread flowers at the end of winter, are covered in spring. [7] Sapodia, curd fruit that have already arrived in late winter ripen in spring: and so is jujube. [8] Star fruit, whose season is from April to October, starts arriving in spring. [9] Rose apple also arrives in April. [10] Farmers grow sweet potato and peanuts in sandy soil in

the spring. [11] Ironically, watermelon and jackfruit and litchis arrive no earlier than the middle of April! [12]
The dry season continues; the lakes, ponds and rivers dry up further. [13] Shing (stinging catfish), climbing perch, African catfish, and other smaller fish are easy to catch. [14] Some lakes and water ponds that dry up in the summer and turn into festival venues for children who race to scoop up the fish with bamboo baskets. [15]

36. Which sentence in the second paragraph is least relevant to the main idea of the third paragraph?

    a. 5
    b. 6
    c. 8
    d. 9

37. Which of the following changes to sentence 12 would focus attention on the main idea of the second paragraph?

    a. Ironically, watermelon and jackfruit and litchis arrive earlier than the middle of April!

    b. Interestingly, watermelon and jackfruit and litchis arrive no earlier than the middle of April!

    c. Surprisingly, even watermelon, jackfruit and litchis arrive by the middle of April!

    d. Unfortunately, watermelon and jackfruit and litchis arrive no earlier than the middle of April!

38. Which sentence is not consistent with the author's purpose?

    a. 15
    b. 10
    c. 13
    d. 14

Directions: Select the correct version of the sentence.

39. When James went in his room, he found that his clothes had been put in the closet.

    a. When James went into his room, he found that his clothes had been put in the closet.

    b. None of the choices are correct.

    c. When James went into his room, he found that his clothes had been put into the closet.

    d. When James went in his room, he found that his clothes had been put into the closet.

40. After you lay the books on the counter, you may lay down for a nap.

    a. The sentence is correct.

    b. After you lie the books on the counter, you may lay down for a nap.

    c. After you lay the books on the counter, you may lie down for a nap.

    d. After you lay the books on the counter, you may lay down for a nap.

41. Don would never of thought of that book, but you could have reminded him.

    a. Don would never have thought of that book, but you could have reminded him.

    b. None of the choices are correct.

    c. Don would never have thought of that book, but you could of have reminded him.

    d. Don would never of thought of that book, but you could of reminded him.

42. Mrs. Foster learned me many things, but I was taught the most by Mr. Wallace.

a. Mrs. Foster taught me many things, but I learned the most from Mr. Wallace.

b. The sentence is correct.

c. Mrs. Foster learned me many things, but I learned the most from Mr. Wallace.

d. None of the choices are correct.

43. He did not have to loose the race; if only his shoes weren't so loose!

a. He did not have to loose the race; if only his shoes weren't so lose!

b. He did not have to lose the race; if only his shoes weren't so loose!

c. The sentence is correct.

d. None of the choices are correct.

44. My best friend said, "Always Count your Change."

a. My best friend said, "always count your change."

b. The sentence is correct.

c. My best friend said, "Always count your change."

d. None of the choices are correct.

45. The Victorian Era was in the nineteenth century.

a. The sentence is correct.

b. The victorian era was in the nineteenth century.

c. The Victorian Era was in the Nineteenth century.

d. The Victorian era was in the Nineteenth century.

46. I prefer pepsi to Coke.

    a. I prefer pepsi to coke.
    b. The sentence is correct.
    c. I prefer Pepsi to Coke.
    d. None of the choices are correct.

47. I always have french fries with my coke.

    a. The sentence is correct.
    b. I always have french fries with my Coke.
    c. I always have French Fries with my Coke.
    d. None of the choices are correct.

48. The blue Jays are my favorite team.

    a. The blue jays are my favorite team.
    b. The sentence is correct.
    c. The Blue Jays are my favorite team.
    d. None of the choices are correct.

49. The Southwest is the best part of the country.

    a. The sentence is correct.
    b. The southwest is the best part of the country.
    c. The southwest is the est part of the Country.
    d. None of the choices are correct.

Mathematics

1. A map uses a scale of 1:100,000. How much distance on the ground is 3 inches on the map if the scale is in inches?

    a. 13 inches
    b. 300,000 inches
    c. 30,000 inches
    d. 333.999 inches

2. Divide 9.60 by 3.2.

    a. 2.50
    b. 3
    c. 2.3
    d. 6.4

3. Subtract 456,890 from 465,890.

    a. 9,000
    b. 7,000
    c. 8,970
    d. 8,500

4. Estimate 46,227 + 101,032.

    a. 14,700
    b. 147,000
    c. 14,700,000
    d. 104,700

5. Find the square of 25/9

   a. 5/3
   b. 3/5
   c. 7 58/81
   d. 15/2

6. Which one of the following is less than a third?

   a. 84/231
   b. 6/35
   c. 3/22
   d. b and c

7. Which of the following numbers is the largest?

   a. 1
   b. √2
   c. 3/2
   d. 4/3

8. 15/16 x 8/9 =

   a. 5/6
   b. 16/37
   c. 2/11
   d. 5/7

9. Driver B drove his car 20 km/h faster than the driver A, and driver B travelled 480 km 2 hours before driver A. What was the speed of driver A?

   a. 70 km/hr.
   b. 80 km/hr.
   c. 60 km/hr.
   d. 90 km/hr.

Practice Test Questions 2

10. If a train travels at 72 kilometers per hour, how far will it travel in 12 seconds?

    a. 200 meters
    b. 220 meters
    c. 240 meters
    d. 260 meters

11. Tony bought 15 dozen eggs for $80. 16 eggs were broken during loading and unloading. He sold the remaining eggs for $0.54 each. What is his percent profit?

    a. 11%
    b. 10%
    c. 13%
    d. 12%

12. In a class of 83 students, 72 are present. What percent of students are absent?

    a. 12%
    b. 13%
    c. 14%
    d. 15%

13. In a local election at polling station A, 945 voters cast their vote out of 1270 registered voters. At polling station B, 860 cast their vote out of 1050 registered voters and at station C, 1210 cast their vote out of 1440 registered voters. What was the total turnout including all three polling stations?

    a. 70%
    b. 74%
    c. 76%
    d. 80%

14. Estimate 5205 ÷ 25

   a. 108
   b. 308
   c. 208
   d. 408

15. 7/15 – 3/10 =

   a. 1/6
   b. 4/5
   c. 1/7
   d. 1 1/3

16. Susan wants to buy a leather jacket that costs $545.00 and is on sale for 10% off. What is the approximate cost?

   a. $525
   b. $450
   c. $475
   d. $500

17. 11/20 ÷ 9/20 =

   a. 99/20
   b. 4 19/20
   c. 1 2/9
   d. 1 1/9

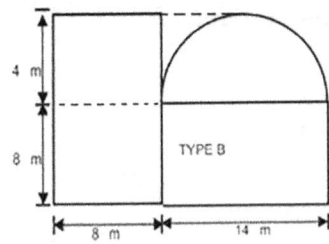

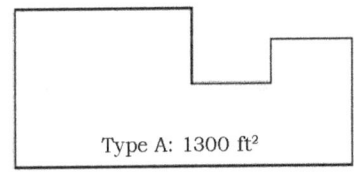

Type A: 1300 ft²

Note: Figure not drawn to scale

18. The price of houses in a certain subdivision is based on the total area. Susan is watching her budget and wants to choose the house with the lowest area. Which house type, A (1300 ft2) or B, should she choose if she would like the house with the lowest price? (1 m² = 10.76 ft² & π = 22/7)

    a. Type B is smaller 140 ft²
    b. Type A is smaller
    c. Type B is smaller at 855 ft²
    d. Type B is larger

19. Draw a reflection of the rectangle ABCD with the given mirror line m.

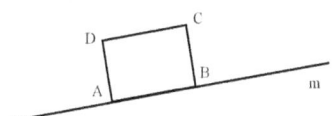

20. Draw a reflection of the quadrilateral ABCD in the coordinate plane if the mirror line is y-axis.

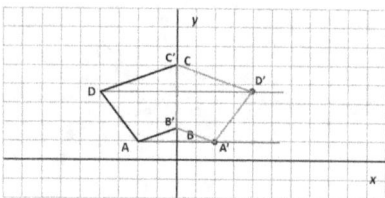

21. Using the quadratic formula, solve the quadratic equation: $0.9x^2 + 1.8x - 2.7 = 0$

    a. 1 and 3
    b. -3 and 1
    c. -3 and -1
    d. -1 and 3

22. Subtract polynomial $5x^3 + x^2 + x + 5$ from $4x^3 - 2x^2 - 10$.

    a. $-x^3 - 3x^2 - x - 15$
    b. $9x^3 - 3x^2 - x - 15$
    c. $-x^3 - x^2 + x - 5$
    d. $9x^3 - x^2 + x + 5$

23. Find x and y from the following system of equations:

$(4x + 5y)/3 = ((x - 3y)/2) + 4$
$(3x + y)/2 = ((2x + 7y)/3) -1$

    a. (1, 3)
    b. (2, 1)
    c. (1, 1)
    d. (0, 1)

24. Using the factoring method, solve the quadratic equation: $x^2 + 12x - 13 = 0$

    a. -13 and 1
    b. -13 and -1
    c. 1 and 13
    d. -1 and 13

25. Using the quadratic formula, solve the quadratic equation: $((x^2 + 4x + 4) + (x^2 - 4x + 4)) / (x^2 - 4) = 0$.

    a. It has infinite numbers of solutions
    b. 0 and 1
    c. It has no solutions
    d. 0

26. Turn the following expression into a simple polynomial:

$5(3x^2 - 2) - x^2(2 - 3x)$

    a. $3x^3 + 17x^2 - 10$
    b. $3x^3 + 13x^2 + 10$
    c. $-3x^3 - 13x^2 - 10$
    d. $3x^3 + 13x^2 - 10$

27. Solve $(x^3 + 2)(x^2 - x) - x^5$.

    a. $2x^5 - x^4 + 2x^2 - 2x$
    b. $-x^4 + 2x^2 - 2x$
    c. $-x^4 - 2x^2 - 2x$
    d. $-x^4 + 2x^2 + 2x$

28. $9ab^2 + 8ab^2 =$

  a. ab^2
  b. $17ab^2$
  c. 17
  d. $17a^2b^2$

29. Factor the polynomial $x^2 - 7x - 30$.

  a. $(x + 15)(x - 2)$
  b. $(x + 10)(x - 3)$
  c. $(x - 10)(x + 3)$
  d. $(x - 15)(x + 2)$

30. If a and b are real numbers, solve the following equation: $(a + 2)x - b = -2 + (a + b)x$

  a. -1
  b. 0
  c. 1
  d. 2

31. If $A = -2x^4 + x^2 - 3x$, $B = x^4 - x^3 + 5$ **and** $C = x^4 + 2x^3 + 4x + 5$, **find** $A + B - C$.

  a. $x^3 + x^2 + x + 10$
  b. $-3x^3 + x^2 - 7x + 10$
  c. $-2x^4 - 3x^3 + x^2 - 7x$
  d. $-3x^4 + x^3 + x^2 - 7x$

32. $(4Y^3 - 2Y^2) + (7Y^2 + 3y - y) =$

  a. $4y^3 + 9y^2 + 4y$
  b. $5y^3 + 5y^2 + 3y$
  c. $4y^3 + 7y^2 + 2y$
  d. $4y^3 + 5y^2 + 2y$

33. Turn the following expression into a simple polynomial: $1 - x(1 - x(1 - x))$

    a. $x^3 + x^2 - x + 1$
    b. $-x^3 - x^2 + x + 1$
    c. $-x^3 + x^2 - x + 1$
    d. $x^3 + x^2 - x - 1$

34. $7(2y + 8) + 1 - 4(y + 5) =$

    a. $10y + 36$
    b. $10y + 77$
    c. $18y + 37$
    d. $10y + 37$

35. Richard gives 's' amount of salary to each of his 'n' employees weekly. If he has 'x' amount of money then how many days he can employ these 'n' employees.

    a. $sx/7n$
    b. $7x/nx$
    c. $nx/7s$
    d. $7x/ns$

36. Factor the polynomial $x^2 - 3x - 4$.

    a. $(x + 1)(x - 4)$
    b. $(x - 1)(x + 4)$
    c. $(x - 1)(x - 4)$
    d. $(x + 1)(x + 4)$

37. Solve the inequality: $(2x + 1)/(2x - 1) < 1$.

a. $(-2, +\infty)$
b. $(1, +\infty)$
c. $(-\infty, -2)$
d. $(-\infty, 1/2)$

38. Using the quadratic formula, solve the quadratic equation:

$(a^2 - b^2)x^2 + 2ax + 1 = 0$

a. $a/(a + b)$ and $b/(a + b)$
b. $1/(a + b)$ and $a/(a + b)$
c. $a/(a + b)$ and $a/(a - b)$
d. $-1/(a + b)$ and $-1/(a - b)$

39. Turn the following expression into a simple polynomial: $(a + b)(x + y) + (a - b)(x - y) - (ax + by)$

a. $ax + by$
b. $ax - by$
c. $ax^2 + by^2$
d. $ax^2 - by^2$

40. Given polynomials $A = 4x^5 - 2x^2 + 3x - 2$ **and** $B = -3x^4 - 5x^2 - 4x + 5$, **find** $A + B$.

a. $x^5 - 3x^2 - x - 3$
b. $4x^5 - 3x^4 + 7x^2 + x + 3$
c. $4x^5 - 3x^4 - 7x^2 - x + 3$
d. $4x^5 - 3x^4 - 7x^2 - x - 7$

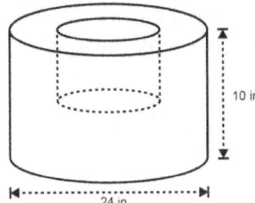

Note: Figure not drawn to scale

41. What is the volume of the above solid made by a hollow cylinder that is half the size (in all dimensions) of the larger cylinder?

    a. 1440π in^3

    b. 1260π in^3

    c. 1040π in^3

    d. 960π in^3

42. Find x if $\log_{1/2} x = 4$.

    a. 16

    b. 8

    c. 1/8

    d. 1/16

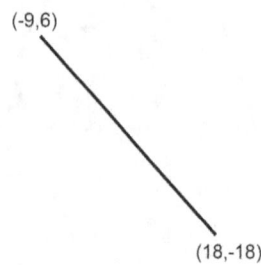

43. What is the slope of the line above?

    a. -8/9
    b. 9/8
    c. -9/8
    d. 8/9

44. Draw a reflection of the triangle ABC with the given mirror line m.

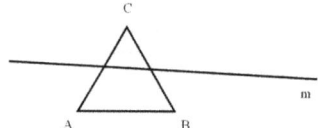

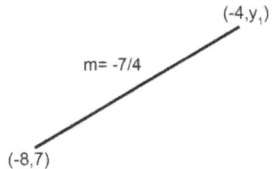

45. With the data given above, what is the value of y_1?

    a. 0
    b. -7
    c. 7
    d. 8

46. The area of a rectangle is 20 cm². If one side increases by 1 cm and other by 2 cm, the area of the new rectangle is 35 cm². Find the sides of the original rectangle.

    a. (4,8)
    b. (4,5)
    c. (2.5,8)
    d. b and c

47. Solve $\log_{10} 10{,}000 = x$.

    a. 2
    b. 4
    c. 3
    d. 6

48. What is the distance between the two points?

    a. ≈19
    b. 20
    c. ≈21
    d. ≈22

49. If in the right triangle, a is 12 and sinα=12/13, find cosα.

    a. -5/13
    b. -1/13
    c. 1/13
    d. 5/13

50. Find the solution for the following linear equation: 1/(4x - 2) = 5/6

    a. 0.2
    b. 0.4
    c. 0.6
    d. 0.8

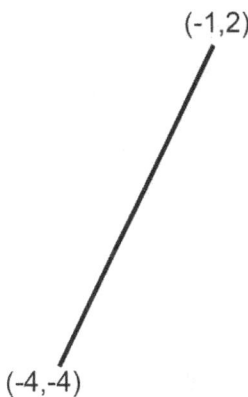

51. What is the slope of the line above?

    a. 1
    b. 2
    c. 3
    d. -2

52. How much water can be stored in a cylindrical container 5 meters in diameter and 12 meters high?

    a. 235.65 m³
    b. 223.65 m³
    c. 240.65 m³
    d. 252.65 m³

53. If members of the sequence {an} are represented by $a_{n+1} = -a_{n-1}$ and $a_2 = 3$ and, find $a_3 + a_4$.

    a. 2
    b. 3
    c. 0
    d. -2

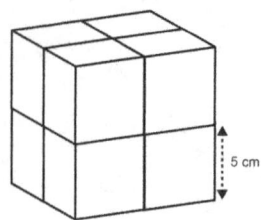

Note: Figure not drawn to scale

54. The figure above is composed of cubes. What is the volume?

    a. 125 cm³
    b. 875 cm³
    c. 1000 cm³
    d. 500 cm³

55. Solve

x √5 - y = √5
x - y √5 = 5

    a. (0, -√5)
    b. (0, √5)
    c. (-√5, 0)
    d. (√5, 0)

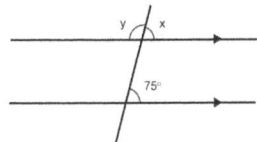

56. What is the value of the angle y?

   a. 25°
   b. 15°
   c. 30°
   d. 105°

57. Using the right triangle's legs, calculate (sinα + cosβ)/(tgα + ctgβ).

   a. a/b
   b. b/c
   c. b/a
   d. a/c

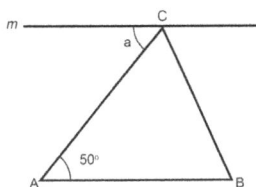

Note: Figure not drawn to scale

58. If the line *m* is parallel to the side AB of △ABC, what is angle *a*?

   a. 130°
   b. 25°
   c. 65°
   d. 50°

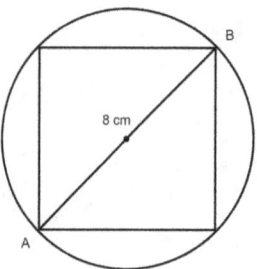

Note: Figure not drawn to scale

59. What is area of the circle?

a. 4 π cm²
b. 12 π cm²
c. 10 π cm²
d. 16 π cm²

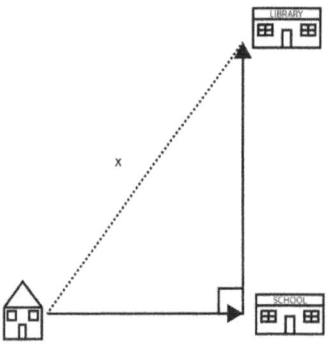

Note: Figure not drawn to scale

60. Every day starting from his home Peter travels due east 3 kilometers to the school. After school he travels due north 4 kilometers to the library. What is the distance between Peter's home and the library?

    a. 15 km
    b. 10 km
    c. 5 km
    d. 12 ½ km

Part IV - Social Studies

US History

1. Why was the "Gilded Age" called the Gilded Age?

    a. the California Gold Rush happened during it

    b. Gold was the major status symbol at the time

    c. There was a class of super-rich who enjoyed a lavish life-style, while there were many in extreme poverty

    d. Gangsters would gild enemies that were rich and/or greedy

2. What was the "Great Migration" of the United states in the early 1900s and late 1800s?

    a. Many blacks moving out of the South

    b. Large groups of European immigrants moving to the East Coast of the United States through Ellis Island

    c. Asians immigrating to the West Coast of the United States

    d. The last large movement of Native Americans to reservations

3. What created woman's suffrage in the United States?

   a. The Seneca Falls Convention

   b. The 18th Amendment

   c. The 19th Amendment

   d. The Jeannette Rankin Law

4. Who built the Panama Canal?

   a. The French

   b. The United States

   c. The Spanish

   d. Both A and B

5. What was the Open Door Policy?

   a. All countries would lower tariffs for more open markets

   b. Anyone could propose an idea to the president through the mail

   c. China would be open to trade with all countries

   d. A name coined for how people would go from government positions to being employed by the companies that lobbied them when they retired

6. What did the Federal Reserve Act do?

   a. Gave legal authority to issue U.S. Dollars

   b. Set up a government bank

   c. All banks had to keep at least 10% of their capital liquid

   d. Took United States assets out of private hands and put it in public trusts

7. What contributed to the United States joining World War I?

    a. The bombing of Pearl Harbor

    b. Alliances with Britain and France

    c. German U-boats torpedoing United States ships

    d. Both B and C

8. What did the Dawes Plan do?

    a. Gave aid in the form of tools and materials to Europe for reconstruction

    b. Gave money to Germany to pay war reparations to the Allies

    c. Facilitated the immigration of displaced persons at the end of World War I to the United States in exchange for a certain amount of low paid labor

    d. Gave money to countries who promised to fight communism

9. What was the start of the Great Depression?

    a. Prohibition

    b. The stock market collapse of 1929

    c. Germany defaulting on its loans to the United States after World War I

    d. The Dust Bowl

10. What did World War II unquestionably do for the Economy?

    a. End the Great Depression

    b. Reduce unemployment

    c. Exacerbate the Great Depression

    d. Choices A and B are still up to debate

World History

11. Which leaders were considered "The Big Three" of the Allied countries?

    a. Adolf Hitler, Benito Mussolini and Fumimaro Konoe

    b. Franklin Roosevelt, Winston Churchill and Charles de Gaulle

    c. Joseph Stalin, Franklin Roosevelt and Winston Churchill

    d. Joseph Stalin, Harry Truman and Winston Churchill

12. What was the Non-Aligned Movement?

    a. A bloc of nations that did not align itself with the United States or Soviet Union

    b. A bloc of nations the United States set up to stand against communism

    c. A movement within the United States to become isolationist once again

    d. A movement within the United states to be more benevolent world-wide instead of taking advantage of third world countries

13. What is MAD?

    a. Mutually Assured Defense

    b. Military Attack Defense

    c. Mutually Assured Destruction

    d. Massive Attack Destruction

Practice Test Questions 2

14. What was the Berlin Blockade?

    a. The First Major Crisis of the Cold War

    b. The Soviet Union stopped allowing aid to get to Berlin

    c. The cause for the Berlin Airlift

    d. None of the above

15. What was Détente?

    a. A "cooling down" period of the Cold War

    b. A "warming up" period of the Col War

    c. A period in which the United States was unsure who the leader of Soviet Russia was

    d. B and C

16. What was the motive of the Great Game between Russia and Great Britain during the New Imperialism colonization of Asia?

    a. To secure clear paths to countries like India, Iran and Afghanistan

    b. To financially exhaust each others countries

    c. To establish trade routes across Asia to Japan and Korea

    d. To be the first to secure trade agreements with most of Asia

17. What was one thing achieved with the Glorious Revolution in Great Britain in 1688?

    a. A Catholic monarch was removed from the throne

    b. A new social order demanding economic equality

    c. New industrial machines that lowered the cost of goods

    d. The standardization of education which allowed everyone to go to school

18. What was the main industry of the Industrial Revolution?

    a. Glass

    b. Paper

    c. Textiles

    d. Gas lighting

19. Which was the first European colony to declare its independence?

    a. Haiti

    b. The United States

    c. Chile

    d. Mexico

20. Which event is considered to be the start of the French Revolution?

    a. The rise of Napoleon Bonaparte

    b. The Woman's March on Versailles

    c. The passing of The Declaration of the Rights of Man and of the Citizen

    d. The storming of the Bastille

Civics and Goverment

21. The main purpose of dividing the government into three branches is

    a. so that no one branch could become too powerful.

    b. so that at least one branch could survive in case of an attack.

    c. to triple the strength of the government.

    d. to take away power from the military.

22. What is the minimum age to serve in the House of Representatives?

    a. 35
    b. 30
    c. 25
    d. 18

23. How does a bill become a law?

    a. It passes through the Senate and is then signed by the President

    b. It is signed by the President and is then passed by Parliament

    c. It passes through both houses of Congress and is vetoed by the President

    d. It passes through both houses of Congress and is signed by the President

24. How can congress override a presidential veto?

    a. With a 2/3 majority vote
    b. With a simple majority vote
    c. With a reconciliation bill
    d. There is no way to override a presidential veto

25. How is an amendment added to the Constitution?

    a. With a majority vote in Congress and the President's signature

    b. With 3/4 of the states ratifying it

    c. With a 2/3 majority vote in Congress

    d. With a majority of the popular vote

26. How many days (excluding Sundays) does the President have to sign a bill into law?

    a. 10
    b. 5
    c. 30
    d. 90

27. How many senators represent each state?

    a. 2
    b. 3
    c. it depends on the state's geographical size
    d. it depends on the size of the state's population

28. Whose vote breaks a tie in the Senate?

    a. The President
    b. The Vice President
    c. The Speaker of the House
    d. The Supreme Court

29. How many congressmen represent each state?

    a. 2
    b. 3
    c. It depends on the state's geographical size
    d. It depends on the size of the state's population

30. The U.S. Constitution designed the legislature to be bicameral. What does bicameral mean?

    a. There are two political parties
    b. There are three branches of government
    c. There are two levels of government: state and federal
    d. There are two houses of Congress

Economics

31. What does the Securities and Exchange Commission regulate?

    a. Agriculture

    b. Homeland Security

    c. The national budget

    d. The stock market

32. Federal income tax is

    a. Paid every time you buy something

    b. Paid through fees for government services

    c. Due annually, although it is normally deducted from every paycheck

    d. Due when you receive a government service

33. Which of the following is a good example of a public good?

    a. A park

    b. A plumber

    c. An airline

    d. A taxi

34. Sales tax is

    a. Paid every time you buy something

    b. Paid through fees for government services

    c. Due annually, although it is normally deducted from every paycheck

    d. Due when you receive a government service

35. Which of the following are exempt from federal taxes?

    a. Large corporations

    b. Small businesses

    c. Athletes

    d. Religious institutions

36. The federal government gets its funding by

    a. Taxation

    b. Selling goods

    c. Investing in stocks

    d. Donations

37. During the Great Depression, Keynesian economics was employed to

    a. raise taxes and decrease government spending.
    b. lower taxes and decrease government spending.
    c. raise taxes and increase government spending.
    d. lower taxes and increase government spending.

38. Bank deposits are guaranteed by the

    a. SEC.
    b. FDA.
    c. HUD.
    d. FDIC.

39. If a country's imports have more value than its exports, it is said to have a

    a. trade surplus.
    b. trade deficit.
    c. balance of trade.
    d. globalized economy.

40. What is a tariff?

   a. A tax on imports
   b. A fee for government services
   c. A guaranteed bank deposit
   d. A stock

Geography

41. In which direction has the mainland U.S. expanded since the American Revolution?

   a. northward

   b. southward

   c. eastward

   d. westward

42. Which of the following will humans not normally avoid?

   a. cold weather

   b. warm weather

   c. deserts

   d. high altitudes

43. Immigrants to the U.S. have always

   a. been welcomed with open arms by the native-born population

   b. been enslaved

   c. been discriminated against before finding equality

   d. come from Latin America

44. **Diffusion which moves a trend from one leader to another throughout a geographic area is known as**

    a. expansion diffusion

    b. stimulus diffusion

    c. relocation diffusion

    d. hierarchical diffusion

45. **What country has the U.S. military occupied from 2001 until 2011?**

    a. Afghanistan

    b. Iraq

    c. Israel

    d. Lebanon

46. **The science of mapmaking is**

    a. archaeology

    b. cartography

    c. geography

    d. GPS

47. **What is environmental determinism?**

    a. countries establishing rules to determine land usage

    b. human devastation of the environment

    c. environments have pre-determined uses which can only be altered by man

    d. climate and landforms are responsible for differences in human culture

48. Limited resources generally lead to

   a. a dense population

   b. exploitation by industrial businesses

   c. a trade route

   d. a scattered population

49. Which region of the U.S. has the fastest growing population?

   a. the northeast

   b. the southeast

   c. the northwest

   d. the Midwest

50. A farmer that produces enough food for his or her family and nothing more is known as a

   a. Subsistence farmer.

   b. Entrepreneur.

   c. Businessman.

   d. Migrant farm worker.

Part V - Science

Physical Science

1. What will be the coefficient of Magnesium chloride after balancing of the given equation

$Mg + HCL \rightarrow MgCl_2 + HCL$

   a. 1

   b. 4

   c. 2

   d. Equation cannot be balanced

2. Which of the following is not true of electromagnetic radiations?

    a. Radio waves have higher frequency than UV rays

    b. Electromagnetic radiations are produced by deceleration of charged particles

    c. Electromagnetic radiations are not affected by gravity

    d. All of the above

3. The speed of light decreases and the frequency increases when:

    a. Light is diffracted

    b. Light enters from one material medium to vacuum

    c. Light enters from vacuum into a material medium

    d. Light is refracted

4. Put the following in order of decreasing frequency: radio waves, X-rays, visible waves and gamma-rays.

    a. Radio waves < X-rays < Visible waves < Gamma rays

    b. Radio waves > Visible waves > X-rays > Gamma rays

    c. Gamma rays> X-rays> Visible waves > Radio waves

    d. Radio waves > X-rays > Visible waves > Gamma rays

5. Which of the following are used in medical imaging?

    a. Radio waves

    b. X-rays

    c. Visible rays

    d. Microwaves

6. Which of the following is not an application of electro-magnetic radiations?

   a. CAT scan
   b. Dental radiograph
   c. Ultrasound
   d. Both a and b

7. Which of the following has application in nuclear medicine, cancer treatment and sterilization?

   a. X-rays
   b. Soft x-rays
   c. Gamma- rays
   d. UV-rays

8. Interference of light indicates:

   a. Light travels with high speed
   b. It lies in electromagnetic spectrum
   c. It is a wave-phenomenon
   d. It doesn't conserves energy

9. Young's double slit experiment two slits were used :

   a. To vary intensity of light
   b. To reduce the resistance
   c. To create path difference
   c. To vary the wavelength

10. Which statement best explains transmutation?

a. Conversion of one element to another

b. Radioactive decay changes atoms of one element to another

c. Gamma decay causing the conversion of one element to another

d. a and b

11. What is the simplest unit of any compound?

a. Atom

b. Proton

c. Molecule

d. Compound

12. What results when acid reacts with a base?

a. A weak acid

b. A weak base

c. A salt and water

d. Hydrogen

13. What are the horizontal rows of the periodic table are known as?

a. Groups

b. Periods

c. Series

d. Columns

14. When do oxidation and reduction reactions occur?

a. One after the other

b. In separate reactions

c. In the product side of the reaction

d. Simultaneously

15. What are most of the elements on the periodic table can be classified as?

    a. Nonmetals

    b. Metals

    c. Metalloids

    d. Gas

16. During the formation of a Chemical Bond, Overall potential energy of the system

    a. Does not Change

    b. Increases

    c. Decreases

    d. None of these

17. Which of the following molecules has a coordinate bond?

    a. NH_4Cl

    b. $NaCl$

    c. HCl

    d. $AlCl_3$

18. If all the reactants in a chemical reaction are completely used, which of the statements about reactants and products is definitely true.

    a. Physical state of products is different as compared to reactants

    b. Density of products is equal to density of reactants

    c. Total mass of reactants is equal to total mass of products

    d. Molecular structure of products is more complex as compared to reactants

19. Half-life of a radioactive substance is

a. Half of the time required by entire substance to decay.

b. Time taken by the given substance to decrease by half.

c. Calculated through T=mc2

d. None of the above

20. Which of the three radiations (Alpha, Beta, Gamma) does not carry an electric charge?

a. Alpha

b. Beta

c. Gamma

d. None of the above

Life Science

21. What are considered to be the four fundamental forces of nature?

a. Gravity, electromagnetic force, weak nuclear force, and strong nuclear force

b. Gravity, electromagnetic force, negative nuclear force, and positive nuclear force

c. Polarity, electromagnetic force, weak nuclear force, and strong nuclear force

d. Gravity, chemical magnetic force, weak nuclear force, and strong nuclear force

22. What is the diagram that is used to predict an outcome of a particular cross or breeding experiment?

    a. Genetic puzzle
    b. Genome project
    c. Hybrid theorem
    d. Punnett square

23. Which of these statements about mechanical energy is/are true?

    a. Mechanical energy is the energy that is possessed by an object due to its motion or due to its position.

    b. Mechanical energy can be either kinetic energy (energy of motion) or potential energy (stored energy of position).

    c. Objects have mechanical energy if they are in motion

    d. All of the above.

24. What is the difference, of any, between kinetic energy and potential energy?

    a. Kinetic energy is the energy of a body resulting from heat while potential energy is the energy possessed by an object that is chilled.

    b. Kinetic energy is the energy of a body resulting from motion while potential energy is the energy possessed by an object by virtue of its position or state, e.g., as in a compressed spring.

    c. There is no difference between kinetic and potential energy; all energy is the same.

25. What are the differences, if any, between chemical changes and physical changes?

a. During a physical change, some aspect of the physical properties of matter are altered, but the identity of the substance remains constant. Chemical changes involve the alteration of both a substance's composition and structure.

b. During a chemical change, some aspect of the physical properties of matter are altered, but the identity of the substance remains constant. Physical changes involve the alteration of both a substance's composition and structure.

c. During a physical change, no aspects of the physical properties of matter are altered, but the identity of the substance remains constant. Chemical changes involve the alteration of both a substance's composition and structure.

d. There is no substantive difference between chemical and physical changes.

26. A_____ is a process that transforms one set of chemical substances to another; the substances used are known as _____ and those formed are _____.

a. A chemical change is a process that transforms one set of chemical substances to another; the substances used are known as products and those formed are reactants.

b. A biological change is a process that transforms one set of chemical substances to another; the substances used are known as reactants and those formed are products.

c. A chemical change is a process that transforms one set of chemical substances to another; the substances used are known as reactants and those formed are products.

d. A chemical variation is a process that transforms one set of chemical substances to another; the substances used are known as reactants and those formed are products.

Practice Test Questions 2

27. _____ is the most abundant element in the Earth's crust and appears on the Atomic Table as the letter ___.

    a. Nitrogen, N
    b. Oxygen, O
    c. Silicon, Si
    d. Sodium, Na

28. Which of these statements about metals are true?

    a. A metal is a substance that conducts heat and electricity.
    b. A metal is shiny and reflects many colors of light, and can be hammered into sheets or drawn into wire.
    c. All of these statements are true.
    d. About 80% of the known chemical elements are metals.

29. The _____ _____ of an element equals the number of protons in an atomic nucleus, and, along with the element symbol is one of two alternate ways to label an element.

    a. Atomic unit
    b. Atomic number
    c. Atomic orbital
    d. Nuclear number

30. Which of the statements about quantum theory is/are false?

a. Quantum theory is concerned with the emission and absorption of energy by matter and with the motion of material particles.

b. Quantum mechanics, a system based on quantum theory, has superseded Newtonian mechanics in the interpretation of physical phenomena on the atomic scale.

c. In quantum theory, energy is treated solely as a continuous phenomenon, while matter is assumed to occupy a very specific region of space and to move in a continuous manner.

d. Quantum theory states that energy is held to be emitted and absorbed in tiny, discrete amounts called quantum.

31. Newton's laws of motion consist of three physical laws that form the basis for classical mechanics. Which of the following is/are not included in these laws?

a. Unless acted on by a force, a body at rest stays at rest.

b. Unless acted on by a force, a body in motion will change direction and gradually slow until it eventually stops.

c. To every action, there is an equal and opposite reaction.

d. A body acted on by a force will accelerate in the same direction as the force at a magnitude that is directly proportional to the force.

32. Electricity is a general term encompassing a variety of phenomena resulting from the presence and flow of electric charge. Which of the following statements about electricity is/are true?

    a. Electrically charged matter is influenced by, and produces, electromagnetic fields.

    b. Electric current is a movement or flow of electrically charged particles.

    c. Electric potential is a fundamental interaction between the magnetic field and the presence and motion of an electric charge.

    d. All of the statements are true.

33. Which of these statements about light energy is/are true?

    a. Light consists of electromagnetic waves in the visible range.

    b. The fundamental particle or quantum of light is a photon.

    c. A and B are true.

    d. None of the statements are true.

34. Which statement is false?

    a. Hydra are an autotroph

    b. Planaria are heterotroph

    c. Animals are heterotrophs

    d. Insectivorous plants are both heterotrophs and autotrophs

35. Which organelle plays most important role in aerobic respiration?

    a. Nucleus

    b. Mitochondria

    c. Golgi apparatus

    d. Cell membrane

36. All maintain homeostasis EXCEPT:

    a. Thermoregulation

    b. Osmoregulation

    c. Excretion

    d. None of the above

37. Mode of inheritance is a manner in which a particular trait is passed on to next generation. Which inheritance mode will a disease have if a heterozygous individual shows phenotype for that disease?

    a. Autosomal dominant

    b. Autosomal recessive

    c. Y- linked

    d. Both a and c

38. Which of the following cases cannot be ignored in phenomenon of natural selection?

    a. Mutation that is hereditary

    b. Mutation that plays role in survival

    c. Mutation that is hereditary and plays role in survival

    d. Mutation which makes an individual different than others in population

39. Herbivores are_____

  a. Producers
  b. Primary consumers
  c. Secondary consumers
  d. Both a and b

40. If a mutation on X chromosome causes a disease which only affects a male child. This inheritance is called:

  a. Sex linked inheritance
  b. Sex limited inheritance
  c. Co- dominant inheritance
  d. Dominant inheritance

Earth and Space Science

41. Which of the following will have most detrimental effect due to acidity on the environment?

  a. Acidic fog
  b. Acid rain (HNO_3)
  c. Acid rain (H_2SO_4)
  d. Acid rain (H_2CO_3)

42. Pick the false statement:

  a. Natural rain is slightly acidic
  b. Hydride of sulfur is main cause of acid rain
  c. Dissolved CO2, SO4 and NO2 can cause acid rain
  d. Coal burning power plants are 7cause of acid rain

43. Which of the followings best describes pollution?

   a. Introduction of contaminating substances into the environment

   b. Introduction of substances which will have adverse effects on the living beings

   c. Introduction of harmful substances into the environment

   d. Introduction of matter or energy into the environment which is harmful for living beings.

44. Abundance of which of the following light elements in the universe is thought to support the Big Bang Model of Origin?

   I) Hydrogen
   II) Oxygen
   III) Helium
   IV) Nitrogen

   a. I & II
   b. I & III
   c. II & III
   d. I, II & IV

45. Which of the following phenomenon can be considered a direct explanation of Newton`s 3rd Law of motion?

   a. Moon orbiting around the earth
   b. Falling of a Meteor
   c. Expansion of the Universe
   d. A Rocket Taking Off

46. An astronomer working in a space station observes light emitted from a stationary star. After a while, the star starts moving away from the space station (Red-Shift) at a high speed while still emitting the light. What will the light seen by the astronomer be, compared to the light observed earlier?

    a. Higher frequency and shorter wavelength

    b. Lower Frequency and Longer wavelength

    c. Same Frequency and wavelength

    d. Higher Frequency and Longer wavelength

47. Which of the following is a part of the abiotic carbon cycle?

    a. Animals

    b. Plants

    c. Fossil fuels

    d. Water

48. The Carbon cycle is not influenced by:

    a. Green houses

    b. Urbanization

    c. Solar energy

    d. Power plants

49. In hydrologic cycle, water sublimates from:

    a. Oceans

    b. Plants

    c. Glaciers

    d. All of the above

50. Pick the incorrect sequence for hydrologic cycle:

a. Evaporation/ transpiration→condensation→precipitation→ ground water

b. Ground water→ evaporation/transpiration → condensation→ precipitation

c. Evaporation→condensation→ transpiration→precipitation→ ground water

d. Evaporation→ condensation→precipitation→ ground water

Answer Key

Reading Comprehension

1. B
We can infer an important part of the respiratory system are the lungs. From the passage, "Molecules of oxygen and carbon dioxide are passively exchanged, by diffusion, between the gaseous external environment and the blood. This exchange process occurs in the alveolar region of the lungs."

Therefore, one primary function for the respiratory system is the exchange of oxygen and carbon dioxide, and this process occurs in the lungs. We can therefore infer that the lungs are an important part of the respiratory system.

2. C
The process by which molecules of oxygen and carbon dioxide are passively exchanged is diffusion.

This is a definition type question. Scan the passage for references to "oxygen," "carbon dioxide," or "exchanged."

3. A
The organ that plays an important role in gas exchange in amphibians is the skin.

Scan the passage for references to "amphibians," and find the answer.

4. A
The three physiological zones of the respiratory system are Conducting, transitional, respiratory zones.

5. A
Helen's parents hired Anne to teach Helen to communicate.

Choice B is incorrect because the passage states Anne had trouble finding her way around, which means she could walk.

6. B
The correct answer because that fact is stated directly in the

passage. The passage explains that Anne taught Helen to hear by allowing her to feel the vibrations in her throat.

7. A
We can infer that Anne is a patient teacher because she did not leave or lose her temper when Helen bit or hit her; she just kept trying to teach Helen.

Choice B is incorrect because Anne taught Helen to read and talk. Choice C is incorrect because Anne could hear. She was partially blind, not deaf. Choice D is incorrect because it does not have to do with patience.

8. B
The passage states that it was hard for anyone but Anne to understand Helen when she spoke.

Choice A is incorrect because the passage does not mention Helen spoke a foreign language. Choice C is incorrect because there is no mention of how quiet or loud Helen's voice was. Choice D is incorrect because we know from reading the passage that Helen did learn to speak.

9. A
Low blood sugar occurs both in diabetics and healthy adults.

10. B
None of the statements are the author's opinion.

11. A
The author's purpose is the inform.

12. A
The only statement that is not a detail is, "A doctor can diagnosis this medical condition by asking the patient questions and testing."

13. B
This passage describes the different categories for traditional stories. The other choices are facts from the passage, not the main idea of the passage. The main idea of a passage will always be the most general statement. For example, choice A, Myths, fables, and folktales are not the same thing, and each

describes a specific type of story. This is a true statement from the passage, but not the main idea of the passage, since the passage also talks about how some cultures may classify a story as a myth and others as a folktale.
The statement, from choice B, Traditional stories can be categorized in different ways by different people, is a more general statement that describes the passage.

14. B
Choice B is the best choice, categories that group traditional stories according to certain characteristics.

Choices A and C are false and can be eliminated right away. Choice D is designed to confuse. Choice D may be true, but it is not mentioned in the passage.

15. D
The best answer is choice D, traditional stories themselves are a part of the larger category of folklore, which may also include costumes, gestures, and music.

All the other choices are false. Traditional stories are part of the larger category of Folklore, which includes other things, not the other way around.

16. D
The best answer is D, traditional stories themselves are a part of the larger category of folklore, which may also include costumes, gestures, and music.
All the other choices are false. Traditional stories are part of the larger category of folklore, which includes other things, not the other way around.

17. B
The correct answer can be found in the fourth sentence of the first paragraph.

Choice A is incorrect because repenting begins the day AFTER Mardi Gras. Choice C is incorrect because you can celebrate Mardi Gras without being a member of a Krewe. Choice D is incorrect because exploration does not play any role in a modern Mardi Gras celebration.

18. A
The second sentence is the last paragraph states that Krewes are led by the Kings and Queens. Therefore, you must have to be part of a Krewe to be its King or its Queen.

Choice B is incorrect because it never states in the passage that only people from France can be Kings and Queen of Mardi Gras. Choice C is incorrect because the passage says nothing about having to speak French. Choice D is incorrect because the passage does state that the Kings and Queens throw doubloons, which is fake money.

19. C
The first sentences of BOTH the 2nd and 3rd paragraphs mention that French explorers started this tradition in New Orleans.

Choices A, B and D are incorrect because they are just names of cities or countries listed in the 2nd paragraph.

20. C
In the final paragraph, the word spectator is used to describe people who are watching the parade and catching cups, beads and doubloons.

Choices A and C are incorrect because we know the people who participate are part of Krewes. People who work the floats and parades are also part of Krewes. D is incorrect because the passage makes no mention of people who do not celebrate Mardi Gras.

21. A
Secede means to break away from because the 11 states wanted to leave the United States and form their own country.

Choice B is incorrect because the states were not accomplishing anything   Choice C is incorrect because the states were trying to leave the USA not join it. Choice D is incorrect because the states seceded before they lost the war.

22. B
Look at the dates in the passage. The shots were fired on

April 12 and Congress declared war on April 14.

Choice A is incorrect because the dates show clearly which happened first. Choice C is incorrect because the passage states that Lincoln was against slavery. Choice D is incorrect because it never mentions who was or was not at Fort Sumter.

23. C
The passage clearly states that Lee surrendered to Grant after the capture of the capital of the Confederacy, which is Richmond.

Choice A is incorrect because the war continued for 2 years after Gettysburg. Choice B is incorrect because that battle is not mentioned in the passage. Choice D is incorrect because the capture of the capital occurred after the march to the sea.

24. A
When the passage said that the North had abolished slavery, it implies that slaves were no longer allowed to be had in the North. In essence slavery was banned.

Choice B is incorrect because it makes no sense relative to the context of the passage.

25. A
The author is enjoying the daffodils very much and so we can infer that he is a lover of nature.

26. C
The mood of this poem is happy. From the last line,

And then my heart with pleasure fills,
And dances with the daffodils.

27. D
Sprightly means happy and full of life. From the lines before and after sprightly, we can see it means happy.

Ten thousand saw I at a glance,
Tossing their heads in sprightly dance.

The waves beside them danced, but they
Out-did the sparkling waves in glee:

28. C
Joyful is the best answer. Happy is a possible answer, but joyful is better. Jocund means jovial, exuberant, light-hearted; merry and in high spirits. From the poem,

Ten thousand saw I at a glance,
Tossing their heads in sprightly dance.

The waves beside them danced, but they
Out-did the sparkling waves in glee:

29. D
This question tests the reader's summarization skills. The question is asking very generally about the message of the passage, and the title, "Ways Characters Communicate in Theater," is one indication of that. The other choices A, B, and C are all directly from the text, and therefore readers may be inclined to select one of them, but are too specific to encapsulate the entirety of the passage and its message.

30. B
The paragraph on soliloquies mentions "To be or not to be," and it is from the context of that paragraph that readers may understand that because "To be or not to be" is a soliloquy, Hamlet will be introspective, or thoughtful, while delivering it. It is true that actors deliver soliloquies alone, and may be "solitary" (A), but "thoughtful" (B) is more true to the overall idea of the paragraph. Readers may choose choice C because drama and theater can be used interchangeably and the passage mentions that soliloquies are unique to theater (and therefore drama), but this answer is not specific enough to the paragraph in question. Readers may pick up on the theme of life and death and Hamlet's true intentions and select that he is "hopeless" (D), but those themes are not discussed either by this paragraph or passage, as a close textual reading and analysis confirms.

31. C
This question tests the reader's grammatical skills. Choice B seems logical, but parenthesis are actually considered to be

a stronger break in a sentence than commas are, and along this line of thinking, actually disrupt the sentence more. Choices A and D make comparisons between theater and film that are simply not made in the passage, and may or may not be true. This detail does clarify the statement that asides are most unique to theater by adding that it is not completely unique to theater, which may have been why the author didn't chose not to delete it and instead used parentheses to designate the detail's importance (C).

32. C
This question tests the reader's vocabulary and contextualization skills. A may or may not be true, but focuses on the wrong function of the word "give" and ignores the rest of the sentence, which is more relevant to what the passage is discussing. Choices B and D may also be selected if the reader depends too literally on the word "give," failing to grasp the more abstract function of the word that is the focus of choice C, which also properly acknowledges the entirety of the passage and its meaning.

33. A
The first speaks to romantic love, a boy has for Annabelle Lee.

Choice B is incorrect; the first passage is romantic love, the second divine love. Choice C is incorrect; while the first passage alludes to young love the second passage makes no distinction,

34. B
This is correct because a careful reading will show in the last line, she is in a tomb, and has died.

Choice A is incorrect; while this could be correct, it is not the most correct and accurate answer, because she has died. Choice C incorrect; the past tense is for a specific reason and not to do with style.

35. B
Divine love is unchanging and therefore unconditional.

Choice A is incorrect; romantic love can be conditional. Choice

C incorrect, the second passage is correct.

36. B
He loves the man, his enemy, and the unnamed woman.

Choices A, C and D are incorrect; he loves the man, his enemy, and the unnamed woman.

37. D
This question tests the reader's summarization skills. The other answers A, B, and C focus on portions of the second paragraph that are too narrow and do not relate to the specific portion of text in question. The complexity of the sentence may mislead students into selecting one of these answers, but rearranging or restating the sentence will lead the reader to the correct answer. In addition, A makes an assumption that may or may not be true about the intentions of the company, B focuses on one product rather than the idea of the products, and C makes an assumption about women that may or may not be true and is not supported by the text.

38. B
This question tests reader's attention to detail. If a reader selects A, he or she may have picked up on the use of the word "debate" and assumed, very logically, that the two are at odds because they are fighting; however, this is simply not supported in the text. Choice C also uses very specific quotes from the text, but it rearranges and gives them false meaning. The artists want to elevate their creations above the creations of other artists, thereby showing that they are "creative" and "innovative." Similarly, choice D takes phrases straight from the text and rearranges and confuses them. The artists are described as wanting to be "creative, innovative, individual people," not the women.

39. A
This question tests reader's vocabulary and summarization skills. This phrase, used by the author, may seem flippant and dismissive if readers focus on the word "whatever" and misinterpret it as a popular, colloquial term. In this way, choices B and C may mislead the reader to selecting one of them by including the terms "unimportant" and "stupid,"

respectively. Choice D is a similar misreading, but doesn't make sense when the phrase is at the beginning of the passage and the entire passage is on media messages. Choice A is literarily and contextually appropriate, and the reader can understand that the author would like to keep the introduction focused on the topic the passage is going to discuss.

40. A
This question tests a reader's inference skills. The extreme use of the word "all" in choice B suggests that every single advertising company are working to be approachable, and while this is not only unlikely, the text specifically states that "more" companies have done this, signifying that they have not all participated, even if it's a possibility that they may some day. The use of the limiting word "only" in choice C lends that answer similar problems; women are still buying from companies who do not care about this message, or those companies would not be in business, and the passage specifies that "many" women are worried about media messages, but not all. Readers may find choice D logical, especially if they are looking to make an inference, and while this may be a possibility, the passage does not suggest or discuss this happening. Choice A is correct based on specifically because of the relation between "still working" in the answer and "will hopefully" and the extensive discussion on companies struggles, which come only with progress, in the text.

41. C
This question tests the reader's summarization skills. The entire passage is leading up to the idea that the president of the US may not have had grounds to assert his Fourteen Points when other countries had lost so much. Choice A is pretty directly inferred by the text, but it does not adequately summarize what the entire passage is trying to communicate. Choice B may also be inferred by the passage when it says that the war is "imminent," but it does not represent the entire message, either. The passage does seem to be in praise of FDR, or at least in respect of him, but it does not in any way claim that he is the smartest president, nor does this represent the many other points included. Choice C is then the obvious answer, and most directly relates to the closing sentences which it rewords.

42. C

This question tests the reader's summarization skills. The entire passage is leading up to the idea that the president of the US may not have had grounds to assert his Fourteen Points when other countries had lost so much.

Choice A is pretty directly inferred by the text, but it does not adequately summarize what the entire passage is trying to communicate. Choice B may also be inferred by the passage when it says that the war is "imminent," but it does not represent the entire message, either. The passage does seem to be in praise of FDR, or at least in respect of him, but it does not in any way claim that he is the smartest president, nor does this represent the many other points included. Choice C is then the obvious answer, and most directly relates to the closing sentences which it rewords.

43. C

This question tests the reader's attention to detail. The passage does state that choices A and B are true, and while those statements are in proximity to the explanation for why the war started, they are not the actual reason given. Choice D is a mix up of words used in the passage, which says that the largest powers were in play but not that this fact somehow started the war. The passage does make a direct statement that a domino effect started the war, supporting choice C as the correct answer.

44. A

This question tests the reader's understanding of functions in writing. Throughout the passage, it states that leaders of other nations were hesitant to accept generous or peaceful terms because of the grievances of the war, and the great loss of life was chief among these. While the passage does touch on the devastation of deadly weapons (B), the use of this raw, emotional fact serves a larger purpose, and the focus of the passage is not the weapons. While readers may indeed consider who lost the most soldiers (C) when so many countries were involved and the inequalities of loss are mentioned in the passage, there is no discussion of this in the passage. Choice D is related to choice A, but choice A is more direct and relates more to the passage.

Practice Test Questions 2

45. B
This question tests the reader's vocabulary skills. Choice A may seem appealing to readers because it is phonetically similar to "catalyzed," but the two are not related in any other way. Choice C makes sense in context, but if plugged in to the sentence creates a redundancy that doesn't make sense. Choice D does also not make sense contextually, even if the reader may consider that funds were needed to create more weaponry, especially if it was advanced.

46. C
To be infamous means to be remembered for an evil or terrible action. Therefore, the word infamy means to remember a bad or terrible thing.

Choice A is incorrect because being famous is not the same as being infamous.

47. C
Each other answer set contains the name of at least one country that was not part of the AXIS powers.

48. D
This is stated in the passage.

Choice A is not correct because there was no indication that Japan would attack San Diego. Choice B is not correct because the attack on Pearl Harbor was a surprise. Choice C is not correct because Roosevelt was not planning to attack Japan.

49. C
The passage clearly states that Japan planned a surprise attack. They chose that early time to catch the U.S. military off guard.

Choice A is not correct because the military does not sleep late. Choice B is not correct because there is no law against bombing countries.

50. B
Here is the passage with the oldest to youngest trees

The earliest trees were [1] tree ferns and horsetails, which grew in forests in the Carboniferous period. Tree ferns still survive, but the only surviving horsetails are no longer in tree form. Later, in the Triassic period, [2] conifers and ginkgos, appeared, [3] followed by flowering plants after that in the Cretaceous period

Language Arts

1. C
There was one light house keeper, and he disappeared.

Choice A is incorrect because the paragraph makes it clear that it was one person keeping the light house. Choice B is incorrect because there is no other mention of a shipwreck. Choice D is incorrect because the light house keeper was not imprisoned on the island, but plausible because he did disappear.

2. B
Choice B is the best choice because it flows from the previous events and explains the urgency with which a new light house keeper is needed.

Choice A is incorrect because the light house was very important in helping ships navigate. Choice C is incorrect; this does not flow; there is no apparent reason for the locals to despise the light house. Choice D is incorrect; this does not flow from the previous events and is very unrealistic.

3. A
Choice A opens the paragraph explaining that the battle went back and forth.

Choice B is incorrect because the battle was not lopsided; it was even. Choice C is incorrect because it opens the paragraph in the first person. Choice D is incorrect because it is clear from the rest of the paragraph that he does not run away, but stays and observes the battle.

4. C
The youth could not tell from the battle flags flying like

crimson foam in many directions which color of cloth was winning.

Choice A is incorrect because it opens the paragraph in the first person. Choice B is incorrect because the battle was not lopsided; it was even. Choice D is incorrect because this sentence sends the story off in a new direction and into the future while the rest of the paragraph is focused on immediate events. A sentence like this would at least begin a new paragraph, if not a new chapter.

5. D
Choice D opens the paragraph with the topic: Australia and its inhabitants.

Choice A is incorrect because it is clear from the paragraph that Australia was not empty. Choice B is incorrect because no other mention of French is present in the paragraph. C. Incorrect because there is no violent struggle for independence mentioned in the paragraph.

6. B
Choice B ties up the paragraph with a description of how fast Australian history has changed.

Choice A is incorrect because the natives have been largely displaced by Europeans and it is very unrealistic for the majority of people in any country to speak three or more languages. Choice C is incorrect because colonial history is well documented, the history of the natives would be the undocumented history. Choice D is incorrect because the paragraph states that English and Christianity (and western culture) overtook Australia.

7. A
Choice A is correct because it accurately summarizes the rest of the paragraph.

Choice B is incorrect because it is not common sense and the paragraph is more about the history of the discoveries than about understanding atomic structure. Choice C is incorrect because, although 1913 is mentioned, it is not the most important thing in the paragraph. Choice D is incorrect because Neils Bohr is not the only scientist in the paragraph and it takes a while to get to him, so he shouldn't be mentioned in the first sentence.

8. B
Choice B introduces the topic accurately.

Choice A is incorrect because Rutherford's work was not misguided, it has just been modified. Choice C is incorrect because the paragraph does not indicate that scientists have stopped studying the atom. Choice D is incorrect because the paragraph does not indicate that scientists throw out their old work, but that they build upon, and modify it.

9. D
Choice D accurately introduces the main point of the paragraph.

Choice A is incorrect because the team has an automatic invitation to the tournament. Choice B is incorrect because the team did win the game. Choice C is incorrect on both counts: they did win and they are going to the tournament.

10. A
Choice A is correct because the game was close, it was a victory and it marks their first winning season in three years.

Choice B is incorrect because the fans are not used to winning; the paragraph indicates that they have just had three losing seasons. Choice C is incorrect because they do not have to wait for an invitation; the paragraph indicates that they automatically go to the tournament. Choice D is incorrect because they did not lose the game.

11. C
The semicolon is used in a list where the list items have internal punctuation, such as "Key West, Florida."

12. C
The semicolon links independent clauses. An independent

clause can form a complete sentence by itself.

13. A
The semicolon links independent clauses with a conjunction (However).

14. B
The sentence is correct. The semicolon links independent clauses. An independent clause can form a complete sentence by itself.

15. B
Double negative sentence. In double negative sentences, one of the negatives is replaced with "any."

16. A
The third conditional is used for talking about an unreal situation (that did not happen) in the past. For example, "If I had studied harder, [if clause] I would have passed the exam [main clause]. Which is the same as, "I failed the exam, because I didn't study hard enough."

17. D
Present perfect. You cannot use the Present Perfect with specific time expressions such as: yesterday, one year ago, last week, when I was a child, at that moment, that day, one day, etc. The Present Perfect is used with unspecific expressions such as: ever, never, once, many times, several times, before, so far, already, yet, etc.

18. C
Bring vs. Take. Usage depends on your location. Something coming your way is brought to you. Something going away is taken from you.

19. A
The sentence is correct. Went vs. Gone. Went is the simple past tense. Gone is used in the past perfect.

20. B
Fewer vs. Less. 'Fewer' is used with countables and 'less' is used with uncountables.

21. D
Its vs. It's. 'It's' is a contraction for it is or it has. 'Its' is a possessive pronoun meaning, more or less, of 'it,' or belonging to 'it.'

22. D
When using 'however,' place a comma before and after.

23. B
"Who" is the best choice because the sentence refers to a person.

24. A
Past perfect is the correct form because it refers to something that happened in the past (he was the greatest inventor) and is still true today.

25. C
The superlative "hottest" is used when expressing the highest degree, or a degree greater than that of anything it is compared with.

26. C
When comparing two, use 'the taller.' When comparing more than two, use 'the tallest.'

27. B
Here the word "sale" is used as a "word" and not as a word in the sentence, so quotation marks are used.

28. C
His father is a poet and a novelist. It is necessary to use 'a' twice in this sentence for the two distinct things.

29. C
Titles of short stories are enclosed in quotation marks, and commas always go inside quotation marks.

30. B
Present tense, "ran well" is correct. "Ran good" is never correct.

31. D
Punctuation always goes inside quotation marks.

32. D
Suggested changes to sentence 7 to focus attention on the main idea in paragraph 3, "The following season, Pato accomplished his first European ambition by winning the 2009 Series A Young Player of the Year award."

The second paragraph discusses Pato's achievements in Europe. Option D expresses and relates them to his ambition more appropriately than the other options.

33. B
The changes to sentence 1 are, "Although <u>well-known</u> among his fans for the <u>"duck-dance"</u> he performs after scoring, Alexandre Rodrigues da Silva has earned the name "Pato" for his ducky skills with the ball that he uses to <u>outclass</u> his opponent in the field."

The changes needed in the first sentence are related to the use of punctuation. The correct form of "well known" is with a hyphen. "Duck dance," refers to the special dance resembling those of ducks therefore it must be inside quotation mark to emphasize its special meaning. In addition, it must be hyphenated since the noun turns out to be a compound modifier of the original noun "dance." Also, the extended verb "outclass" has been inappropriately hyphenated. All these changes are carried out in option B only.

34. B
Suggested changes to sentence 5 are, "Augmented reality has turned out to be one such idea that soon was incorporated into applications like MapLens, SiteLens, Layar and the AR game ARhrrrr!"

Option B best contributes to the cohesion of the paragraph by addressing the subordinate clause "more avant-garde concepts..." and making it the subject of the next sentence. Other options do not make augmented reality their subject as a "concept" so that they focus the main idea of the paragraph.

35. B

Suggested changes to sentence 4, "This has tempted application developers to explore more avant-garde concepts that offer the possibility to be integrated into their applications."

Vocabulary usage is questionable in this sentence. The word "solicit" is used when someone is inclined to something negative like something against the law, here it is used in the context of something innovative and that has the potential to serve humanity. Also, "capacity" is not something that is "offered" and the noun is not used best in descriptive phrases that involve the passive form. Therefore, they must be replaced. Considering all combinations that are offered in the options, B has the right set of appropriate vocabulary.

36. B

Sentence 6 is the least relevant to the main idea of the second paragraph. "Spring may witness the arrival of season's first rain and of a nor'wester."

All other sentences in the paragraph talk about the trees. Sentence 6 talks about the arrival of rain and thunderstorms.

37. C

Suggested changes to sentence 12 to focus attention on the main idea of the secibd paragraph are, "Surprisingly, even watermelon, jackfruit and litchis arrive by the middle of April!"

The third paragraph discusses the availability of various fruits in spring. Apart from sentence 12, all the sentences do it cohesively. Sentence 12 is somewhat inconsistent with the main idea of the paragraph. It is possible to make it more relevant to the paragraph and add more cohesion between sentences by adjusting it to the form suggested in option C. Addition of "even" coupled with changing the sentence from negative to affirmative brings the focus of the paragraph to this sentence. Other options fail to do this as the negative tone of the language used remains intact in the suggested changes.

38. A
Sentence 15 is not consistent with the author's purpose. "Some lakes and water ponds that dry up in the summer and turn into festival venues for children who race to scoop up the fish with bamboo baskets."

Sentence 15 talks about summer and is the only sentence to do so. This is not consistent with the author's purpose, to describe spring in Bengali.

39. A
In vs. Into. 'In' a room means inside. 'Into' refers to movement or action.

40. C
Lay vs. Lie. Lie requires an object and lay does not. So you can lie down, (no object. and you lay a book on the floor.

41. A
The third conditional is used for talking about an unreal situation (that did not happen) in the past. For example, "If I had studied harder, [if clause] I would have passed the exam [main clause]. Which is the same as, "I failed the exam, because I didn't study hard enough."

42. A
Learn vs. Teach. Learning is what students do, and teaching is what teachers do.

43. B
Lose vs. Loose. Lose is to no longer have, or to lose a race. Loose is not tied or able to move freely.

44. A
Quoted speech is not capitalized.

45. A
The sentence is correct. Periods and events are capitalized but not century numbers.

46. C
Brand names are capitalized.

47. B
Generic terms such as 'french fries' are not capitalized. Brand names are capitalized.

48. C
The names of sports teams, as proper nouns, are capitalized. In this sentence, the full name is capitalized, Blue Jays.

49. A
The sentence is correct. North, South, East, and West when used as sections of the country, but not as compass directions

Mathematics

1. B
1 inch on map = 100,000 inches on ground. So 3 inches on map = 3 x 100,000 = 300,000 inches on ground.

2. B
9.60/3.2 = 3

3. A
465,890 - 456,890 = 9,000.

4. B
46,227 + 101,032 is about 147,000. The exact answer is 147,259.

5. C
$(25/9)^2 = 625/81$

6. D
84/231 = 12/33 > 1/3
6/35 = 1/5 < 1/3
3/22 = 1/7 < 1/3

7. B

$\sqrt{2}$ is the largest number.
Here are the choices:

    a. 1

    b. $\sqrt{2} = 1.414$

    c. $3/22 = .1563$

    d. $4/3 = 1.33$

8. A

First cancel out $15/16 \times 8/9$ to get $5/2 \times 1/3$, then multiply numerators and denominators to get $5/6$.

9. C

We are told that driver B is 20 km/h faster than driver A. So: $V_B = V_A + 20$ where V is the velocity. Also, driver B travelled 480 km 2 hours before driver A. So:

x = 480 km

$t_A - 2 = t_B$ where t is the time. Now we know the relationship between A and B drivers in terms of time and velocity. We need to write an equation only depending on V_A (the speed of driver A) which we are asked to find.

Since distance = velocity•time: $480 = V_A \cdot t_A = V_B \cdot t_B$

$480 = (V_A + 20)(t_A - 2)$

$480 = (V_A + 20)(480/V_A - 2)$

$480 = 480 - 2V_A + 20 \cdot 480/V_A - 40$

$0 = -2V_A + 9600/V_A - 40$ ... Multiplying the equation by V_A eliminates the denominator:

$2V_A^2 + 40V_A - 9600 = 0$ ... Simplifying the equation by 2:

$V_A^2 + 20V_A - 4800 = 0$

$V_{A1,2} = [-20 \pm \sqrt{(400 + 4 \cdot 4800)}] / 2$

$V_{A1,2} = [-20 \pm 140] / 2$

$V_A = [-20 - 140]/2 = -80$ km/h and $V_A = [-20 + 140]/2 = 60$ km/h

We need to check our answers. It is easy to make a table:

t_A	V_A	V_B	t_B	$t_A - t_B$
480/80 = 6		-80 - 20 = -100 B is 20 km/h faster than A. - sign only mentions the direction of the velocity. For magnitude, we need to add -20.	480/100 = 4.8	6 - 4.8 = 1.2 This should be 2!
480/60 = 8	60	60 + 20 = 80	480/80 = 6	8 - 6 = 2 This is correct!

So, V_A = 60 km/h is the only answer satisfying the question.

10. C
1 hour is equal to 3,600 seconds and 1 kilometer is equal to 1000 meters.

Since this train travels 72 kilometers per hour, this means that it covers 72,000 meters in 3,600 seconds.

If it travels 72,000 meters in 3,600 seconds

It travels x meters in 12 seconds

By cross multiplication: x = 72,000 • 12 / 3,600

x = 240 meters

11. A
Let us first mention the money Tony spent: $80

Now we need to find the money Tony earned:

He had 15 dozen eggs = 15•12 = 180 eggs. 16 eggs were broken. So,

Remaining number of eggs that Tony sold = 180 − 16 = 164.

Total amount he earned for selling 164 eggs = 164•0.54 = $88.56.

As a summary, he spent $80 and earned $88.56.

The profit is the difference: 88.56 - 80 = $8.56

Percentage profit is found by proportioning the profit to the money he spent:

8.56•100/80 = 10.7%

Checking the answers, we round 10.7 to the nearest whole number: 11%

12. B
Number of absent students = 83 – 72 = 11

Percentage of absent students is found by proportioning the number of absent students to total number of students in the class = 11•100/83 = 13.25

Checking the answers, we round 13.25 to the nearest whole number: 13%

13. D
To find the total turnout in all three polling stations, we need to proportion the number of voters to the number of all registered voters.

Number of total voters = 945 + 860 + 1210 = 3015

Number of total registered voters = 1270 + 1050 + 1440 = 3760

Percentage turnout over all three polling stations = 3015•100/3760 = 80.19%

Checking the answers, we round 80.19 to the nearest whole number: 80%

14. C
The approximate answer to 5205 ÷ 25 is 208. The exact answer is 208.2.

15. A
A common denominator is needed, a number which both 15 and 10 will divide into. So 14-9/30 = 5/30 = 1/6

16. D
The jacket costs $545.00 so we can round up to $550. 10% of $550 is 55. We can round down to $50, which is easier to work with. $550 - $50 is $500. The jacket will cost about $500.

The actual cost is 545-54.50 = 490.50.

17. C

11/20 x 20/9 = 11/1 x 1/9 = 11/9 = 1 2/9

18. D
Area of Type B consists of two rectangles and a half circle. We can find these three areas and sum them up in order to find the total area:

Area of the left rectangle: (4 + 8)•8 = 96 m²

Area of the right rectangle: 14•8 = 112 m²

The diameter of the circle is equal to 14 m. So, the radius is 14/2 = 7:

Area of the half circle = (1/2)•πr² = (1/2)•(22/7)•(7)² = (1•22•49)/(2•7) = 77 m²

Area of Type B = 96 + 112 + 77 = 285 m²

Converting this area to ft²: 285 m² = 285•10.76 ft² = 3066.6 ft²

Type B is (3066.6 - 1300 = 1766.6 ft²) 1766.6 ft² larger than type A.

19.

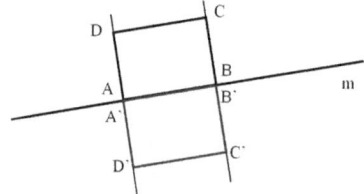

20. B
0.12 + 2/5 + 3/5, Convert decimal to fraction to get 3/25 + 2/5 + 3/5, = (3 + 10 + 15)/25, = 28/25 = 1 3/25

21. B
To solve the equation, we need the equation in the form ax2 + bx + c = 0.

0.9x² + 1.8x - 2.7 = 0 is already in this form.

Practice Test Questions 2

The quadratic formula to find the roots of a quadratic equation is:

$x_{1,2} = (-b \pm \sqrt{\Delta}) / 2a$ where $\Delta = b^2 - 4ac$ and is called the discriminant of the quadratic equation.

In our question, the equation is $0.9x^2 + 1.8x - 2.7 = 0$. To eliminate the decimals, let us multiply the equation by 10:

$9x^2 + 18x - 27 = 0$ ... This equation can be simplified by 9 since each term contains 9:

$x^2 + 2x - 3 = 0$

By remembering the form $ax^2 + bx + c = 0$:

$a = 1, b = 2, c = -3$

So, we can find the discriminant first, and then the roots of the equation:

$\Delta = b^2 - 4ac = (2)^2 - 4 \bullet 1 \bullet (-3) = 4 + 12 = 16$

$x_{1,2} = (-b \pm \sqrt{\Delta}) / 2a = (-2 \pm \sqrt{16}) / 2 = (-2 \pm 4) / 2$

This means that the roots are,

$x_1 = (-2 - 4)/2 = -3$ and $x_2 = (-2 + 4)/2 = 1$

22. A
We are asked to subtract polynomials. By paying attention to the sign distribution; we write the polynomials and operate:

$4x^3 - 2x^2 - 10 - (5x^3 + x^2 + x + 5) = 4x^3 - 2x^2 - 10 - 5x^3 - x^2 - x - 5$

$= 4x^3 - 5x^3 - 2x^2 - x^2 - x - 10 - 5$ ... similar terms written together to ease summing/substituting.

$= -x^3 - 3x^2 - x - 15$

23. C
First, we need to arrange the two equations to obtain the form $ax + by = c$. We see that there are 3 and 2 in the denominators of both equations. If we equate all at 6, then we can cancel all 6 in the denominators and have straight equations:

Equate all denominators at 6:

$2(4x + 5y)/6 = 3(x - 3y)/6 + 4 \cdot 6/6$ ... Now we can cancel 6 in the denominators:

$8x + 10y = 3x - 9y + 24$ ... We can collect x and y terms on left side of the equation:

$8x + 10y - 3x + 9y = 24$

$5x + 19y = 24$ ... Equation (I)

Let us arrange the second equation:

$3(3x + y)/6 = 2(2x + 7y)/6 - 1 \cdot 6/6$ ... Now we can cancel 6 in the denominators:

$9x + 3y = 4x + 14y - 6$ ... We can collect x and y terms on left side of the equation:

$9x + 3y - 4x - 14y = -6$

$5x - 11y = -6$ ... Equation (II)

Now, we have two equations and two unknowns x and y. By writing the two equations one under the other and operating, we can find one unknown first, and find the other next:

$\quad 5x + 19y = 24$

$\underline{-1/\ 5x - 11y = -6}$ ... If we substitute this equation from the upper one, 5x cancels -5x:

$\quad 5x + 19y = 24$

$\underline{-5x + 11y = 6}$ ... Summing side-by-side:

$5x - 5x + 19y + 11y = 24 + 6$

$30y = 30$ ... Dividing both sides by 30:

$\quad y = 1$

Inserting y = 1 into either of the equations, we can find the value of x. Choosing equation I:

$5x + 19 \cdot 1 = 24$

$5x = 24 - 19$

$5x = 5$ ... Dividing both sides by 5:

$x = 1$

Practice Test Questions 2   295

So, x = 1 and y = 1 is the solution; it is shown as (1, 1).

24. A
$x^2 + 12x - 13 = 0$ ... We try to separate the middle term 12x to find common factors with x^2 and -13 separately:

$x^2 + 13x - x - 13 = 0$ ... Here, we see that x is a common factor for x^2 and 13x, and -1 is a common factor for -x and -13:

x(x + 13) - 1(x + 13) = 0 ... Here, we have x times x + 13 and -1 times x + 13 summed up. This means that we have x - 1 times x + 13:

(x - 1)(x + 13) = 0

This is true when either, or both, the expressions in the parenthesis are equal to zero:

x - 1 = 0 ... x = 1

x + 13 = 0 ... x = -13

1 and -13 are the solutions for this quadratic equation.

25. C
First, we need to simplify the equation:
$((x^2 + 4x + 4) + (x^2 - 4x + 4)) / (x^2 - 4) = 0$

$(x^2 + 4x + 4 + x^2 - 4x + 4) / (x^2 - 4) = 0$ ... 4x and -4x in the numerator cancel each other.

Note that $x^2 - 4$ is two square difference and is equal to $x^2 - 2^2 = (x - 2)(x + 2)$:

$(2x^2 + 8)/((x - 2)(x + 2)) = 0$

The denominator tells us that if x - 2 or x + 2 equals to zero, there will be no solution. So, we will need to eliminate x = 2 and x = -2 from our solution which will be found considering the numerator:

$2x^2 + 8 = 0$

$2(x^2 + 4) = 0$

$x^2 + 4 = 0$

$x^2 = -4$ ... We know that, a square cannot be equal to a negative number. Solution for the square root of -4 is not a real number, so this equation has no solution.

26. D
We need to distribute the factors to the terms inside the related parenthesis:

$5(3x^2 - 2) - x^2(2 - 3x) = 15x^2 - 10 - (2x^2 - 3x^3)$

$= 15x^2 - 10 - 2x^2 + 3x^3$

$= 3x^3 + 15x^2 - 2x^2 - 10$ ... similar terms written together to ease summing/substituting.

$= 3x^3 + 13x^2 - 10$

27. B
We need to distribute the factors to the terms inside the related parenthesis:

$(x^3 + 2)(x^2 - x) - x^5 = x^5 - x^4 + (2x^2 - 2x) - x^5$

$= x^5 - x^4 + 2x^2 - 2x - x^5$

$= x^5 - x^5 - x^4 + 2x^2 - 2x$ ... similar terms written together to ease summing/substituting.

$= -x^4 + 2x^2 - 2x$

28. B
To simplify the expression, we need to find common factors. We see that both terms contain the term ab^2. So, we can take this term out of each term as a factor:

$9ab^2 + 8ab^2 = (9 + 8) ab^2 = 17ab^2$

29. C
$x^2 - 7x - 30 = 0$ ... We try to separate the middle term $-7x$ to find common factors with x^2 and -30 separately:

$x^2 - 10x + 3x - 30 = 0$ ... Here, we see that x is a common factor for x^2 and $-10x$, and 3 is a common factor for $3x$ and -30:

$x(x - 10) + 3(x - 10) = 0$ ... Here, we have x times x - 10 and 3 times x - 10 summed up. This means that we have x + 3 times x - 10:

$(x + 3)(x - 10) = 0$ or $(x - 10)(x + 3) = 0$

30. A
We need to simplify the equation by distributing factors and then collecting x terms on one side, and the others on the other side:

$(a + 2)x - b = -2 + (a + b)x$

$ax + 2x - b = -2 + ax + bx$

$ax + 2x - ax - bx = -2 + b$ ... ax and -ax cancel each other:

$2x - bx = -2 + b$ ... we take -1 as a factor on the right side:

$(2 - b)x = -(2 - b)$

$x = -(2 - b)/(2 - b)$ ... Simplifying by 2 - b:

$x = -1$

31. C
We are asked to find A + B - C. By paying attention to the sign distribution; we write the polynomials and operate:

$A + B - C = (-2x^4 + x^2 - 3x) + (x^4 - x^3 + 5) - (x^4 + 2x^3 + 4x + 5)$

$= -2x^4 + x^2 - 3x + x^4 - x^3 + 5 - x^4 - 2x^3 - 4x - 5$

$= -2x^4 + x^4 - x^4 - x^3 - 2x^3 + x^2 - 3x - 4x + 5 - 5$ ... similar terms written together to ease summing/substituting.

$= -2x^4 - 3x^3 + x^2 - 7x$

Remove parenthesis
$4Y^3 - 2Y^2 + 7Y^2 + 3Y - Y =$
add and subtract like terms, $4Y^3 + 5Y^2 + 2Y$

32. D
To simplify, we remove parenthesis:

$(4y^3 - 2y^2) + (7y^2 + 3y - y) = 4y^3 - 2y^2 + 7y^2 + 3y - y$ ... Then, we operate within similar terms:

$= 4y^3 + (-2 + 7)y^2 + (3 - 1)y = 4y^3 + 5y^2 + 2y$

33. C
To obtain a polynomial, remove the parenthesis by distributing the related factors to the terms inside the parenthesis:
$1 - x(1 - x(1 - x)) = 1 - x(1 - (x - x \cdot x)) = 1 - x(1 - x + x^2)$

$= 1 - (x - x \bullet x + x \bullet x^2) = 1 - x + x^2 - x^3$ ... Writing this result in descending order of powers:

$= - x^3 + x^2 - x + 1$

34. D
To simplify the expression, remove the parenthesis by distributing the related factors to the terms inside the parenthesis:

$7(2y + 8) + 1 - 4(y + 5) = (7 \bullet 2y + 7 \bullet 8) + 1 - (4 \bullet y + 4 \bullet 5)$

$= 14y + 56 + 1 - 4y - 20$

$= 14y - 4y + 56 + 1 - 20$ ... similar terms written together to ease summing/substituting.

$= 10y + 37$

35. D
We understand that each of the n employees earn s amount of salary weekly. This means that one employee earns s salary weekly. So; Richard has ns amount of money to employ n employees for a week.

We are asked to find the number of days n employees can be employed with x amount of money. We can do simple direct proportion:

If Richard can employ n employees for 7 days with ns amount of money,

Richard can employ n employees for y days with x amount of money ... y is the number of days we need to find.

We can do cross multiplication:

$y = (x \bullet 7)/(ns)$

$y = 7x/ns$

36. A
$x^2 - 3x - 4$ ... We try to separate the middle term -3x to find common factors with x^2 and -4 separately:

$x^2 + x - 4x - 4$ ... Here, we see that x is a common factor for x^2 and x, and -4 is a common factor for -4x and -4:

Practice Test Questions 2

= x(x + 1) - 4(x + 1) ... Here, we have x times x + 1 and -4 times x + 1 summed up. This means that we have x - 4 times x + 1:

= (x - 4)(x + 1) or (x + 1)(x - 4)

37. D
We need to simplify and have x alone and on one side in order to solve the inequality:

(2x + 1)/(2x - 1) < 1

(2x + 1)/(2x - 1) - 1 < 0 ... We need to write the left side at the common denominator 2x - 1:

(2x + 1)/(2x - 1) - (2x - 1)/(2x - 1) < 0

(2x + 1 - 2x + 1)/(2x - 1) < 0 ... 2x and -2x terms cancel each other in the numerator:

2/(2x - 1) < 0

2 is a positive number; so,

2x - 1 < 0

2x < 1

x < 1/2 ... This means that x should be smaller than 1/2 and not equal to 1/2. This is shown as (-∞, 1/2).

38. D
To solve the equation, we need the equation in the form $ax^2 + bx + c = 0$.

$(a^2 - b^2)x^2 + 2ax + 1 = 0$ is already in this form.

The quadratic formula to find the roots of a quadratic equation is:

$x_{1,2} = (-b \pm \sqrt{\Delta}) / 2a$ where $\Delta = b^2 - 4ac$ and is called the discriminant of the quadratic equation.

In our question, the equation is $(a^2 - b^2)x^2 + 2ax + 1 = 0$.

By remembering the form $ax^2 + bx + c = 0$: $a = a^2 - b^2$, $b = 2a$, $c = 1$

So, we can find the discriminant first, and then the roots of the equation:

$\Delta = b^2 - 4ac = (2a)^2 - 4(a^2 - b^2) \cdot 1 = 4a^2 - 4a^2 + 4b^2 = 4b^2$

$x_{1,2} = (-b \pm \sqrt{\Delta}) / 2a = (-2a \pm \sqrt{4b^2}) / (2(a^2 - b^2)) = (-2a \pm 2b) / (2(a^2 - b^2))$

$= 2(-a \pm b) / (2(a^2 - b^2))$ ... We can simplify by 2:

$= (-a \pm b) / (a^2 - b^2)$

This means that the roots are,

$x_1 = (-a - b) / (a^2 - b^2)$ ... $a^2 - b^2$ is two square differences:

$x_1 = -(a + b) / ((a - b)(a + b))$ ... $(a + b)$ terms cancel each other:

$x_1 = -1/(a - b)$

$x_2 = (-a + b) / (a^2 - b^2)$ ... $a^2 - b^2$ is two square differences:

$x_2 = -(a - b) / ((a - b)(a + b))$ ... $(a - b)$ terms cancel each other:

$x_2 = -1/(a + b)$

39. A
To simplify, we need to remove the parenthesis and see if any terms cancel:

$(a + b)(x + y) + (a - b)(x - y) - (ax + by) = ax + ay + bx + by + ax - ay - bx + by - ax - by$

By writing similar terms together:

$= ax + ax - ax + bx - bx + ay - ay + by + by - by$ ... + terms cancel - terms:

$= ax + by$

40. C
We are asked to add polynomials A + B. By paying attention to the sign distribution; we write the polynomials and operate:

$A + B = (4x^5 - 2x^2 + 3x - 2) + (-3x^4 - 5x^2 - 4x + 5)$

= $4x^5 - 2x^2 + 3x - 2 - 3x^4 - 5x^2 - 4x + 5$ ... Writing similar terms together:

= $4x^5 - 3x^4 - 2x^2 - 5x^2 + 3x - 4x - 2 + 5$ ... Operating within similar terms:

= $4x^5 - 3x^4 - 7x^2 - x + 3$

41. B
Total Volume = Volume of large cylinder - Volume of small cylinder

Volume of a cylinder = area of base • height = $\pi r^2 \cdot h$

Total Volume = $(\pi \cdot 12^2 \cdot 10) - (\pi \cdot 6^2 \cdot 5) = 1440\pi - 180\pi$

= 1260π in^3

42. D
$\log_{1/2} x = 4$ ... We know that $\log_a a^b = b \cdot \log_a a = b \cdot 1 = b$
$\log_{1/2} x = \log_{1/2}(1/2)^4$ ... Now, we can remove $\log_{1/2}$ terms since both sides have this function applied:

$x = (1/2)^4$

$x = 1^4/2^4$

$x = 1/16$

43. A
If we know the coordinates of two points on a line, we can find the slope (m) with the below formula:

$m = (y_2 - y_1)/(x_2 - x_1)$ where (x_1, y_1) represent the coordinates of one point and (x_2, y_2) the other.

In this question:

$(-9, 6) : x_1 = -9, y_1 = 6$

$(18, -18) : x_2 = 18, y_2 = -18$

Inserting these values into the formula:

$m = (-18 - 6)/(18 - (-9)) = (-24)/(27)$ ... Simplifying by 3:

$m = -8/9$

44.

We reflect points A, B and C against the mirror line m at the right angle and we connect the new points A', B' and C'. The process is the same even though the points of the triangle are not on the same side the of the mirror line.

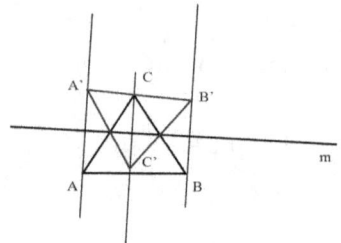

45. A

If we know the coordinates of two points on a line, we can find the slope (m) with the below formula:

$m = (y_2 - y_1)/(x_2 - x_1)$ where (x_1, y_1) represent the coordinates of one point and (x_2, y_2) the other.

In this question:

$(-4, y_1) : x_1 = -4, y_1 =$ we will find

$(-8, 7) : x_2 = -8, y_2 = 7$

$m = -7/4$

Inserting these values into the formula:

$-7/4 = (7 - y_1)/(-8 - (-4))$

$-7/4 = (7 - y_1)/(-8 + 4)$

$7/(-4) = (7 - y_1)/(-4)$ ... Simplifying the denominators of both sides by -4:

$7 = 7 - y_1$

$0 = -y_1$

$y_1 = 0$

46. D

The area of a rectangle is found by multiplying the width to the length. If we call these sides with "a" and "b"; the area is = a•b.

We are given that a•b = 20 cm² ... Equation I

One side is increased by 1 and the other by 2 cm. So new side lengths are "a + 1" and "b + 2."

The new area is (a + 1)(b + 2) = 35 cm² ... Equation II

Using equations I and II, we can find a and b:

ab = 20

(a + 1)(b + 2) = 35 ... We need to distribute the terms in parenthesis:

ab + 2a + b + 2 = 35

We can insert ab = 20 to the above equation:

20 + 2a + b + 2 = 35

2a + b = 35 - 2 - 20

2a + b = 13 ... This is one equation with two unknowns. We need to use another information to have two equations with two unknowns which leads us to the solution. We know that ab = 20. So, we can use a = 20/b:

2(20/b) + b = 13

40/b + b = 13 ... We equate all denominators to "b" and eliminate it:

40 + b² = 13b

b² - 13b + 40 = 0 ... We can use the roots by factoring. We try to separate the middle term -13b to find common factors with b² and 40 separately:

b² - 8b - 5b + 40 = 0 ⋯ Here, we see that b is a common factor for b² and -8b, and -5 is a common factor for -5b and 40:

b(b - 8) - 5(b - 8) = 0 Here, we have b times b - 8 and -5 times b - 8 summed up. This means that we have b - 5 times b - 8:

(b - 5)(b - 8) = 0

This is true when either or both of the expressions in the parenthesis are equal to zero:

b - 5 = 0 ... b = 5

b - 8 = 0 ... b = 8

So we have two values for b which means we have two values for a as well. In order to find a, we can use any equation we have. Let us use a = 20/b.

If b = 5, a = 20/b → a = 4

If b = 8, a = 20/b → a = 2.5

So, (a, b) pairs for the sides of the original rectangle are: (4, 5) and (2.5, 8). These are found in (b) and (c) answer choices.

47. B
$\log_{10} 10,000 = x$ ... We know that $\log_a a^b = b \cdot \log_a a = b \cdot 1 = b$

$\log_{10} 10,000 = \log_{10} 10^x$ Now, we can remove $\log_{1/2}$ terms since both sides have this function applied:

$10,000 = 10^x$

$10^4 = 10^x$ If bases are the same, powers are the same:

4 = x

x = 4

48. D
The distance between two points is found by $= [(x_2 - x_1)^2 + (y_2 - y_1)^2]^{1/2}$

In this question:

(18, 12) : $x_1 = 18$, $y_1 = 12$

(9, -6) : $x_2 = 9$, $y_2 = -6$

Distance $= [(9 - 18)^2 + (-6 - 12)^2]^{1/2}$

$= [(-9)^2 + (-18)^2]^{1/2}$

$= (9^2 + 2^2 \cdot 9^2)^{1/2}$

$= (9^2(1 + 5))^{1/2}$ ... We can take 9 out of the square root:

= 9•6^(1/2)

= 9√6

= 9•2.45

= 22.04

The distance is about 22 units.

49. D
To understand this question better, let us draw a right triangle by writing the given data on it:

Note: Figure not drawn to scale

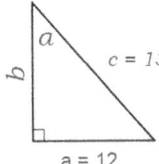

The side opposite angle a is named by a.

sin a = length of the opposite side / length of the hypotenuse = 12/13 is given.

cos a = length of the adjacent side / length of the hypotenuse = b/13

We use the Pythagorean Theorem to find the value of b:

(Hypotenuse)² = (Opposite Side)² + (Adjacent Side)²

c² = a² + b²

13² = 12² + b²

169 = 144 + b²

b² = 169 - 144

b² = 25

b = 5

So;

cos a = b/13 = 5/13

50. D
1/(4x - 2) = 5/6 ... We can cross multiply:

5(4x - 2) = 1•6 ... Now, we distribute 5 to the parenthesis:

20x - 10 = 6 ... We need x term alone on one side:

20x = 6 + 10

20x = 16 ... Dividing both sides by 20:

x = 16/20 ... Simplifying by 2 and having 10 in the denominator provides us finding the decimal equivalent of x:

x = 8/10 = 0.8

51. B
If we know the coordinates of two points on a line, we can find the slope (m) with the below formula:

$m = (y_2 - y_1)/(x_2 - x_1)$ where (x_1, y_1) represent the coordinates of one point and (x_2, y_2) the other.

In this question:

$(-4, -4) : x_1 = -4, y_1 = -4$

$(-1, 2) : x_2 = -1, y_2 = 2$

Inserting these values into the formula:

$m = (2 - (-4))/(-1 - (-4)) = (2 + 4)/(-1 + 4) = 6/3$ ... Simplifying by 3:

m = 2

52. A
The formula of the volume of cylinder is the base area multiplied by the height. As the formula:

Volume of a cylinder = $πr^2h$. Where π is 3.142, r is radius of the cross sectional area, and h is the height.

We know that the diameter is 5 meters, so the radius is 5/2 = 2.5 meters.

The volume is: V = 3.142•2.5^2•12 = 235.65 m^3.

53. C
We are given that,

$a_2 = 3$

$a_{n+1} = -a_{n-1}$

Let us insert n = 2:

$a_3 = -a_4$ ... If we carry a_4 to left side:

$a_3 + a_4 = 0$ ... We were asked to find this. Without using $a_2 = 3$, which would not be useful in this question; we reached this result.

54. C
The large cube is made up of 8 smaller cubes with 5 cm sides. The volume of a cube is found by the third power of the length of one side.

Volume of the large cube = Volume of the small cube•8

= $(5^3) \cdot 8$ = 125•8

= 1000 cm^3

There is another solution for this question. Find the side length of the large cube. There are two cubes rows with 5 cm length for each. So, one side of the large cube is 10 cm.

The volume of this large cube is equal to 10^3 = 1000 cm^3

55. A
First write the two equations one under the other. Our aim is to multiply equations with appropriate factors to eliminate one unknown and find the other, and then find the eliminated one using the found value.

$-\sqrt{5}$ / $x\sqrt{5} - y = \sqrt{5}$ ... If we multiply this equation by $\sqrt{5}$, y terms will cancel each other:

$\underline{x - y\sqrt{5} = 5}$

$-x\sqrt{5}\sqrt{5} + y\sqrt{5} = -\sqrt{5}\sqrt{5}$ ... using $\sqrt{5}\sqrt{5} = 5$:

$\underline{x - y\sqrt{5} = 5}$

$-5x + y\sqrt{5} = -5$

$\underline{x - y\sqrt{5} = 5}$ ... Summing side-by-side:

$-5x + y\sqrt{5} + x - y\sqrt{5} = -5 + 5$ ... $+ y\sqrt{5}$ and $- y\sqrt{5}$, -5 and + 5 cancel each other:

$-4x = 0$

x = 0

Now, using either of the equations gives us the value of y. Let us choose equation 1:

x√5 - y = √5

0√5 - y = √5

-y = √5

y = -√5

The solution to the system is (0, -√5)

56. D

As shown in the figure, two parallel lines intersecting with a third line with angle of 75°.

x = 75° (corresponding angles)

x + y = 180° (supplementary angles) ... inserting the value of x here:

y = 180° - 75°
y = 105°

57. B

To understand this question better, let us draw a right triangle by writing the given data on it:

Note: Figure not drawn to scale

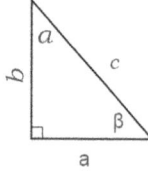

The side opposite to angle α is named by a.
The side opposite to angle β is named by b.
The hypotenuse which is the opposite side to 90° angle is named by c.

We are asked to find (sinα + cosβ)/(tgα + ctgβ).

As general formulas:

sinx = length of the opposite side / length of the hypotenuse cosx = length of the adjacent side / length of the hypotenuse

tgx = length of the opposite side / length of the adjacent side

ctgx = length of the adjacent side / length of the opposite side

So, in this question;

sinα = a/c, cosβ = a/c, tgα = a/b, ctgβ = a/b

Inserting all known values:

(sinα + cosβ)/(tgα + ctgβ) = (a/c + a/c)/(a/b + a/b) = (2a/c)/(2a/b) = (2a/c)(b/2a) Simplifying by 2a:

= b/c

58. D
Two parallel lines (m & side AB) intersected by side AC. This means that 50° and a angles are interior angles. So:
a = 50° (interior angles).

59. D
We have a circle given with diameter 8 cm and a square located within the circle. We are asked to find the area of the circle for which we only need to know the length of the radius that is the half of the diameter.

Area of circle = πr^2 ... r = 8/2 = 4 cm

Area of circle = $\pi \cdot 4^2$

= 16π cm² ... As we notice, the inner square has no role in this question.

60. C
We see that two legs of a right triangle form by Peter's movements and we are asked to find the length of the hypotenuse. We use the Pythagorean Theorem:
(Hypotenuse)² = (Adjacent side)² + (Opposite side)²

h² = a² + b²

We know that a and b are 3 km and 4 km. So,

$h^2 = 3^2 + 4^2$

$h^2 = 9 + 16$

$h^2 = 25$

$h = \sqrt{25}$

$h = 5$ km

Part IV - Social Studies

US History

1. C
The Gilded Age was a satire given by Mark Twain about how the super-rich were a thin gold varnish covering up societies' woes.

Choice A is incorrect; the California Gold Rush happened before the Gilded Age.

Choice B is incorrect; while having gold was a status symbol it was not the reason why the time period was called the Gilded Age.

Choice D is incorrect; gangsters were never known for gilding their enemies.

2. A
A black exodus from the South to the Midwest intensified during the end of reconstruction and the start of Jim Crow laws.

Choice B is incorrect; while European immigrants were immigrating in large numbers during this time period this was not a name given to it.

Choice C is incorrect; Asian immigrants were immigrating during this time period and suffered a lot of discrimination through a general hostility to their culture and through official means by way of the Chinese Exclusion Act and the Gentleman's agreement.

Choice D is incorrect; the creation of reservations ended in the mid-1800s under President Hays, new reservation land would not be added until 1934 under the Indian Reorganization Act.

3. C
With the 19th Amendment Women's Suffrage came into national law in 1919.

Choice A is incorrect; the Seneca Falls Convention was the first women's rights conventions, it did not actually create any laws though.

Choice B is incorrect; the 18th Amendment to the United States Constitution prohibited the manufacture, sale, transport, import, or export of alcoholic beverages.

Choice D is incorrect; Jeannette Rankin was the first women senator in the United States, before all women had the right to vote, but she never had a law named after her.

4. D
Both the French and the United States contributed to building the Panama Canal, though there was about a decade where there was no construction.

Choice A is incorrect; while the French did start construction of the Panama Canal in 1881, they did not complete it.

Choice B is incorrect; the United States finished the Panama Canal in 1914, but they did not start the construction.

Choice C is incorrect; the Spanish did not contribute to building the Panama Canal.

5. C
Secretary of State John Hay proposed the Open Door Policy to his European counterparts to abate any conflict between powers over China in the future.

Choice A is incorrect; no countries willingly lowered tariffs significantly during the early 20th century when the Open Door Policy took effect.

Choice B is incorrect; President Mckinley did not accept ideas from everyone when the Open Door Policy took effect.

Choice D is incorrect; the revolving door is the name coined for people going from government positions to industry positions they were supposed to regulate and vice versa.

6. A
Before the Federal Reserve Act, banks did not have the authority to put money into, or take money out of circulation.

Choice B is incorrect; there has not been a government bank in the United States since 1836, the Second Bank of the United States.

Choice C is incorrect; laws have been fluid over the years on how much cash a bank must have liquid, and will probably continue to be so.

Choice D is incorrect; The United States has taken assets out of private hands and put them in public trusts, but the Federal Reserve Act did not do this.

7. C
The Germans had a submarine blockade of Great Britain and torpedoed many ships, both merchant and passenger liners, angering many Americans and was a major factor in America entering the war.

Choice A is incorrect; the bombing of Pearl harbor is what led the United States into World War II.

Choice B is incorrect; the United States was not allied with either Britain or France.

8. B
To allow the Allies to pay off their debts to the United States, the United States loaned money to Germany so that they could pay off their reparations to the Allies.

Choice A is incorrect; this is the Marshall Plan after World War II.

Choice C is incorrect; the United Sates actually slowed down immigration to the United States instead of increasing it.

Choice D is incorrect; this is the Truman Doctrine after World War II.

9. B
The United States stock market collapse of 1929 caused the downfall of many financial institutions and the start of the Great Depression.

Choice A is incorrect; Prohibition started in the 1920s, the Great Depression did not start until 1929.

Choice C is incorrect; while Germany did default on its loans to the United States after World War I, the Great Depression occurred several years after this event.

Choice D is incorrect; the Dust Bowl happened during the Great Depression, it did not precipitate it.

10. B
World War II reduced unemployment with so many working-class men in the armed forces, and jobs were available for anyone able to take them.

Choice A is incorrect; the Great Depression ended with the start of World War II, but the economy was already recovering, so there is some doubt as to whether it helped end the depression.

Choice C is incorrect; World War II did not exacerbate the Great Depression because the Great Depression ended with the onset of World War II.

Choice D is incorrect; only the ending of the Great Depression is up for debate.

World History

11. C
Russia, the United States and Great Britain where considered "The Big Three" Allied countries.

Choice A is incorrect; these were the three main leaders of the Axis powers.

Choice B is incorrect; France was not part of "The Big Three" Allied forces.

Choice D is incorrect; Harry Truman was the US president at the end of WWII, but Franklin Roosevelt was the main WWII president.

12. A
The Non-Aligned Movement was a group of nations that wanted to be neutral in the Cold War.

Choice B is incorrect; the United States helped create a few blocs of nations to oppose communism, but none were the Non-Aligned Movement.

Choice C is incorrect; the movement for the United States to become isolationist once again was very small, and not the Non-Aligned Movement.

Choice D is incorrect; there were movements within the United States to become a more worldly benevolent power, but none were called the Non-Alignment Movement.

13. C
Mutually Assured Destruction (MAD) is a doctrine of military strategy and national security policy in which a full-scale use of high-yield weapons of mass destruction by two or more opposing sides would cause the complete annihilation of both the attacker and the defender.

Choice A is incorrect; MAD refers to nuclear weapons, an offensive weapon rather than a defensive one.

Choice B is incorrect; while military in nature that was not the acronym.

Choice D is incorrect; while a good description of what were to happen, this is not the acronym.

14. D
None of the answers are correct.

Choice A is incorrect; while true, it is not the only right answer.

Choice B is incorrect; the Soviet Union stopped aid from getting to Berlin to force the allies to allow them to supply Berlin and thereby gain control of the city, but that is not the only correct answer.

Choice C is incorrect; the Berlin Airlift was able to surpass the quantity of cargo that regularly reached Berlin before the blockade, but it is not the only correct answer.

15. A
Détente is the easing of hostility or strained relations, especially between countries. Here, it refers to was a period during the middle of the Cold War in which both the United States and the Soviet Union were on cordial terms, and actively trying to lessen tensions.

Choice B is incorrect; there were a couple "warming up" periods in which the world came very close to nuclear war, but these were not Détente.

Choice C is incorrect; the United States usually knew who was the head of the Soviet Union and it never became an issue when they did not.

Choice D is incorrect; neither C nor B are correct.

16. A
By controlling Central and Southern Asia, other countries would be easily accessible.

Choice B is incorrect; neither country was trying to financially exhaust the other.

Choice C is incorrect; neither country was trying to trade with Japan.

Choice D is incorrect; Britain and Russia were not competing for trade in Asia.

17. A
The Catholic King James II of England was overthrown by the Protestant William of Orange.

Choice B is incorrect; the Glorious Revolution did not achieve economic equality.

Choice C is incorrect; implementation of industrial machines was during the Industrial Revolution.
Choice D is incorrect; the Glorious Revolution did not impact education.

18. C
Increased productivity due to the cotton gin, power looms, the flying shuttle and the spinning jenny made textile production the leading industry of the Industrial Revolution

Choice A is incorrect; glass was produced, but it was not the main industry.

Choice B is incorrect; paper was produced, but it was not the main industry.

Choice D is incorrect; gas lighting was produced, but it was not the main industry.

19. B
The United States was the first European colony to declare its independence from Britain in 1776.

Choice A is incorrect; Haiti declared its independence from France in 1804.

Choice C is incorrect; Chile was independent of Spain by 1831.

Choice D is incorrect; Mexico was independent of Spain by 1831.

20. D
The storming of the Bastille happened in July, 1789 and is considered the flash point of the French Revolution.

Choice A is incorrect; Napoleon's rise to power is considered to be the end of the French Revolution.

Choice B is incorrect; the March on Versailles happened during the French Revolution when people were upset with the high price of bread.

Choice C is incorrect; this document was passed in France in August, 1789.

Civics and Government

21. A
The main purpose of dividing government is to prevent one branch from becoming too powerful, and a dictatorship taking hold.

Choice B is incorrect; but may sound plausible to someone unfamiliar with divided government.

Choice C is incorrect; dividing the government does not strengthen it.

Choice D is incorrect; the military has little to do with this.

22. C
The minimum age to serve in the House of Representatives is 25.

Choice A is incorrect; 35 is the age for president.

Choice B is incorrect; 30 is the age for Senators.

Choice D is incorrect; 18 is the age of majority.

23. D
A bill becomes law when it passes through both houses of Congress and is signed by the President.

Choice A is incorrect; a bill must pass through the House and the Senate, and then it can be signed by the President.

Choice B is clearly incorrect because Parliament is part of the English government.

Choice C is incorrect; a veto negates the passage of a law.

24. A
Congress can override a presidential veto with a two-thirds majority vote.

Choice B is incorrect; a simple majority vote is required to pass a bill.

Choice C is incorrect; reconciliation is a legislative process of the United States Senate intended to allow consideration of a budget bill with debate limited to twenty hours under Senate rules. Reconciliation also exists in the United States House of Representatives, but because the House regularly passes rules that constrain debate and amendment, the process has had a less significant impact on that body.

Choice C is partly true, however, choice A is a much better choice.

Choice D is incorrect; a veto can be overridden.

25. B
An amendment added to the constitution with three-quarters of the states ratifying it.

Choice A is incorrect; this is the process for a regular bill.

Choice C is incorrect; this is the process to override a veto.

Choice D is incorrect; virtually nothing is decided by national popular vote.

26. A
The president has 10 days (excluding Sundays) to sign a bill into law.

27. A
Each state is represented by two senators.

Choice C is incorrect; but may seem plausible due to house representation being proportional.

Choice D is incorrect; the size of the state's population determines house representation.

28. B
The Vice President is considered president of the Senate, and their vote breaks a tie.

Choice A is incorrect; the President stays separate from congress.
Choice C is incorrect; the Speaker of the House stays separate from the Senate.

Choice D is clearly incorrect because the Supreme Court does not legislate.

29. D
The number of congressmen that represent each state depends on the state's population.

Choice A is incorrect; each state has 2 senators.

Choice C is incorrect but may seem plausible due to representation being proportional to population.

30. D
The U.S. Constitution specifies a bicameral legislature, which means having two branches or chambers.

Choice A is incorrect but may seem plausible due to the prefix bi-.

Choice B is clearly incorrect because bi- means two.

Choice C is incorrect by definition and because there are many levels of government: city, county, state, federal.

Economics

31. D
The Securities and Exchange Commission, SEC, regulates The stock market.

Choice A is incorrect; the FDA regulates agriculture.

Choice B is incorrect; the Department of Homeland Security is charged protecting the United States from terrorist attacks.

Choice C is incorrect; congress determines the national budget.

32. C
Federal income tax is due annually, although it is normally deducted from every paycheck.

Choice A is incorrect; sales tax is paid every time you buy something.

Choice B is incorrect; fees are distinct from taxes.

Choice D is incorrect; income tax is distinct from government services.

33. A
A park is a good example of a public good. A public good is a commodity or service that is provided without profit to all members of a society, either by the government or a private individual or organization.

Choices B, C and D are incorrect; a plumber, an airline and a taxi are examples of private services.

34. A
Sales tax is paid every time you buy something.

Choice B is incorrect; fees are distinct from taxes.

Choice C is incorrect; sales tax is paid when you buy something, not annually.

Choice D is incorrect; sales tax is distinct from government services.

35. D
Religious institutions are not subject to federal taxes.

Choices A and B are incorrect; large corporations and small businesses are subject to taxes.

Choice C is incorrect; Athletes are private citizens and are subject to taxes.

36. A
The federal government gets its funding by taxation.
Choice B is incorrect; the government does not sell goods.

Choice C is incorrect; the government rarely invests in stocks.

Choice D is incorrect; the government rarely receives donations.

37. C
During the Great Depression, Keynesian economics prescribed lower taxes and increasing government spending to stimulated the economy.

Choice A is incorrect; this is the opposite of the Keynesian approach.

Choice B is incorrect; government spending was increased during the Great Depression.

Choice C is incorrect; taxes were not raised during the Great Depression.

38. D
Bank deposits are guaranteed by the Federal Deposit

Insurance Corporation.

Choice A is incorrect; the SEC regulates the stock market.

Choice B is incorrect; the FDA regulates food and drugs.

Choice C is incorrect; HUD is the department of Housing and Urban Development.

39. B
If a country's imports have more value than its exports, it is said to have a trade deficit.

Choice A is incorrect; a trade surplus is the opposite.

Choice C is incorrect; the balance of trade is the difference between imports and exports.

Choice D is incorrect; globalization simply refers to the connectedness of the world's economies.

Geography

40. A
A tariff is a tax on imports.
Choice B is incorrect; a tariff is a tax on imports.

Choice C is incorrect; tariffs have little to do with bank deposits.

Choice D is incorrect; tariffs are not related to stocks.

41. D
The U.S. has expanded westward all the way to the Pacific Ocean since the American Revolution.

Choice A is incorrect; Canada is to the north.

Choice B is incorrect; the Caribbean and Mexico were and are to the south.

Choice C is incorrect; the Atlantic Ocean was and is to the east.

42. B
Humans do not normally avoid warm weather.

Choice A is incorrect; humans try to avoid cold weather.

Choice C is incorrect; deserts cannot support very much life.

Choice D is incorrect; high altitudes cannot support much life.

43. C
Immigrants to the U.S. have always always been discriminated against before finding equality.

Choice A is incorrect; the native-born population tends not to welcome immigrants.

Choice B is clearly incorrect; slavery has been illegal since 1863.

Choice D is incorrect; immigrants have come from all over the world.

44. D
Diffusion, which moves a trend from one leader to another throughout a geographic area is known as hierarchical diffusion.

Choice A is incorrect; expansion diffusion is the diffusion of people.

Choice B is incorrect but plausible; stimulus diffusion pertains to ideas, but not necessarily to leaders.
Choice C is incorrect; relocation diffusion skips over certain areas.

45. A
The U.S. military occupied Afghanistan since 2001 until June 2011.

Choice B is incorrect; Iraq was invaded in 2003 and U.S. forces have officially left.

Choice C is incorrect; the U.S. has never occupied Israel.

Choice D is incorrect; the US. sent troops to Lebanon in the 1980s, but did not occupy Lebanon.

46. B
The science of mapmaking is called cartography.

Choice A is incorrect; archaeology is the study of human activity in the past.

Choice C is incorrect; geography is a field of science dedicated to the study of the lands, the features, the inhabitants, and the phenomena of the Earth.

Choice D is incorrect; GPS stands for Global Positioning System.

47. D
Environmental determinism is the theory that climate and landforms are responsible for differences in human culture.

Choice A is incorrect; but plausible due to the word "determine."

Choice B is incorrect; human devastation of the environment is an environmental influence on humans.

Choice C is incorrect; this may be true but it is irrelevant to the question.

48. D
Limited resources generally lead to a scattered population, since the area cannot support many people.

Choice A is incorrect; a dense population needs more resources.

Choice B is incorrect; industrial businesses look for an abundance of resources.

Choice C is incorrect; a trade route may appear but this is irrelevant to the question.

49. B
The southeast region of the U.S. has the fastest growing population.

50. A
Subsistence agriculture is self-sufficiency farming in which the farmers focus on growing enough food to feed themselves and their families. The typical subsistence farm has a range of crops and animals needed by the family to feed and clothe themselves during the year.

Choice B is incorrect; entrepreneurs start businesses.

Choice C is incorrect; businesspeople sell things.

Choice D is incorrect; migrant farm workers are employees of other farmers.

Science

Physical Science

1. A
The equation Mg + HCL -> $MgCl_2$ + HCL
will produce one molecule of $MgCl_2$ will be produced.
The coefficient (the number preceding the compound) will be 1.

2. D
None of the choice are correct. UV radiations have higher frequency than radio waves (Choice A), EM radiations are produced by acceleration of charged particles and these radiations are massless but are affected by gravity, (Choices B and C).

3. C
The speed of light decreases and the frequency increases

when light enters from vacuum into material medium.

Choices A and D are incorrect since when light is diffracted to refracted speed and frequency are not affected. When light enters from material medium into a vacuum, the speed increases and the frequency is decreases, so option B is also incorrect.

4. B
In order of decreasing frequency:
Radio waves > Visible waves > X-rays > Gamma rays.

Radio waves have highest frequency here, then the order of decreasing frequency will be: visible rays, X-rays and gamma rays.

5. B
Soft X-rays are used in medical imagining technology.

The other choices are incorrect, as radio waves, visible rays and microwaves either cannot penetrate the body or are damaging.

6. C
Ultrasound is not an application of electromagnetic radiations. Sound waves with a frequency above the upper limit of human hearing are used for detection. CAT scan and dental radiographs are generated by X-rays, hence choice C is not an application of EM radiations.

7. C
Gamma- rays are used to kill living organisms by process of irradiation and are used a lot in sterilizing medical equipment.

They are also used for cancer treatment when these rays are directed onto tumor cells. Radioisotopes emitting gamma rays are used in nuclear medicine .

So, choice C is the best choice. Other radiations, x-rays, soft x-rays and uv-rays are not reported to have all these applications.

8. C
Interference of light indicates it is a wave-phenomenon: waves may enhance or diminish the effect of each other when they interfere or overlap. Light waves follow pattern of interference which is evident of light as a wave phenomenon.

Choices A and B cannot be predicted by interference of light. Choice C is an incorrect statement.

9. C
Young's double slit experiment two slits were used to create path difference: path difference is necessary for the phenomenon of interference (constructive and destructive waves) to occur.

Choices A and D are incorrect because slits will not vary the intensity or wavelength, moreover wavelength has to be the same in this experiment. Choice B is irrelevant.

10. D
Choices A and B best explains transmutation. Transmutation is defined as conversion or change of atoms of one element into another element through radioactive decay or nuclear reaction. Choice D is the best option.

Choice C is incorrect because gamma decay do not cause transmutation.

11. A
Atom is the basic or fundamental par of any matter or element.

12. C
When acid and base react, they neutralize each other properties to form salt and water.

13. B
The horizontal rows from right to left of the periodic table are known as periods and elements on a row share the same number of electron shells.

14. D
Oxidation and reduction reactions are each just half of a

redox reaction and both occur simultaneously, because the exact electrons lost in oxidation is what is gained in reduction.

15. B
The elements on the periodic table can be classified as metals, metalloids and non-metals. Most of the elements on the table can be classified as metals.

16. C
A quantity of energy, equal to the difference between the energies of the bonded atoms and the energies of the separated atoms, is released, usually as heat. That is, the bonded atoms have a lower energy than the individual atoms do

17. A
A co-ordinate bond is a covalent bond (a shared pair of electrons) in which both electrons come from the same atom.

18. C
According to law of conservation of mass option c is best possible.

Choices A, B and C are not the best options as the physical state of product and reactant might be same, the density of both might be different, and the molecular structure of product can be simpler.

19. B
The half-life is the time required by a substance to decrease in quantity by half. It is calculated by $N_t = N_o \times (1/2)^{t/h}$.

20. C
Gamma rays are neutral. Alpha rays bend towards cathode and are positively charged. Beta rays bend towards anode and are negatively charged.

Life Science

21. A
The four fundamental forces of nature are, gravity, electromagnetic force, weak nuclear force, and strong

nuclear force.

Note: Electromagnetic force is more commonly known as electricity.

22. D
A Punnett square resembles a game of tic-tac-toe, in which the genotypes of the parents gametes are entered first, so that subsequent combinations can be calculated.

23. D
All the statements are true.
    a. Mechanical energy is the energy that is possessed by an object due to its motion or due to its position.

    b. Mechanical energy can be either kinetic energy (energy of motion) or potential energy (stored energy of position).

    c. Objects have mechanical energy if they are in motion

24. D
Potential energy is the energy of a body resulting from motion while kinetic energy is the energy possessed by an object by virtue of its position or state, e.g., as in a compressed spring.

25. A
During a physical change, some aspect of the physical properties of matter are altered, but the identity of the substance remains constant. Chemical changes involve the alteration of both a substance's composition and structure.

Note: Examples of physical changes include breaking glass, cutting wood and melting ice. Sometimes, the process can be easily reversed. Restoration of the original form is not possible following a chemical change.

26. C
A chemical change is a process that transforms one set of chemical substances to another; the substances used are known as reactants and those formed are products.

27. B
Oxygen is the most abundant element in the Earth's crust and appears on the Atomic Table as the letter O.

28. C
All of these statements are true.

> a. A metal is a substance that conducts heat and electricity.
> b. A metal is shiny and reflects many colors of light, and can be hammered into sheets or drawn into wire.
> d. About 80% of the known chemical elements are metals.

29. C
The atomic number of an element equals the number of protons in an atomic nucleus, and, along with the element symbol is one of two alternate ways to label an element.

30. C
The following statement is false,
In quantum theory, energy is treated solely as a continuous phenomenon, while matter is assumed to occupy a very specific region of space and to move in a continuous manner.

31. B
The following is not included in Newton's laws of motion, Unless acted upon by a force, a body in motion will change direction and gradually slow until it eventually stops.

This answer is related to Newton's 1st law of motion which states that: Unless acted upon by a force, a body at rest stays at rest, and a moving body continues moving at the same speed in a straight line.

32. D
All of the statements are true.

> a. Electrically charged matter is influenced by, and produces, electromagnetic fields.
> b. Electric current is a movement or flow of electrically

charged particles.

c. Electric potential is a fundamental interaction between the magnetic field and the presence and motion of an electric charge.

33. C
A and B are true.

a. Light consists of electromagnetic waves in the visible range.

b. The fundamental particle or quantum of light is a photon.

Note: Light energy is the only visible form of energy. A light bulb is a device that uses electrical energy to create electromagnetic energy in the form (in part) of visible light and heat.

34. A
Hydra are an autotroph - this statement is false, Hydra are heterotrophs.

35. B
Mitochondria. ATP production and respiratory chain reactions occur in mitochondrial membrane, making it important in cellular respiration.

Choices A, B and C may play minor roles.

36. D
None of the above: all the mentioned processes maintains homeostasis. Thermoregulation maintains body temperature. Osmoregulation maintains water content and excretion gets rid of body wastes and maintain stable body condition.

37. D
Choices A and C as males are heterozygous (XY) hence there is a possibility of y-linked as well as x-linked diseases appearing in males, moreover, autosomal dominant diseases will also appear in an individual heterozygous for that disease.

Choice B is incorrect as autosomal recessive disease will appear in homozygous individual only.

38. C
Mutation that is hereditary and plays role in survival. Mutation should improve adaptability and survival of individual and should be heritable.

Choices A and B are not the best option because mutation should have a positive effect, should improve chance of survival and should be hereditary.

Choice D is also not the best option as other factors are also involved.

39. B
Herbivores consume plants (i.e producers), so they are the primary consumers.

Choice C is incorrect as secondary consumers consume herbivores. Choice D is incorrect because only choice B is correct.

40. B
A mutation on X chromosome causes a disease which only affects a male child is called a sex limited inheritance. A disease due to a defect in X chromosome should also affect female progeny, but if it doesn't effect females, and it is limited to males only, it is known as sex limited inheritance.

Choice A is incorrect because if the disease appears in both male and female children, based who receives the defective chromosome, it is called a sex linked inheritance.

Choice C is incorrect. Co-dominant inheritance means both alleles express independently, so, the disease should appear in the female progeny too.

Choice D is incorrect because in dominant inheritance, the female progeny XX, should show symptoms of disease as well.

Earth and Space Science

41. A
Acidic fog will cause the most damage as pH of acid fog is very low. pH of 1.7 has been recorded for acidic fog.

Choices B, C and D are not the best choices as acidic fog has the lowest pH among the choices.

42. B
The false statement is, Hydride of sulfur is main cause of acid rain . Hydride of sulfur is SH_2 is not the cause of aicd rain, it's the oxide of sulfur i.e. SO_2, hence this is the false choice, and all other choices are true.

43. D
All choices define pollution, but choices A and C are incomplete as they do not specify that contaminants/substances are harmful to whom?

Choice B explains that substances are harmful to living beings, but does not explain the type of substances, therefore, choice D is the best choice as it defines that substances may be matter or energy, and their introduction to the environment will be harmful to all living things.

44. B
The abundance of the "light elements" Hydrogen and Helium found in the observable universe are thought to support the Big Bang model of origins.

45. D
Explosions in a chamber create pressure that pushes gases out of a rocket. This in turn produces thrust that pushes the rocket forward.

46. B
As per Doppler's effect, when a source is moving away from the observer (Red shift), the observed frequency is lower than the actual frequency and hence observed wavelength will be longer than the actual wavelength.

47. C

Fossil fuels are part of abiotic carbon cycle. Although biotic and abiotic carbon cycles overlap, fossil fuels are only part of abiotic carbon cycle.

Animals and plants are part of biotic carbon cycle. Plants are part of abiotic carbon cycle, but fossil fuel is the best choice.

48. C

Solar energy does not affect the carbon cycle directly. Green houses need carbon dioxide enrichment for plant growth, urbanization leads to increased atmospheric carbon dioxide, burning fossil fuels has the same effect. Therefore, all these influence carbon cycle directly except solar energy.

49. C

Sublimation is a process where solids are directly converted to a vapor state (gaseous form). Water in the form of ice in glaciers sublimates to form clouds. Oceans and plants sublimate (evaporation i.e. liquid to gaseous state).

50. C

Condensation (cloud formation) will lead to precipitation (rain/ snow) but transpiration cannot lead to precipitation without condensation process hence, choice c is an incorrect sequence of events in hydrologic cycle. All other sequences are correct.

Conclusion

CONGRATULATIONS! You have made it this far because you have applied yourself diligently to practicing for the exam and no doubt improved your potential score considerably! Getting into a good school is a huge step in a journey that might be challenging at times but will be many times more rewarding and fulfilling. That is why being prepared is so important.

Study then Practice and then Succeed!

Good Luck!

FREE Ebook Version

Download a FREE Ebook version of the publication!

Suitable for tablets, iPad, iPhone, or any smart phone.

Go to
http://tinyurl.com/

TASC® Test Strategy!

Learn to increase your score using time-tested secrets for answering multiple choice questions!

This practice book has everything you need to know about answering multiple choice questions on the TASC®!

You will learn 12 strategies for answering multiple choice questions and then practice each strategy with over 45 reading comprehension multiple choice questions, with extensive commentary from exam experts!

Also included are strategies and practice questions for basic math, plus math tips, tricks and shortcuts!

Maybe you have read this kind of thing before, and maybe feel you don't need it, and you are not sure if you are going to buy this Book.

Remember though, it only a few percentage points divide the PASS from the FAIL students.

Even if our multiple choice strategies increase your score by a few percentage points, isn't that worth it?

https://www.createspace.com/4720329

Endnotes

Reading Comprehension passages where noted below are used under the Creative Commons Attribution-ShareAlike 3.0 License

http://en.wikipedia.org/wiki/Wikipedia:Text_of_Creative_Commons_Attribution-ShareAlike_3.0_Unported_License

[1] Infectious disease. In *Wikipedia*. Retrieved November 12, 2010 from http://en.wikipedia.org/wiki/Infectious_disease.
[2] Thunderstorm. In *Wikipedia*. Retrieved November 12, 2010 from en.wikipedia.org/wiki/Thunderstorm.
[3] Meteorology. In *Wikipedia*. Retrieved November 12, 2010 from en.wikipedia.org/wiki/Outline_of_meteorology.
[4] Cloud. In *Wikipedia*. Retrieved November 12, 2010 from http://en.wikipedia.org/wiki/Clouds.
[5] U.S. Navy Seal. In *Wikipedia*. Retrieved November 12, 2010 from en.wikipedia.org/wiki/United_States_Navy_SEALs.
[6] Respiratory System. In *Wikipedia*. Retrieved November 12, 2010 from en.wikipedia.org/wiki/Respiratory_system.
[7] Mythology. In *Wikipedia*. Retrieved November 12, 2010 from en.wikipedia.org/wiki/Mythology.
[8] Tree. In *Wikipedia*. Retrieved November 12, 2010 from en.wikipedia.org/wiki/Tree.

www.ingramcontent.com/pod-product-compliance
Lightning Source LLC
Chambersburg PA
CBHW060941230426
43665CB00015B/2024